RECLAIM YOUR ROOTS,
LIVE A LEGA

ANCIENT-FUTURE
UNITY

COMPILED BY ♀ DANIELLE ASHÉ ♀ JANE ASTARA ASHLEY
WITH ESSAYS FROM 26 BLACK FEMININE LEADERS

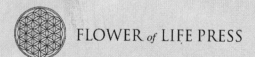

FLOWER *of* LIFE PRESS

PRAISE

"We need trustworthy and truthful voices, voices that have been missing from literature, to reunite us. 'Nurturing the Neglected Inner Me' by Mirabelle Adamu opens this important collection of Black women's stories. The reader arrives in the United States of America from Cameroon, with Mirabelle, ready to build her future by attending Howard University. The journey ahead includes much more than the hard work of earning a doctorate of pharmacy. It involves the challenges and calamities of the human experience and the transformational opportunities provided when we choose to become the protagonist of our own life. Mirabelle dives deep into personal growth, facing her own inner shadow and undoing the ancestral and cultural patterns that limited her so that she can create her most authentic and humanitarian life."

—Kim Douglas, author of *High Desert: A Journey of Survival and Hope,*
CEO, Write to Unite

"POW! her-full! I love the soulful cry of freedom that rang throughout this essay! The depth of Anim Bey's feeling painted a poignant picture of her journey to re-member and accept herself in all of her Divinity. Through witnessing her experience, there is healing for us all."

—Rev. Tonya D. Parker, Creatrix of Mind Body & Soul Food, author of *Diary of a Witch's Daughter, ABC Your Way from Danger to Opportunity: Spiritual Activism in Changing Times,* and *ABC Your Way from Distress to De-Stress: A Holistic Guide for Home-based Workers*

"Treneti is at the forefront of embodying a completely new way of being and creating in service to the Sovereignty of all. She expands the mind to new possibilities through her unique artistic expression that bridges worlds. Her personal story, music and poetry invoke ancestral resilience, a deepened connection with our infinite nature and a homecoming to our soul's truth. Her devotion to the Muse is awe-inspiring and her words of wisdom guide us back to the power we hold within this present moment."

—Shakti Mayumi

"Lindsey Cameron's story is an unflinching, yet tender, retelling of the ten days she spent at the bedside of her dying father. Since he is unable to make amends for his past wrongdoings, she makes them for him—retracing the highs and lows of their own painful past, and reaching out to the people he had wounded through the years. This is a powerful and touching story of redemption created from a fierce will . . . and a fierce love."

—Paige Britt, author of *The Lost Track of Time* and *Why Am I Me?*

"Her words, although unfamiliar to my so-called civilised mind, sing to my soul like a familiar soothing nursery rhyme. I am not a black woman, and yet the resonance of experience with Coco's words bridges an ancient 'primitive, savage, and uncivilised' chasm with an unbreakable bond of love between our human hearts. Coco says it all; what I feel through the vibration of her words is our mutual devotion to one another, if we can surrender enough to listen to our inner wisdom and get out of our own way, then humanity can begin to heal our collective wounds that separated us. This chapter is not just reclaiming the roots for black women, it's reclaiming the roots for the feminine that runs through all of us, whatever our sex or ethnic origin."

—Katie Mottram, author of *Mend the Gap*, founder of www.emergingproud.com, Emerging Proud Press Pocket Books of Hope, producer of www.a-call-to-awakening.com

"Good people deserve good things! 'Moment in a Hurricane' should be a whole book. The transparency of life in a rural world makes deliverance achievable. This chapter is the kind of empowering story that inspires people to use their talents to give back to the community. It was also written together well. The words and the flow of the story kept me reading. I wanted more. The question is, what happens next? 'Moment in a Hurricane' is a great read."

—Trinell Parrish-Brown

"Jocelyn Gordon weaves the stories of wounds, the lineage of mothers, nature, and healing that leads us inward towards a path to explore our own stories and to reclaim our power. This book is inspiration that is needed for these times so that we may remember our wholeness, celebrate our ancestors and reclaim our birthright of freedom."

—Tracee Stanley, bestselling author of *Radiant Rest: Yoga Nidra for Deep Relaxation* and *Awakened Clarity and Empowered Life Self-Inquiry Oracle* and Founder Empowered Life Circle

"Jackie Graves transmits her personal, often painful journey in words poetically gorgeous, while simultaneously awakening in the reader the universal desire to shed one's pain and move toward the liberation of one's soul. . . through narrative that is fearlessly honest and genuine. Please read this: you will be transformed by its distilled beauty and strength, you will feel healed by the wisdom and perspicacity of this author, you will feel in your gut the very essence of writing as art."

—Wendy Lipp, Publisher, Prashanti Press

"Katia Herrera is a BRILLIANT artist who explores the realms of cosmic phenomena and combines it with Afrocentrism. She embraces her culture unapologetically and expresses her thoughts through visual art as well as written literature. Katia's writings highlight the mental transformations that a person goes through while discovering Knowledge of Self. This is a great inspiring read for ALL!"

—Bro. Lyle, author of *Self Liberation for The Melanated People*

"Wow—there are moments when words touch you as an incantation from the divine, as a transmission of energy that moves you to the core. Libra Mayo has delivered such an offering in her poem—'Written on Fire.' It is a jeweled and dazzling gift—that at once is sumptuous and arresting—for it calls us to all to awaken. Take time to immerse yourself in this potent beauty: 'Turning inside out and outside in Activating light language that pours from my lips like honey.' Yes I taste the honey . . . and encourage you to as well. . ."

—Elayne Kalila Doughty, MA, MFT, Ordained Priestess, Psychotherapist, Sacred Ecstatic Activist, Gatekeeper and Focalizer of the Priestess Presence Temple

"'Look At Me: A Reflection Forward' by Stacè Middlebrooks is a must-read for all who know deep in their souls that it is possible for us to reflect to the outside world an authentic image of our whole selves, our intellect, power, and our magic! Stacè's journey from corporate life to creating her own company is less about taking a risky transition (although it was that) and more a reflection on embracing our intuitive, sacred work and empowering others to do the same. There can never be enough Black women role models who stand out as successful leaders in corporations, as entrepreneurs, mentors, coaches, spiritual guides, and rarely do we find one who has done it all, knows the cost, and is willing to share her story. Thank you Stacè for sharing yours."

—Marilyn Nagel, Co-Founder, Chief Advocacy Officer, RISEQUITY, CEO, Ready-Aim-Aspire

"Ivey Moore reveals a deeper look into the foods we eat, the true weight they carry, and how it's all linked to the trauma we may have experienced throughout our lineage. She encourages us to partake in the 'Real Soul Food' to lighten our Karmic loads, heal our-selves, heal our past, and create healing for our future generations. This book is a must-read for anyone ready to create huge healing shifts for themselves and their lineage. Ivey gives solid advice in this book to help you do just that."

—Latrice Folkes Jones, Holistic Life & Business Coach, Vegan Chef, author of the *Lifeit Detox*

"Nyakuiy's story brought tears to my eyes as I read about her, and her family's forced pilgrimage from the sacred homelands of their people, the Nuer, into the 'standard white American way'—a journey that led her away from Self and back again to rediscover and reclaim her birthright: the divinity within her. Nyakuiy's story is unique and yet it is every indigenous person's story. It is the story of every person who has ever been cut off from their ancestral lineage, from their true origins of Divine Co-Creators—taught to believe in the religious and societal dogma of conform-or-die. Nyakuiy has taken back her name and in so doing, reclaimed her-Self and her mighty indigenous heritage. Her story inspires hope, strength and courage, and serves as a loving reminder that there is immense power in allowing yourself to be exactly who you are."

—Jennifer Juvenelle, author of *Daughter of Belia*

"Tiara Shardé offers an important and potent path to cultural, family, and individual healing through the body's capacity for sensual pleasure. She throws off the concrete slabs that cover our ancestors' secrets and replaces the misguided religious spiritual bypass of someone else doing your work for you, with a guide to cultivating the divine feminine energy that can metabolize and transform it on your own. Her call to align with our divinity through pleasure, ecstasy, and joy is essential to moving out of pathology, secrecy, and suffering into health, love, and co-creation."

—Bruce and Leah Kalish, Television/Film Actor, Writer and Producer, Family Constellation Facilitators, LA

"Lettie Sullivan is one of the most important emerging voices in the realm of anti-racism and women's empowerment. She has a unique way of unifying all people and helping readers transcend pain. The authors in this book are creating a new paradigm of healthy, loving relationships with each other and our planet. A must-read!"

—Sara Connell, bestselling author of *Bringing In Finn*

"Oh, what a beautiful web you weave. I thoroughly enjoyed reading this book. The complexities of a melanated queen simply trying to navigate the oceans of life. Strong, bold, intelligent, talented, beautiful, and oh so vulnerable at the same time. Simply wanting to be seen and recognized not for who they think you are but for who you are. This speaks to generations of unaddressed trauma. Generations of people suffering in silence, fractured families, often too proud to reveal their vulnerabilities. 'PTSD wha dat? No! No treatment for you and me, still we rise.' Brilliant."

—Lin Strong

"Authentic, raw, and uninhibited, Jermira's journey is one of self-reflection, growth, and resilience. She shows us how an inner change in a single individual can cause a change in her environment. She reveals how her practice of Nichiren Buddhism with the Soka Gakkai International has allowed her to not be a victim of her past but rather step into her future and take actions that liberate her from the shackles of her own destiny. I was deeply moved and encouraged by her journey."

—Lisa Barnes Young, PhD

"From a nightmarish dystopia close to our current reality, to a young planet where ancient memories thrive in pits of bio-illuminated plasma, Chante Zupancic's 'Yin the Beginning' grounds the reader's body while blowing their mind. A soothing meditation on the power of blackness, yin energy, and the imagination, the story is medicine for our era of social and climate collapse: 'We didn't know we had the map inside our skin, inside our blood, within our voice. . . nothing is ever truly lost, just reimagined.'"

—Kate Duva

FLOWER *of* LIFE PRESS

Ancient-Future Unity: Reclaim Your Roots, Liberate Your Lineage, Live a Legacy of Love

Copyright © 2021 Flower of Life Press, LLC

Book design by Kirsten Livingston, kliving63@gmail.com
Cover Design by Astara J. Ashley, floweroflifepress.com
Cover artwork by Katia Herrera, creativepowerr@gmail.com

To contact the publisher, visit floweroflifepress.com
Library of Congress Control Number: Available upon request.

Flower of Life Press, Old Saybrook, CT.
ISBN-13: 978-1-7371839-2-1
Printed in the United States of America

This book is dedicated to every person
whose voice has ever been suppressed—

May you find liberation
in sharing your authentic truth

Contents

The Emergence of
Ancient-Future Unity

BY DANIELLE ASHÉ

"If you find a book you really want
to read but it hasn't been written yet,
then you must write it."

—*TONI MORRISON*

When I received the vision for this project, I was in awe of its multidimensionality.

Ancient-Future Unity was inspired by my experience as a Flower of Life Press co-author in a collaborative book called, *Set Sail: Shine Your Radiance, Activate Your Ascension, Ignite Your Income, Live Your Legacy.*

During my journey to becoming a published author, I envisioned how beautiful it would be to create a collaborative book that featured the voices of black women and women of color.

As all of the pieces and layers revealed themselves, a truly evolutionary picture of infinite potential and possibility began to form:

Sisterhood
Collaboration
Co-creation
Community
New Economy
Entrepreneurship
Healing
Legacy
Lineage
Leadership
Diversity
Expression
Power
Representation
Solidarity. . .

and so much more.

This vision wove together so many threads—in a way that I had never seen before.

The beginning of a movement, the rise of a new paradigm.

An experiment with a mind of its own, that at times required us to step out of the way and let the Divine lead.

As the #BlackLivesMatter and the anti-racism movement came to the forefront of current affairs, I felt that these social movements were not addressing many of the deeper aspects of the human condition necessary to bridge the factions, not only between races, but also among black women.

After years of personal study and practice in the fields of social justice, spirituality, and consciousness, this felt like the perfect time to move forward with this project.

It is the richness and complexity of our diverse, lived experiences and the courage to share our stories that contain the power to bring our hearts closer together, on a personal level that runs deeper than the impact of systemic racial policies, ideologies, frameworks, or social theories.

This book is a celebration of the diverse perspectives and lived experiences of black women coming together in unity and solidarity.

As we join forces to share our stories and expand our reach with this message of unity, we've envisioned the book rippling outwards, like the symbol of the Flower of Life, with limitless expansion: from book circles, to libraries, to classrooms.

This felt like a similar intention to the anthologies that I read in my "Reading Black Women's Writing" course in college, with stories that changed my life and helped me to better understand myself and the world.

Ancient-Future Unity was designed to create a sacred container for each author to grow as a leader.

Each woman who contributed a story to this collection underwent her own initiation as she reflected upon what stories she would reveal and how to put her lived experience into words.

For most of the co-authors, publishing their words alongside the words of other women was an initiation into deeper truth and claiming more of their creative power.

For some, it was a journey of worthiness.

For some, it was a journey of sisterhood.

For some, it was a journey of self-discovery.

For some, it was a professional opportunity.

For some, it was about legacy.

For some, it was all of the above.

This is an anthology that can be passed down from generation to generation as a way of sharing and preserving our stories and the timeless, universal wisdom that they carry.

It also ignites the possibility that the daughters or granddaughters of the authors published in this first edition will also be published in this series someday, and so on, and so on.

One of the most magical things about collaborative books is seeing how the title of the book comes to life for each author and becomes the thread that weaves all of the stories together. The titles are chosen early on and tend to directly and/or indirectly influence each of the authors' stories and their journey.

The title for this book came through loud and clear and speaks to what is emerging and most alive within the collective consciousness. Similar themes had been at the forefront of my own journey, but little did I know that I would be initiated to fully embody the meaning behind these words. As the title of "Ancient-Future" came to me, it felt incomplete. . . and then Astara brought in the word "unity"—and the rest is *herstory*.

Whoever you are and wherever you are, our prayer and intentions are that the truth of our stories will touch your heart and Soul.

We offer this book as a catalyst to activate the frequency of ancient-future unity internally and externally, individually and collectively, as an invitation for you to also Reclaim your Roots, Liberate your Lineage, and Live a Legacy of Love.

I am deeply grateful to Astara for holding the container to birth this book, for her team at Flower of Life Press, and for each of the co-authors who said yes as we all held this vision and underwent the publishing process through the most significant historical event of our time—a global pandemic that has impacted each and every one of us in ways that we could never have anticipated.

We are all truly honored to have captured our stories and completed this book together, to now be able to share this gift with you.

Learn more at: **lovedanielleashe@gmail.com**

Rediscovering the Soul of My Purpose

BY MIRABELLE ADAMU

When I arrived at the JFK airport in the United States of America on a very cold snowy day in January 2000, I barely recalled the fourteen-hour journey from my home country of Cameroon. It was the first time I took a plane, and I didn't talk to anyone other than the agents at the airports and immigration. I had contracted a head cold a day before my departure, and everything was just a blur as I was already late for classes. I was an international student heading to Howard University to study Pharmacy because there was no pharmacy school in Cameroon.

I hadn't seen my mother in seven years, but she picked me up from the airport, and we took the train to Brooklyn. She seemed like a stranger to me. I only spent the weekend in New York City and I had to take the bus the next day to Washington, D.C. My mother had arranged for a friend to pick me up from the bus station and take me to the campus where I would be staying. I had no time to process the change in environment, school, food, people, accent, and myself. All I was conditioned to do was adjust and do well in school.

As a single mother and a babysitter in New York, my mother did a great job, at least from my perspective. My baby sister was three years old, and this was the first time I saw her. I couldn't understand her fast American accent. And it took me a while to adjust my ears to the varying American accents that I would encounter. Now I seriously wonder how my mother intended to pay for my tuition at Howard University without any scholarship or loans.

Howard University required a bank statement of $25,000, but my mother only had $10,000 in her savings account. She spoke with her employer and they were very kind to write an affidavit of support that she worked for them, and they also attached a bank statement of $25,000. That was how I got admitted into Howard University. I completed my pre-pharmacy requirements but was late to submit my pharmacy application, which is only done once a year. So, I had to wait a year before I could start the professional program. Waiting a year was not an option for me as an international student, so I had to move back to New York to live with my mother. I transferred to Long Island University (LIU) and took some humanities classes just to maintain my student visa.

After a year at LIU, my mom could not continue paying my tuition so we decided that I would complete the pharmacy technician program, work, and continue school. By the grace of God, my mother's employer again stepped in and decided to sponsor me for the four professional years of the Pharmacy program at LIU. I graduated from a six-year professional Pharmacy program with a doctorate and no debt or student loans. That was pure Divine grace working through me, but I did not know it. It is now that I see and understand the impact of student debt and the loan crisis in America.

I got married right out of Pharmacy school and was a busy diplomatic housewife in Africa. We lived in Kenya for ten years, then Ethiopia for two years. I'd say I grew up in Kenya, which is where I ventured into the all-consuming world of infertility, in-vitro fertilization, miscarriages, adoption, and finally my son. When my partnership of fourteen years fell apart and I moved to Pine Ridge Indian Reservation in South Dakota in 2017, I was at the deep end of my shadow self and could barely breathe. I knew relationships were supposed to change as we grow and evolve, but mine was stuck in time. There were a lot of personal traumas that I hadn't taken the time to delve into, and it was all surfacing and needing to be acknowledged. I didn't know how—and neither did my emotionally-avoidant ex-husband. So, we ended up divorcing, and I made it my sole mission to heal myself and move out of the state of victimhood. I had forgotten who I was and my purpose in life. I had forgotten the kindness and graciousness shown to me when I first moved to this country. I had forgotten what it means to love and to serve humanity from a place of love. I was living a soulless, superficial life filled with material possessions while trying to find myself and my higher purpose by looking to others for answers.

Moving to work at Pine Ridge was the best decision I ever made personally. It was remote and very far away from my family and friends. I remember feeling a sense of freedom when I first arrived. The wide endless fields, clear blue skies, my own first apartment, a job with wonderful colleagues, and the spirit of the land. I could feel it all. But the reality of my divorce came crashing as I lost both my son *and* my little sister whom I adopted with my ex-husband.

I discovered my inner strength, my power to let go, and forgive and move on. Initially, I saw a therapist. Then I dove into self-help books, podcasts, and YouTube videos. The *aha* moment came when I realized I could not help myself if I didn't know or acknowledge what the problem was. So, I started with my shadow self. I realized that I had been in denial and dishonoring myself for a very long time by not listening to my intuition, feeling like a victim, not knowing how to set boundaries, and by not speaking up and showing up for *me*.

This was the first time I learned to be with myself without any outside influence or agenda. I started listening to Teal Swan videos on YouTube and some of them resonated with me. Then I stumbled upon *The Gene Keys: Embracing Your Higher Purpose* by Richard Rudd and was immediately drawn to it. I loved the contemplative part and learning how to do the inner work by myself. It was not pleasant in the beginning because I had to face my own shadows alone. I had to figure out what nourishes my soul, how I need to be loved, what I was willing to compromise in my life, and deepen my love for nature. I started recognizing patterns of ancestral energy blocks in my family lineage. I was supported in this process by my new tribe and wonderful friend, Susan Beautiful Bald Eagle.

In the process of nurturing myself back to a whole person, I healed the relationship with my mother, which was always fragile and full of blame. I also am more loving to myself and my needs. Letting go of blame, guilt, and shame helped me forgive my father and my ex-husband. As a child, I had no baseline of what a healthy emotional relationship should look like, so I was busy seeking it outside.

In a quest to avoid the mistakes of my parents and to seek security, which I never had as a child, I entered into wrong relationships that were emotionally unfulfilling and I ended up inflicting more scars on myself while holding on tight to a relationship structure built on a shaky foundation. And crumble it did, in a heap of emotional exhaustion. As an introverted child, I was always daydreaming—it was the only time I could forget what was happening around me. I vowed to myself to always speak up about my needs, although this is still a work in progress. In my culture, we are primed to take care of others from a very young age. As a child, you are expected to take care of your younger siblings or cousins. As you grow older, you are expected to continue taking care of them *and* also your parents plus other relatives that need help, usually financially. However, we fail to educate the young ones and youth about knowing their bodies and protecting themselves from danger. As a result, I see and understand what many youths are going through, especially those from unstable homes or those without any positive role models.

One of the lessons I learned from *The Gene Keys* is around my willpower. I have strong willpower, although I need to learn to use it correctly. In the past, I pushed myself mentally to achieve whatever I thought was best for me without listening to my body and intuition. I was in a hurry to accomplish all the material things that I desired as a child. My body was already beginning to give me signals that I ignored: polycystic ovarian syndrome (PCOS), difficulty getting pregnant, miscarriages, and threats of premature delivery. Apart from the physical manifestations of forcing my will, I felt emotionally unsupported and unloved.

My career has always been sporadic as I figured out how to balance a diplomatic life in Africa. Most diplomatic wives either choose to stay home or find a local job with their home Embassies where they can utilize their soft skills to perform other duties. I had just graduated with a Doctorate Degree in Pharmacy, but could not work anywhere in Africa because each country requires licensure. This is the same nuisance that foreign-born practitioners encounter when they emigrate to America regardless of their work experience. I decided to study for a Master's Degree in Public Health so it would be easier to be of service. I enjoy working, and I love exploring different aspects of my job. Working as a pharmacist is very specialized, while working as an Epidemiologist is broader, which I find interesting. At some point in my career, I will really love to be able to combine both career paths so I can better serve in the public health field in a unique way. I studied Pharmacy in the United States, but my love for public health came about while my family was based in Kenya, East Africa. We lived in a small town called Kisumu in Nyanza Province right by Lake Victoria. It's a beautiful town with the Luo dialect being the predominant language spoken. I worked in more than twenty healthcare centers collecting HIV data to evaluate the impact of anti-retroviral therapy (ART) in the area from 2005 to 2009. The findings from the research led to the scale-up of ART services within the region, which was great to witness. This was my first experience seeing the impact of public health work, and I loved it.

Although I enjoyed working, I somehow felt that I had to follow my spouse at the time since he was the primary breadwinner. He was working for the U.S. government, stationed abroad, and as his dependent, I could not find a good-paying job out there. It was during this time that I started feeling anxious about my purpose in life. Initially, my main goal was to establish a safe and secure home for my family. Then I realized I wanted to work and earn a salary that was equivalent to my services.

I started working with the humanitarian non-governmental organization Doctors Without Borders/Medicins Sans Frontieres (MSF). I loved the selfless work that they do globally to provide basic healthcare services to vulnerable populations. It was during this time that I realized I'm a humanitarian at heart—but I still needed to figure out how to balance my love for humanitarian work while supporting myself. However, as I continued changing who I was and discovering my passions, my marriage didn't change. It was stable while I was a stay-at-home mother, but when I went back to work, I realized that my marriage wasn't evolving along with me. It was stagnant.

As I learn to slow down and take pauses in my life, I am more observant of my energy, which in turn helps me to be more patient and intentional with decisions, responses, and choices. The art of contemplation has helped me own the responsibilities of nurturing myself from my childhood wounds and connect back to Source, where I always felt disconnected. I see my life now as the different seasons that I have passed through and will continue to transform without being frightened. I am a tiny part of the whole universe.

By being fully connected to my being and Source, I embrace all my past fears, hurts, disappointments, rejections, failures, rage, anger, lies, infidelities, guilt, shame, and envy. I see where they were coming from, I acknowledge them, and let them go.

I see how interconnected I am to everything and everyone and the impact my decisions and choices have on the whole. Now, I see it more clearly through the sacrifices my mother made to uplift the entire family from poverty and illiteracy. I see it through the love and support of Sarah and Chris, who chose to sponsor me through four years of Pharmacy school. I see it through Benta, who welcomed, loved and cared for me in Kenya when I was struggling with marital infidelity and a difficult pregnancy. I see it through my best friends when we share experiences openly without fear, guilt, shame, or fear of rejection. I feel it through my ancestors from the pain, strength, and resilience that they shouldered in their lifetime. Now, I see it in everything and everyone around me. My greatest hope is to integrate this new awareness into my everyday life at work, with family and friends, and in future relationships.

Mirabelle Adamu works at the Pine Ridge Indian Reservation in South Dakota. She is a humanitarian at heart and passionate about health equity for all World citizens regardless of creed, color, gender, or nationality. As a very curious being, Mirabelle is interested in energy flow and healing. She believes that as humans, we have not yet started exploring the great potential of the human body/mind capacity as a species. As we become more aware of our nobility and inherent powers, many conditions that afflict humanity, such as diseases, greed, fear, and extremes of wealth and poverty will be eradicated.

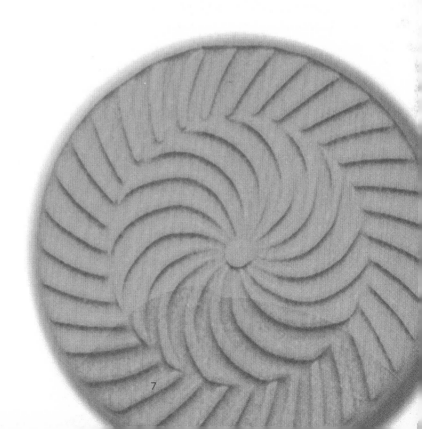

Being Labeled Black, Lesbian, and Conscious!

BY REV. ANIM BEY

Growing up was a bittersweet experience. There's so much I can list in between these blank pages that it could fill your heart with rage and force a burning need to vindicate. But I don't want to send you into tantrums that are to be overcome so that the development of my journey can be highlighted. I'm not here to insert a tug-of-war into your heart or to initiate you to judge what is deemed as fair or unfair in my journey. Each character who played a role in my life's story has intuitively agreed before incarnation into the flesh to usher me onward to my current status. As impossible as it may seem, before my incarnation into the physical realm, I agreed to go *through the fire* too. So now I'm here! I say through the fire because the growing process has an equal impact on both me, the antagonist, and them, the protagonists. It is within each moment of conjunction that we learn either how to expand or how to contract through our core premise. Someone moves forward and someone stays complacent to process a new order or way of being. That's the fire, which I'm okay with. My only concern with this fire is to show how the labels weigh heavy on my free spirit. What I come to share is the illumination of the transformation process.

At this moment, someone reading this is wishing they could tell their story out loud. Somewhere across the hemisphere, there's a voice trapped in the ethers and suspended in space by the curses that they themselves agreed to due to their own lack of inner guidance or self-acknowledgment.

I've come to free you! If you are the one, know that your voice is heard. I am a vessel created by you to vibrate your freedom in a time of need. Know that there is nothing greater than You: The Soul/Sol! My place here is to simply document my truth in writing (right-ing/riting) and to liberate myself in you.

Before now, I didn't think my experiences were relevant enough to bring into the public's collective consciousness. There were times I felt less than myself based on someone else's perspective of how I should be compared against who I AM. Often I silenced my voice as a way of peacemaking. It took me some time to shake off the world's conditioning to embrace that I'm not much of a trained actress; I can't fake not being hurt when I am. Sure, I can laugh to mellow the pain, but there's a part of me that carries a sword to cease any transmission of insecurities inwardly or outwardly. So, I write to liberate myself in you. My lesson on this plane is to embrace my whole being against all odds, and it can feel damn good when realized. My journey is not to slow down for anyone's recognition but to live my truth so that I shed light on subjects that have been hidden in plain sight for those who are willing to look closely.

Today, I walk inebriated by my higher guides, knowing that it is imperative to be authentic in order to navigate my own narrative. However, if the truth of others along my journey resides in facts that may not be recognizable by their own self-doubt, self-hatred, or personal frustrations, let it be so. I invoke the spirit of true self-love so that they may transmute any low vibrating thought-forms to its highest integrity. More so, I come to express the absolute truth of any matter, as the truth itself, nothing more or less. The people who once owned my discomfort, afflictions, and tribulations were all actors who played a role in helping me to accept my inner God-dess. I use the title *Goddess* not because it's the latest form of colloquialism that I could insert to grab your attention, but because it embodies both the masculine and feminine aspects of who we are, God-dess. It took these opposing, yet contrasting forces in my life to allow me to be included in this book, writing to you about being labeled Black, lesbian, and conscious—an ancient lifestyle brought back into the awareness of humanity for future recognition.

If one looks closely, they will see by their own self-assurance that titles are nothing more than codes that can serve as a barrier between the conscious and the subconscious mind to perpetuate continued separation outside of Divine reasoning. It truly takes one to know him—or herself—to know that titles are to be respected as a projection of someone else's coding and may or may not be related to who you fully are or able to comprehend. When I came to this acceptance, I recognized how to bypass codes in order to see myself accordingly. Our physical forms are minuscule in comparison to the greatness of who we really are.

As I write to you in my female form, my masculine energy comes out to dance with the cosmos to document what many have been misinterpreted, bastardized, and shunned due to the rejection of appearances. It is baffling that through all of the impactful events on this earthly plane, the world continues to be blinded by titles, appearances, and empty words that yield no resolution to our collective insanity.

You may be wondering, what on God's green earth is she talking about?! Well, first let me backtrack to my childhood so that I can come full circle with the message encoded in my title. As stated, growing up was a bittersweet experience. As a child, gender never mattered to me. To me, it was an animated concept that had no validation in my world. What I resonated with as a child is that energy took form over the body. So, the body was the last thing to be accepted. However, what was clear is that forcing sexuality on anyone is just as diabolical as rape and there are limitations to be respected. So, why would I choose this experience, you ask? Same as you choose to wake up and to live another day. To illuminate, to overcome, to master your lower vibration, and to take ownership of your natural self.

Growing up, I was taught male is male, and female is female, and that a male and a female are supposed to be together and no other way. My intuition was stating otherwise. Consequently, in my confusion about my differences, I tested the world's theory and then my own. I came to realize that the hype of being with anyone for any particular reason was an absurd concept, yet I lived the absurdity anyway. As I noticed the conflict in my heart, I stumbled upon the knowledge that I was born in a time where the divine masculine energy had been weakened and struggled to keep his mother alive, so she duplicated her son in me. As I was growing into this acceptance, word of mouth dictated the arrest of my development before I could speak.

Somehow, those low vibrations swarmed in my world as it did in theirs. This was a bright light moment when I saw the world as if I was going out of my body only to re-enter anew. My own body was being taken over like property and handed to whoever called it near. I combed my adolescence over a thousand times to figure out what was the final blow to initiate such a dramatic internal transformation. I walked on in my journey slowly re-membering myself.

Partially grounded in my being, Spirit took me to another place in my heart called *codependency*—a place where emotional needs paraded and masked themselves as whatever they deemed to be. During this critical time in my life, I craved the nurturing of a woman, and by the age of thirteen, I called my first experience near. This is when I understood Universal Principles. I knew I had the ability to craft my world the way I saw fit. This is what I was gifted with, as were you. My task was to master my "Fe." The initiation into womanhood led the calling for me to replicate myself at the age of twenty-three. This is the time my womb harnessed its purest energy and attracted a willing partner near. Dancing to my call was the right male energy needed at that time. He was the one to bring me Light from Above. And so he did!

A few months after the birth of our Son, I was forced to face the lack of my partner's upbringing with my lack of experience in a male and female connection. I chose to learn how to connect with the Divine Male in his innocence by raising our young King, so that he may help heal the wounds of scorned men worldwide. Please do not pervert my message to mean anything more than what's stated. Instead, picture a male so comfortable with himself that speaking against any group other than himself is merely beneath his intelligence. That's my Son/Sun. That's the power of the Womb-Man, God-ess, and the Divine un-divided.

You see, everything about myself, I tested against the proclaimed "right way" and found my true divine way of being. This is not to say that what you serve is correct or incorrect. I'm just simply saying, what I was taught and what was for me were two different routes. And no one could teach me that. I had to walk through the fire that came in the form of crude remarks, abusing, and being abused, occasionally called among the whispers *another dumb black homeless girl,* and being attacked and left for dead on the streets, all in order to find my Light.

My light, as you wonder, is to know that I AM not black. I do not see beings as if I'm picking out a crayon from the box. I AM Born of MY ANCESTORS' spirit, manifested in a DIVINE VESSEL that allows the assimilation of the Sun's rays to vibrate through my DNA. My Light is to resonate all frequencies on one vibe, so that you may know the truth in you when you see me. Any restrictions that you perceive in my presence are that of indentured thoughts steeped in captivity and bondage, which is not related to any of my Descent. I come to keep the sacred covenant sacred, so to define my experience by anyone's standards is a misnomer, just like the physical forms to which we ascribe.

For that awareness alone has earned me the title of Lesbian. Sworn by some to be at the bottom of the totem pole and has even been cast as one with sexual prowess, here to consume all women in the world. Know that the creation of all life is a sexual act and the ongoing of it is intimate by nature. So to deem me as separate from the divine act of life is artificial by far. My journey is not to consume any woman by sexual seduction but to appeal to her total being by letting her know she is free to live and manifest her truth on all levels. She is the manifester of life, and NO ONE outside of herself has the power to take that away or capture her Divine Essence for themselves.

For that, I, as a woman have become a sport to Les Miserables. For centuries, they have hunted but never could find a more favorable comparison to "my kind." As the old adage spoken by my Grandmothers, Eardy May Green, Polly Ann Norward, and Joan Scurry, "there is nothing new under the Sun." So, the world must therefore accept that with my presence. Instead, violence and separation have become the most popular response favored throughout history, but they have not provided any solutions to date. Or is the world looking for solutions?

My light is not for the taking. It's never given as an option to solve anyone's personal conflict. I'm simply sharing it to help guide you toward self-acceptance and to know you must succumb to the truth of yourself in order to elevate and illuminate. Some go peacefully, some not as willingly. Either way, it's a journey that cannot be ignored or denied. And it took me to reproduce my sol reflection in my Son to understand this closely.

The sacredness of my true being is an ancient practice only known to a few. It is passed around by many names but understood by only those who are divinely selected. This art is so sacred that I will not give a title to prevent further botchery. The nature of it has been dissected over millennia by those looking for a cheap thrill while others wish to strike gold. Its true name has been kept from the tongues of man, so that spoken language is dissolved on the tongues of those who dare to defy its boundaries. Therefore, my light reaches through the dark corners of many minds to help them understand the meaning of ANIM. I AM here to bring you into your light, so that fear no longer resides within your cellular memory. Meanwhile, allowing its healing to radiate throughout the planet. Understand, I AM not dependent on physical stimulation from a woman or a man to sustain my purpose but can use my sexual power to take others beyond this realm to find their light within. And for that, they label me a Conscious Black Lesbian Woman.

Founding Minister of Ankh Ministries, **Anim "Torrie C." A. Bey** is an Ordained Metaphysical Minister, Reiki Master, Ra Sekhi Practitioner, and Certified Medium. She combines her skills as a digital, visual, and musical artist with her intuitive abilities and talent for creating healing products with Earth Mother's gifts. She is the producer and host of Planet 9 Radio, formally known as HMi Radio. Under her Spiritual product line, she provides Reiki/Ra Sekhi and intuitive  readings, ear candling, spiritual and ritual consults, powerful meditations, healing teas, candles, personal care products, and metaphysical educational courses. She is a teacher of the Celestial Arts and a 3rd Eye Development coach.

Learn more at: **ankhministries.org**

Special Gift

Level One 3rd Eye Development Course

Inquire by emailing code: AFU

Triggers, Transformation, and Triumph

BY SAMMI BLAQUE

The Future...

Sister let me dance with you

Hand in hand with you

Breasts heaving

Tongues teasing

Veils lifted and leaving

Let me smile with you

Song singing

Lips between our hips

Dripping

This is a reclaiming

We are taking back our joy

Our god-given right to pleasure

On the lips

In between the hips

Sister, I forgive you

When you didn't realize

How they weaponize

Sisterhood

Making us competition
When we stand on the same side
Hand in hand,
Eye to blessed eye.
Let me dance with you,
My Sister!
Come with me
into a promised land
Where we are the milk and honey
And they give us our flowers regularly
Sister. . .
I reclaim US
and celebrate you
Your intellect
The way you weave
Words through time and space. . .
The way you dance
Building up visions of empires
I celebrate you.
Singing praises that lift you to the heavens
So God May kiss you
And your skin darken just a little bit more
I reclaim that Black is a Blessing
And May you
Feel free
for no reason at all
Smile a little longer
Scream a little harder

Laugh a little louder
May you take up space
Filling the room with your aura
Making everyone take notice of
Your beauty
Your essence
Your beautiful yin presence
For no reason at all.
No performance necessary
No prerequisite for praise
Sister, your existence is a blessing
Let your being radiate rays
Of golden light
You are a child of the sun
Mother of the moon
Dearest sister,
this is a reclaiming
Of my love for you.

Trigger Warning.

This is a story of empowerment.

This chapter is dedicated to my Gramma who died January 21, 2021. And though I was an '80s baby, for as long as I can remember my Grandmother was always old. When I was young her curls were dark steely grey, with sterling silver streaks. Her wrinkles were deeply set, earned after years of laughter, tears, and raising eight kids. Growing up in Southern California underneath swaying palm trees, she was the wisest woman I knew. My best friend and my hero. At that age, the sun was always shining in California, and my personality seemed to match perfectly. I was a natural performer who always kept a smile on my face. I was in dance studios for Ballet, Tap, Jazz, and Gymnastics by the time I was three. And though I loved to dance on hardwood floors in front of the mirrors, on stages, or around the house, my favorite place to be was at my Gramma's feet where I would tell her all my secrets. Her hands braided my hair, scratched my back, and stung me with a slap when she deemed necessary. My eyes sparkled with admiration for my Gramma. I used to think she would live forever.

In the early 90s, I started to notice what Gramma said about me. Every day after my mom and older sister had left for the day, my Gramma and I would watch the Price Is Right, Jeopardy, and Wheel of Fortune on our TV; a big wooden box with a turn dial that sat on the carpet. Whenever we watched game shows it seemed like she was always right. I was a sincere, happy kid, who spoke in earnest. I told her that she should go on the shows and win all the money since she always knew all the answers. My Gramma always used to say I was a "fast and smart" child. Though I didn't know exactly what that meant at the time, I could tell by her graveled tone it wasn't a compliment. Confused and throat tight with embarrassment, hearing those words had frozen me. "Didn't she like that I was smart or fast?" I wondered, as I took her words and stuffed them inside of me, hoping I could hide them away.

I was very smart growing up. While my sister acted as a rebel, I was an honor roll student and quickly learned how to overachieve and excel. I spoke and won oratorical contests and received awards at not just a school level but from my district as well. I also saw things that no one else even dreamed of. I had nightmares that no one else could handle. I got initiated into orgasm very young. It's just the dharma of my path. By the age of eleven I was molested by my mother's live-in boyfriend, Don, for two years. Yes, Gramma was right again. I had to grow up real fast. And this cataclysmic event presented me with my first-ever grown-up decision. And I found myself at a crossroads.

Don was the kind of hero that made ladies swoon, and made men get hard-ons in an admiration that bordered on lust. He was over 6-feet tall and over 200 lbs. with a gun collection he loved to show off. He was a veteran of the Los Angeles Police Department and almost lost his life in the line of duty. He loved to tell a story about how the doctors said that if the bullet were up two inches higher he would have died. I remember how he would unbutton his shirt with a chuckle during back-yard barbecues to reveal the scar to the men who wanted to see it. The first time I ever felt seen was by this grown man, who was supposed to be loving and romancing my mother.

The day he preyed on me, I slipped into a familiar trauma response: freeze. I didn't know how to react. I didn't know what to do. Passively, I complied. He took me by the hand and led me. And though I trembled and it shook down to my core, I obediently followed.

From that day forward, my life completely shattered and who I used to be began slipping away. My mind spun like a tornado. What would happen if I exposed this? Would mom believe me? Would anyone believe me? How could I get away?

Around this time, El Niño sent heavy rainfall and devastation to Southern California. Thick grey storm clouds hung over our heads every day, blocking out the sunshine we were all used to. The storms were relentless. I remember sitting next to the window, as rain pelted the glass in front of me. I watched in silence as my mother drove away, leaving me alone with Don again. I was still, and everything was quiet inside and around me. Yet, my heart thumped loudly in my chest, my breath fast and shallow. I couldn't cry. I couldn't run. It was as if I was cemented to the floor. As her car disappeared, I knew what was coming and that it was just the beginning...

While it was raining outside, inside my being I stood rain-soaked at that crossroads without an umbrella. To my right was the road of speaking out and telling my mom and family. Time seemed to stand still as I paused and waited in the rain for the right moment to speak out, when suddenly that moment arrived. My rebellious sister, ten years older than me, had her own moment with Don. He found an excuse to be alone with her and made his move. Running his icy fingertips along her inner thigh as they rode in his black Corvette, he asked if she liked that. Her response was a violent "No." As she told her story I felt this explosive joy and relief. I thought, "Finally! I'll tell Mom, too!"

I thank God for my sister. She had the courage to do what I couldn't. I remember when she came to mom with her story. She stood at the front door, yelling through tears at Mom about what had happened. I watched from the kitchen and stood up, ready to walk up and say "Me, too," when mom said, "I don't believe you. He told me you'd say that. You're always causing trouble." I felt a frosty chill go up my spine, and once again I froze. I felt the anger, betrayal, sadness, and hurt that radiated from my sister. Everything shattered like glass around me, and my heart collapsed as they continued to argue, my mom defending our abuser. I couldn't take hearing my mom say those hurtful things to me, nor the embarrassment. In a flash, I turned to the left and chose the path of silence.

I walked silently along that path every day for two years. And though I chose to walk that path to protect myself from isolation, shame, and embarrassment, I came to see that the secrets I kept inside me ended up isolating me anyway. The secrets fueled the shame and trapped me tighter than I could have ever have imagined. I had no idea how to explain to my mom that my young eleven-year-old body was regularly being ripped open by powerful orgasms at the hands of her boyfriend. I had no idea how to explain that it felt so good, even though I knew it was wrong. We never talked about sex in any meaningful way. And when I brought up the topic of sex or boys, it was quickly shut down. I didn't think I could tell anyone, not her, my sister, or my Gramma. While I once loved taking center stage and capturing everyone's attention, I now longed to disappear. Gramma's comments that I was "fast" started to make sense, and I decided to become invisible.

The thing about invisibility is that it's safe because you're not really showing up. You're like a ghost or specter. It's like playing a background character in a movie where you're supposed to be the star of the show! In dance we have this concept of "marking it," versus "full out." During practice, as you're learning, most of the time you're just marking it. You're committing the routine to memory and blocking out your movements on stage. But once the lights, make-up, and costumes are on, it's show time! That's when you're supposed to dance full out. Leaving it all on the floor for people to enjoy. Maybe you can relate to not playing full out.

For me, after years of abuse and being a ghost, not showing up became a way of life. I let go of any cares I had. I became carefree, but the destructive kind of carefree that has you walk out into traffic without looking both ways first. "What was the point of it all?" I wondered. "Why should I care so much in a world that doesn't care about you or your feelings?" The veils had been stripped away and I saw life for what it was and it all felt so unfair. Suddenly I became a rebel, too. The only thing that mattered to me, and the only thing that kept me committed to coming home every day, was my dog Chaka Zulu. Chaka was a purebred Akita, a gift from Don. Chaka was a loyal and loving friend. His fluffy fur and comforting cuddles kept me sane during that time. Other than caring for him, I just wanted to float through life, forever marking it, without ever truly showing up or performing for anyone.

That became my biggest downfall—the pattern of not caring about myself, not showing up for myself, and not performing to the best of my abilities. After all the California rains and storms cleared away, the only thing left in my world was ice. My heart felt like it had been ripped out and suddenly I was the Tin Man from *The Wizard of Oz*. Cold. Hard as metal. Unfeeling. Numb. Getting stuck so often. I stopped caring. I stopped caring about school. I stopped caring about dance—one of the few natural talents that brought me joy. My life didn't have room for joy anymore. I became a vessel filled part of the way with pain, and a lot of that pain belonged to a full-grown adult male who pushed it inside my skinny 11-year-old body. The hardest part was that I stopped caring about myself.

I was in agony, and nothing mattered anymore. I put myself in dangerous situations—I didn't care if I got hurt. I gave myself away carelessly to other men. I took rides from strangers on the street. Nothing felt real anymore. Not the pain or even the consequences of my actions.

I stopped being me. I started being half me, half pain. Half in, half out. Halfway checked out. Almost never present. Not even knowing what presence was. I lost touch of what I wanted. I ignored what I needed because I didn't think anyone would help me. Soon, I didn't even know what I needed anymore. I lost touch with who I was.

I stopped dancing. I gave up on myself. I quit. I isolated myself. Closing myself off from everything and everyone. Afraid to be hurt. Afraid to be seen. Living in a dark fiery hell of my own making. It was through this secret, silent, shameful pleasure that I lost my voice.

Soon after my 13th birthday, for reasons totally unrelated to me and what I endured for two years, my mom and Don broke up. He left, taking the only refuge I had, my dog Chaka, with him. I felt so confused. At some of my darkest moments the only one who saw me and paid attention to me—the only one who gave me what I wanted the most was my abuser. And deep down. . . while it was happening, I have to admit. . . I enjoyed it. I enjoyed being the center of his world. I enjoyed that he would move heaven and earth to spend time alone with me. I used to watch the bulge in his pants harden and push out as he would call the school and tell them I would be staying home sick today. Just the thought of me and what he was gonna do with me excited him. And I loved it. I loved the attention. It was the thing I wanted most, and what no one else seemed to want to give me.

It ingrained a strange push/pull in me. I grew up performing. . . and while I relished attention, applause, and praise, I didn't want the shame and embarrassment of coming forward about the sexual abuse I suffered. That particular flavor of attention was one I had tried and spit out because I didn't like the taste. It locked me into a weird space of choosing invisibility when the only thing I've ever been good at is being seen. It also confused my emotions. Orgasms are powerful and pleasurable experiences. Don helped me have many orgasms over the years that felt so deliciously good. But the flavor of those experiences left a bad taste in my mouth. I knew they were wrong. Even though my body reacted appropriately to the stimuli, my mind wouldn't let me enjoy it. After abuse, I almost never reached orgasm. And as I continued to grow, I found that I was attracted to tall, muscular men like my abuser. Sex while I was mentally checked out, almost never orgasming, became the norm. The pattern had been laid, and I began living out my karma.

Despite those sexual experiences, I still got married and conceived and gave birth to my daughter. Her emergence was like shining a bright light directly in my eyes after years in the dark; I felt dizzy and blinded by her beauty. She was an angel on Earth. Yet, I knew that I was still stumbling to adjust to the responsibility of motherhood. The turning point came one day when she was less than one year old. She was crying, nothing I did seemed to soothe her. I was struggling to get dinner made, as she demanded my attention. In a moment of frustration, I screamed. My shriek scared her even more, and her cries intensified. I collapsed in a puddle of helplessness and as I did, I saw her face. Suddenly clarity washed over me. I recognized the face she was making. She was in pain—MY pain, to be specific. The pain I put on her. I knew I had to be a better mother for my daughter.

I looked at my relationship with my mother. She was a woman of strong work ethic, and a strong resolve to achieve. I get my taste for adventure and spontaneity from her. And her dreamy sign of Pisces always led her to falling in love with many men, many times throughout her life. She was always a hopeless romantic like that. And when I was a kid, I got that from her too. As much as I love my mother and appreciate all the many ways I am like her, after her relationship with Don, I decided that I most wanted to be myself. I forgave my mom well into my twenties when I finally had the courage to tell her what really happened to me. Apart from choosing to be me, I knew I wanted to be the kind of mom my daughter could come to—a mother who prepared her for the changes that were to come with her body and desires, all while keeping her safe and protected. That was a curse I very deliberately set out to break.

At that point in my journey, I didn't consciously know much about breaking curses. I hadn't been to church in years, so, the only thing I could do was go to my family physician. My husband was a soldier in the United States Army, so Tricare had us covered. But I had to call and wait

25

weeks to even be seen. The packed waiting room always made me feel anxious that me or the baby would catch something, especially in wintertime Colorado Springs. I pushed my daughter's stroller and filled out the paperwork so that I could be seen by the doctor. By the time my name was called my stomach was in knots and I felt really scared.

I was triaged under fluorescent overhead lights. And taken back to see my doctor—a slightly dismissive white man named Chris. Regardless, I explained what was happening, shared my fears, pains, and shameful explosive feelings. Advocating for myself as best I could. He diagnosed me with Postpartum Depression, prescribed me antidepressants, and opiates for the pain. I flirted dangerously with the drugs. More than once, my husband came home to find me passed out while my daughter crawled through the apartment unsupervised. I went back to the doctor—advocating for myself again. Asking to be taken off meds, fearing addiction, and demanding that we find something that works for me!

Dr. Chris relented with a sigh. He recommended therapy. After multiple google searches and phone calls, I found someone who would take my insurance and accept new patients. I scheduled a babysitter and began seeing Dr. Baron. She went to the same university for grad school that I did for undergrad. I saw her for two years, talking in-depth about everything in my past and all my hopes for the future. We talked and talked, and though it was therapeutic being listened to, I was still struggling with my mood, my weight, my marriage, and all the pain that I carried in my body. Pregnancy really cracked me open like an egg, and all my demons seemed to be spilling out. Physically, I was at my heaviest—188 lbs., which for my petite dancer frame was excruciating. I longed for more. I wanted more. I wanted something that would get me there faster. All I knew was that I wanted to be there. I wanted relief! So, I went back to my doctor again.

He sat across from me and studied my face as I spoke. He grabs my chart and begins flipping through pages, looking at all the other recommendations and various medications he's already prescribed. He finally closes the folder with a sign, and says, "Why don't you try something else? You should try yoga." The thought had never occurred to me. I had never taken a yoga class before. But I had taken dance. And I was a good enough dancer, I was confident that I could do it. But I was also skeptical. Meditation, yoga, and all that—It was *woo woo*, and I didn't think it was for me. My spirituality was based in Christianity. Could I really do yoga? What would it mean? I had so many questions. But, my doctor insisted, and honestly, so many things were going wrong that I thought, what could I possibly have to lose? I'm glad I asked because something magical began to happen.

Like magic, before my eyes, my life began to undergo a total transformation. Where once I was angry, reactive, and full of rage, I became calmer and slow to anger. I decided to go all in on yoga—no half-assing it! After a few months of managing my pain with yoga, and with my doctor's blessing, I got off my meds completely. I got into the best shape of my life and lost over 60 lbs. I was skinnier than I was before I got pregnant. And it set me down a path of personal development that had me look at the weeds taking root in my garden and helped me dig down in the dirt and pull them out. Hypnotherapy, Reiki, Tarot, Abraham Hicks, and Meditation became my lifeline. I even delved deeply into inner child work, shadow work, and the Akashic Records. In 2015 it was revealed that I was a bodhisattva in service to the Divine Feminine, and life took an interesting turn, even though I didn't fully understand what it all meant. As my perspective changed, so did I. And that was just the beginning.

Something else really startling emerged from all the psychic clearing and healing I did; it was something I wasn't even intentionally trying to do. My relationships began to change and get better. My husband and I split in the midst of all this transformation, and romantically I turned a corner on the path that revealed a beautiful oasis there for me to explore and enjoy. One day I decided to stop being "good" and start being real. I started meeting men who took me on amazing dates and spoiled me. I started having wonderfully intimate experiences. High value, confident, dominant, alpha men, with vision, intelligence, and grit. CEOs, founders, millionaires, and educated professionals. I had a new date every weekend, and I started to enjoy being seen again. The healing continued to enrich and sweeten my life more and more.

Next thing I know, I manifested a brand-new apartment completely redecorated and sitting next to 700 acres of open, natural forest, while being fucked open to God by ambitious men with big dicks who loved to care for me and buy me gifts. How did I do this? I seriously asked the question because it happened so unintentionally. I wanted to know how I did it! And like I said before, I don't know how to half-ass anything. So, I put my whole ass into figuring out how I was having better relationships, better sex, and just living like a goddess in general. I deepened my devotion to my yoga practice and enrolled at the Institute of Authentic Tantra. I became certified by the American College of Sexological Science, and became a love coach. Everyday my reality confirms my intuitive knowing and the path unfolds beneath my feet with a sweetness like ripe strawberries.

Looking back on my life, I marvel at what had to be overcome to reach this point. I'm often reminded of the Sammi from twenty-two years ago. My eyes mist, because at 11-years-old, feeling isolated and invisible, I don't think she would have ever imagined herself being seen, loved, adored, ravished, and so deeply cared for. I don't think she would have imagined loving sex, let alone talking about it. I don't think she could ever fathom loving herself as much as I do now. Learning to advocate for myself, stand up for myself, hold myself accountable, and become committed to continuous growth became demonstrations of self-love, just as much as bath bombs, and sugar scrubs. Every hurdle was jumped and the transformation made it all worth it in the end.

I went from overweight, angry, brokenhearted, and physically in pain, to living like a goddess. Silk robes, champagne, candlelight, fresh flowers, dance parties, brunch, and date nights. Calm kisses, communication, and healthy co-parenting with my babies. I take pleasure in being a mom, and from being alone. In short, I liberated myself. I let go of everything that weighed me down, and now I'm back to feeling like sunshine and champagne bubbles. I experience the union and ecstasy of the divine from moment to moment. I found a love that I know will last a lifetime; the one with myself.

I want to link hands with one million women who are ready to end their struggle with being "good" so they can start being real. Real with their desires. Real with their dreams. So they can start living them and having them. Women who are tired of not orgasming with their partners. Women with low libido who seemed to lose that spark of desire a while ago. Women who feel like caged birds but are finally ready to be unlocked and sing. Women who wanna get their groove back!

Rare Bird
Hey there, Bird.
You've always been a Rare Bird.
With your feathers flowing
From here to there, Bird.
Once an ugly duckling,
You were told you couldn't fly, Bird.
Nobody liked your color
You was dark and ugly, bird.
Every now and then they asked if you were an Exotic Bird.
They aint neva seen one like you,
That's word.
Looking for your soulmate,
You dance and flap, and twirl.
Looking into the lake
The water reflects so clearly
You find the one you would live
Your life for.
Peacock fan, now goddess it's time to strut.
You prance, and bob,
G'on shake it girl
You are a rare and exotic bird.

© Sammi Blaque

29

Sammi Blaque (She/Her/Goddess) is an award-winning entrepreneur and international love, sex, and relationship expert. She offers no BS relationship advice to spiritualists who want to create conscious relationships and have soul-satisfying sex. She's a Sexologist, yoga teacher specializing in Tantra, and is devoted to helping people make love in all areas of their life. She lives in Colorado, and when she's not talking about sex, you can find her out in nature with her kids, or on the nearest dance floor.

Want to talk about sex with Sammi? Visit **TheVenus.co** to join the conversation!

Special Gift

Trauma is a reality for most. To grow through it, you need healing tools. To support you on your journey I am sharing with you a class I created on EFT (**Emotional Freedom Technique**—better known as Tapping). I share this class with all of my paid clients because it's essential to learn when working deeper with me. Because you're supporting *Ancient-Future Unity*, I am giving away this class at no charge to you! ($97 value)

TheVenus.co/gift

If you want to link hands with me, I invite you to join The Venus Collective. To learn more about joining The Venus Collective, visit **jointhev.co/gift**

Life in Devotion to Creation

BY TRENETI

Infinitely I dance with creation
As infinite as I Am
This dance is eternally liberating
As infinite as I Am
I can never capture the elusiveness
Of this nature
As infinite as I Am
Yet I enjoy chasing her
Long into the night and far within my dreams
For she brings me right here
Every time
As infinite as I Am
These attempts to crystalize myself in finite facets
A muse me.

In Egyptian Arabic the word for artist is fannanah

فنانة انا

The root word for artist is this language is fanaa, and means
infinity. In this sacred ancient language, the artist
is one who creates with infinity.
This resonates with me, deeply.

My whole life I have been in devotion to The Hall of Muses. A place that dwells in the unseen, whispering never-ending fractals of beautiful expressions that can Become. . . if we so chose to allow our vessels to labor and birth them.

My initial relationship with the muses of creativity began when I was a child. I found refuge in creating art. In the temple of my imagination the darkness of the world could not consume me. My communion with art provided a lifeline for me, something I could control, something pure to see myself and God through. Inside the art I found exalted bliss. Five minutes deep in a creative flow can feel like an eternity of interconnectedness. My fascination and obsession with exploring this energy became my antidote, my anti-addiction and my most trustworthy pure spiritual teacher.

The future is now and we are multidimensional Souls that create. There is a myth that teaches young artists that they must choose one form and master it. That if they explore any other forms, they are diminishing their gifts in the initial medium. These forms of art are not called mediums for no reason. They are literally, mediums. . . a bridge between the essence of the muse and it getting into the physical world through us. Different messages and different time periods of our lives call for different mediums, even different muses. They all teach us and heal us in different ways. They all help recollect the pieces of who we really are. The best way to describe the soul is as a techno-color stained glass mosaic with more dimensions that you can count. To think one can explore all of its facets in one form of art is the most basic delusional, linear human thinking one can possibly be possessed by.

We are so much more than we can even comprehend. Over the course of my existence I have proven this to be the truth. I walk the edges of realms and through my artistic expressions I create clear pathways for others to meet me there.

For me, the only thing worth mastering is the art of Being ourselves. Truly. Everything else is a means to that end. With that said I have explored many artistic mediums, fully, deeply, professionally and profoundly. "Go big or go home" is how I have always approached my art. Doing anything else with my time has always brought great physical, mental and emotional agony so monetizing whatever mode of expression that cradles my interest gives me a way to sustain my lifeforce without submitting to the deep entrapments of jobs. I have had my fair share of jobs, don't get me wrong, but those were always moments of recalibration on the journey to harnessing my devotion for The Hall of Muses.

The Dance has always been my primary Muse, all the other Muses that have initiated me feel like extensions of the dance. When I am singing, I am dancing with my vocal cords. When I am producing music, I am creating space for bodies to dwell in their dances. I am also creating the perfect frequency to emanate the dance of my soul to. When I am painting The Dance is what moves the brush and informs the stroke of paint as it runs across the canvas. When I am writing I am dancing with my words on the page, choreographing the movement of your eyes to follow me this direction. . .

. . . And that direction

right

here

To this feeling.

When I am building mandalas on the Earth and I am dancing with the mother. She is showing me how abundant she is and how freely she gives through the stones and plants that she offers to my creation. When I am sculpting beautiful shapes into wire, making adornments and talismans with the minerals of the Earth I am dancing with each bend of the wire and placement of stone. When I grow in my gardens I am dancing with the rhythms of the mother and the patience of her life-giving process. Even in the creation of spaces for people to gather, I am dancing. I am

choreographing an environment that will flow in a certain way to produce a certain dance with the bodies that come to occupy this space.
Even within the most seemingly simple art of being still and holding
space, I am dancing. In this dance, there is always a subtle negotiation,
transference and transmutation of energies occurring.

Voices

She speaks in many voices
The muse has not one face
She hardly has any face at all.
She is more of an energy that wraps herself around you
And whispers, look here.
She moves us and inside of that motion
If we are paying attention, we find ourselves
We learn more about that which created all life
Through the act of creating.
Each muse offers us a key
To unlock another dimension
Of our internal landscape
She consoles us in Soul
Once you drink from the well of her nourishment
You will always return for more.
With her, we heal things that hands cannot reach
With her, we hear things that fall deaf on average ears
With her, we see things too Godly to exist in this world
And with her guidance we bring the essence of these
encounters into manifest.

AN OFFERING

The words that follow this statement are pathways pointing you home to
yourself. Allow them to percolate in your mind. Allow them to unwind
you. Allow them to fuel the spark between you and the act of creating.

Read these poetic musings when you need to feel inspired, centered and connected to what is real. When the amnesia gets you and you forget the big why, let these words bring you back. Read them all or just one at time, as you feel called. If the poem has a * around the title, the words can be found living in a melodic form in one of my songs. Use the key at the end of the chapter to find the names of the songs and stream on your favorite listening platform. Thank you, for receiving.

Simple

A natural return
Meet me in the silence
After the flame of old past
Returns to embers

A faint memory of time burning in the distance
I did not come here to rekindle
I came to redesign

Meet me in the silence
After your heart's gone mad from
Masking these truths
A natural return
is made simple.

Mental Real Estate

Do not waste your time sitting around inside the
minds of others
Being a pawn in their existence, allows them to write your role,
To meet their melodramatic desires.
That sadness is going nowhere
That story is on a loop.
Invest in your own mental real estate
The choice is yours to discover

That happy place none can take
Dwelling within the stillness

Own Savior

Show me
Where it is.
How do I lean in?
Ease around this bend.
Seemingly tight in space again.
Nowhere else to go?
Release enter flow.
As I do less
Justice is able to catch up to me
As I shed the layers of do more
Sudden rapid growth occurs
All in my favor
No other
There can be
No other.
Be thy own savior

Resistance that opens. . .

As I open my heart
I dump out this mess.
It started before the beginning of me
Many wombs ago
Many cycles of chaos later, it still echoes in pain.

For what purpose does it take shape?

The pattern appears to me in the form of a young man trying
to figure himself out. . .
At my expense.

Different faces, same spaces, a little more grace
and a little less patience.
Finally, I see with neutral eyes, very clean.

This is not a wound that can be healed in action.
This is not a wound that can be stitched back
together by a new connection.
Another honeymoon paired with a false sense of 'this one will be
different now,' will do nothing here.
This a wound that has journeyed through time woven
tightly between folds of DNA.
Waiting to be unraveled. . .

A scar of severance, older than mankind,
cyclically converging at the heart.

As I open my heart
I dump out this mess.
The only thing I find wise to resist these days is
gravity pulling my shoulders concave.
I stretch open in resistance, convex.
It makes sense to move in opposition to this.
Because it is the closing and curling in on oneself,
expecting a fatal blow
That attracts it, lets in, so the wounds can activate again.
This time We will stretch in opposition.

Unravel
As I open my heart
I see all those who came before me
A long line of men and women who stumbled over each other
in betrayal, abuse, shame, passion, fear. Resentment, grievance,
debt, violence, peace, love, oppression, beholding, sacrifice,
rebellion, contentment, joy, celebration, perseverance,

resilience, hard choices, faithful synchronicities of all varieties in
pursuit of life, in pursuit of finding the meaning, in pursuit of
filling a void that can only be made whole when we
find our way hOMe.

It started before the beginning of me
This pull towards pain
This void of separation
This dismayed story of loss begins again before it ends.

I took another blow today. . .

Gravity tempts me to cave in
Close down my vessel, lift the icy barricades of
delusional self-protection.

Unravel, press, stretch open in resistance.

To spiral closed is to spiral down.
To spiral down is to become consumed in a vortex of
rippling replays,
Varying characters montaging the same moment.
Until I make the choice. . .
To twist the plot in a new direction making a decision
none before me could,
Prior to conceiving the next generation.
Thus, consumed they became.

I stretch open in resistance; my heart will not be closed today.
Open
I pull my wings back toward my spine.
And pray to God please give me strength.
To keep expanding
Gaining compassion and girth within my wisdom tree.

In the art of radical resilience through radical forgiveness
may I become most masterful.
Here's to a new script in the lineage of my womb.

*Proudly, I stretch open in opposition to carry forth the best of
the mothers and fathers that came before me, not their worst.
May I only embody the strength acquired from our collective
pain without the predisposition to repeat it. May I cradle it in
my arms as a bouquet with our collective wisdom and talents.*

As I open my heart
I pour these energies
In
I imbue myself with codes of excellence
*I awaken the teachings of the rose, her roots wrap around the
edges of my uterus, her thorny bush adorns my center, her petals
bloom the most supple lush flowers in my heart, her fragrance
rises and merges her essence and her wisdom within the
corridors of my mind, it escapes me only to whisper messages of
deep truth through the chambers of my ears.*
It started before the beginning of me
But it ends here. This womb will birth a new cycle.

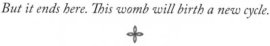

Reclamation Invokes Power
I reclaim my energy across the sands of time
Recollect the pieces fallen scattered across my mind
Whole Again
Complete within my own right
My soul can finally rest inside this temple
Let forgiveness be so simple
In my heart I know we kinfolk
Release the two
Until the one and one
Make three
Union in my energy.
Devoted to the truth
But still enjoy the mystery.
Align

Hone In
Ride the Dragon
Until we Win.
Never afraid to go in the dark
For a light I know I'm the spark.
Let God shine through,
All else be removed
Let God Shine Through
All else be removed.

Believe it to see it

When we look up, we see the stars
When we look down, we see the ground
We see what we are looking for
Believe it and you will see it.

The Initiates

Follow me
To the edge again
Wondering
If you've been listening
Take a chance
Leap before you look
Follow the path
That the masters took

Sphinx
Riddle me
I'll answer
Take me deeper
Mystery keeper
I am ready to see

Space between
My brow line
Open, open breathe

Spirals of green
Unearth between
My sacred wings
Treasures untold hidden
Inside this cave of gold

We are destined to know
And forget it again
Round and round
The wheel we go

Return to center
Return to center
Return to center
Return to center

I know you
Remember us

I know you
Remember trust

You been holding on
To those fears for so long
What if we just jumped
And let 'em all go

Open your hands
Open your hands
Open your healing hands
Feel the energy pouring out and seeping in

Return to center
Return to center

Return to center
Return to center

Return
Return

If Only Then

If I can only
Be present
Where I am presently,
Then there is only one life in me.
Whether my presence is currently in this collectively
perceived realm
Or somewhere all my own
This moment is not recurring
Here is the only place for me
There is no past life
When We are eternally present.
Only ghosts echo in my memories
Modular imprints of what used to be
Subject to manipulation based on
The frequency embracing me
When I cast my inner eye
To glare in its direction.
Even as I describe it
We get swept away
into something that
is not.

If only,
Let's be present

All Said All Done

Lungs
Tongues
When it is all said and done
We will have won.
In breath
In place
Purple nectar, dripping shapes
I find you spinning, opening gates
I swallow to follow you where you lead
Lungs
Tongues
In breath
Between
Syllables,
the potent see.
When it is all said and done
We will have won.

Treneti

SONG KEY:

Reclamation Invokes Power
Poem can be found living as lyrics in the song "Release Work" by Treneti

The Initiates
Poem can be found living as lyrics in the song "The Initiates" by Treneti

Treneti is a vocalist, lyricist, bassist, producer, and visionary. Her artistry is multi-dimensional and keeps the evolutionary journey of human consciousness as a central inquisition in the creative process. When she is not creating music and playing shows, she is working with clients one-on-one and in group courses to  facilitate the rediscovery of authentic expression. With dance as the foundation of her visionary art, career movement always plays a primary role in her expression of sound.

In addition to creating and sharing her own artistic offerings, Treneti is the CEO and Founding Visionary of Soulful Resonance—a mother tree organization centralized in regenerative arts, education and entertainment. Treneti nurtures other multi-dimensional artists and intuitive intelligence educators to embody their gifts and step into the power of their voices as influential instruments of change.

Learn more at **treneti.com, soulfulresonance.com**
IG: @trenetimusic & @soulresonance

Special Gift

Connect with The Initiates in the form of Song:

This song "The Initiates" and many more are available for your listening pleasure at **treneti.com** and when you search Treneti on any major music streaming platform.

Yellow

BY LINDSEY D. CAMERON

Number our days.

Number our days black.

Save one.

Number our days black save one.

Color it yellow.

For hope.

Day 10
December 27, 2010
Temple, TX

"Lindsey," he hoarsely called out, spittle around his mouth, his breath rattling in his chest. His first word in ten days. Shoving away my repulsion to the rotting smell of cold, sweet garlic that oozed out of his pores, I cradled him in my arms, running my hand over his forehead and smoothing his brow.

"Shhh. . . . . ." I murmured, stroking the damp, soft curls that had hung on through all the rounds of chemo. Softly, I start singing in Arabic:

'Allahumma yá Subúhun
yá Quddus
yá Hannánu

yá Mannán.
Farrij Laná Bi'l-Fazli Va'l-Ihsán.
Innaka Rahmanu Mannán[1]

And then silence.

It was over.

Today was yellow.

No matter how many times one says it is "the end" we often don't believe it, squeezing in one last hug, touch, or tender embrace. *"Just five more minutes Mommy!"* the little boy pleads on the swing. *"Just one more day!"* the daughter begs her father, *"Can't you stay with me just one more day?"*

ACT I

Day 0
December 16, 2010
Washington, DC

Casted foot propped onto a coffee table with my wheelchair beside me, I was drifting into a Percocet-induced nightmare when I answered my brother's call.

"Dad was making strange noises, so I went into his room. He wouldn't wake up and was choking. I called 911. They just took him away."

Less than twenty minutes ago my Dad and I had talked. On the phone his voice sounded strong, as usual, and we found something

My father in his police dress uniform circa 1986.

50

to bicker about, as usual. He complained about his three-day headache that his doctors weren't taking seriously. Given his Stage III cancer diagnosis, headaches weren't at the top of the doctor's list of concerns.

My dad (center) on his promotion to Sergeant, circa 1981.

A lifelong DIY-er, he had been chugging coffee and downing twelve Excedrin each day. Given his headache, and to avoid arguing, I decided not to tell him of my bubbling intentions to leave the intelligence community and enter academia. He wouldn't understand why I would want to leave such a "good" job that had always been his dream. We ended the call with an "I love you"—an addendum to our calls since his diagnosis last year.

Twenty minutes later he was gone as I knew him, trapped in a dreamless slumber.

I was the last person to talk to him.

Was his last memory of me?

WINTER, 1986
CHICAGO, IL

My first memory was of him. Sitting on the shiny new red slide in the backyard, in my favorite pink jeans and striped shirt, I watched him walk out the back door and head toward the garage. It was late afternoon, the sun already retreating in the blustery Chicago winter, and I knew he would be gone till morning.

I was always so proud when I saw him in his police uniform. He was a lieutenant. Gray slacks, crisp blue shirt, black leather bomber jacket. His chest and peaked hat emblazoned with the shiny star *"Cameron # 266."* He was protecting our city. Protecting his family. Protecting me.

Sleeping on top of the toy chest and my father's clothes. He had painted the chest to match the rainbow he had painted on the wall. Circa 1988.

Spying me perched on the slide, he came over to say goodbye enveloping me in his arms and Old Spice.

"Be good to your Mom."

I probably started crying before he left. It hurt so much when he was away. Without my dad my mother turned into a shrew, often overwhelmed and exhausted with a full-time job and four kids under the age of six. And then there was me—the oldest—always finding "smart" things to say and her chasing me around the house with an old shoe. Most nights I ended up sleeping on a bed of his clothes, either on top of my toy chest or in his closet, his scent soaking up my tears.

Day 1
December 17, 2010
Temple, TX

"The scans show there's heavy bleeding on the brain. A lot of damage."

The doctor, tall, old, white, and flanked by more than half a dozen residents, calmly ends his statement looking toward, but not quite, at me. His voice is soft but not firm. There is an opening, a space, almost an invitation. He's telling me this doesn't have to be the end. I can push a bit harder and ask for more details about the aneurysm or request more tests. Perhaps the doctor would suggest an exploratory procedure. But I want none of this. Maybe others do just that—selfishly pursue life at all costs, unable to accept the end of a loved-one's life. Indeed, my mother was one of those keeping her mother, lost in Alzheimer's, alive via feeding tubes for over seven years. But not me. Not my Dad. We were ready for death.

As early as eleven, I remember my father being emphatically clear on his wishes.

"Don't keep me alive on some machine. And none of that religion bullshit. When I die—that's it. The worms will start eating my brain," he would say, pointing his fingers to his head, twirling them around like spaghetti on a fork.

Imagine your brain as spaghetti and worms . . .

We kids would squeal, "Ewwwww! Don't say that!!"

"Look, you need to face it; That's what happens when we die. The worms and the spiders come get you." He would then playfully turn his fingers into worms and spiders while we joyfully screamed and ran away.

As the oldest, my siblings turn to me. I am the closest with my father—we have a similar personality and temperament. And I know his wishes.

"Let's remove the life support. He doesn't want to be this way."

Hours later a different doctor, sans entourage, appears to remove the tubing.

"How long does it take?"

"Oh, usually not too long. Maybe an hour or two."

The four children are watching, bristling with anticipation. Only I have laid with the dying before, and I want to make sure my Dad doesn't die alone. My mother, divorced from my father for more than twelve years, opts out of witnessing the transformation, leaving the room in a hurried rush. Death terrifies her.

We sit.

And we wait.

Beep. Beep. Beep.

And wait.

Beep. Beep. Beep

And wait.

Beep. Beep. Beep

And nothing happens.

The monitor rhythmically beats in sync with his strong and steady heart. His breathing remains heavy and regular. Several hours later a different nurse pops her head in,

"It doesn't happen right away. It could take a day or so."

My brother and sister go to a nearby greasy spoon, Baytown Seafood Express. (Over the next ten days, I would eat at Baytown twice a day.) My youngest sister joins my mother in the waiting room to read *Vogue*.

Alone I wait. Slowly the vital signs start changing; my Dad's heart rate slows and his breathing becomes irregular.

Beep . . . .

   Beep . . . .

      Beep . . . .

         Beep . . . .

            Beep . . . .

Like the sun rising over a mountain, Death was taking His time, slowly and surely approaching. My Dad looked so peaceful. Was it supposed to be like this? This man—who had loomed so large in my life—looked like a lost child nestled among fluffy white pillows. He had hurt so many, myself included. Would he find peace in the next world? Or would he be doomed to wander endlessly, atoning for his wrongs?

A scream catches in my throat.

> *Oh god.*
>   *I hope.*
>   *I hope not.*

For years, I yearned for him to atone for my checkered childhood. At times, he was both my best friend and most ferocious enemy.

But that never happened.

The closest thing to an apology I got was "I did those things to protect you and our family," or "No one will love and protect you like I do. I'm your father. Remember, Lindsey, I want only the absolute best for you."

On my bad days I want revenge. For him to feel pain. On my good days I want him to atone. To seek forgiveness and grow. Looking back, I'm still not sure if December 17th, 2010 was a good day or a bad day.

I pray.

"Please God help him make peace. Let him make peace so he's ready to move on in the next world."

Beep. Beep. Beep.

In an instant, all the vital signs in the room changed. His heart beat speeds up and his breathing becomes more regular. The slow peaceful death had been averted. Being no stranger to miracles, I think,

"My prayer worked!"

Eagerly, I look around the room waiting for something else to happen. Maybe my Dad would start speaking and tell me all the things I needed to hear? Maybe he would atone.

Instead my sister comes in with my Caesar salad with shrimp. We watch *The Simpsons.* Then *Southpark.*

Beep. Beep. Beep.

From the beeps, it doesn't sound like my Dad is dying anytime soon. Had I upset the natural order of things? As the night wears on, my family packs up their things to go back to the hotel.

"I'm going to spend the night here. Just in case."

The nurses give me pillows and blankets, as if it is an everyday occurrence to sleep in the same room with a man who is beginning to decay. I'm always cold, so I turn up the heat and settle on the couch.

FEBRUARY 1994
CHICAGO, IL

My Dad introduced me to my first love: country music. Neither of us were Southerners by birth, but there was something about the heart-felt stories set to banjos and fiddles that fed our souls. When he was a kid, my Dad would rush home during lunch break, gobbling down a PB&J and a glass of milk or eggnog in winter, and watch through the magnifier[2] the *Ford Show* and the *Porter Wagoner Show*. His favorite was Tennessee Ernie Ford's haunting lament[3] about a life in the coal mines:

> *You load sixteen tons, what do you get?*
> *Another day older and deeper in debt*
> *Saint Peter, don't you call me 'cause I can't go*
> *I owe my soul to the company store*

I imagine the song reminded my Dad of his father and namesake, Jake Cameron, Sr. Indeed, my Dad's nickname was Chippy—a chip off the old block. My Dad's father got his start scavenging coal that had fallen off railcars and selling it door to door in rural Mississippi, before

My father's father, Jake B. Cameron, Senior. My dad was called Chippy because he shared his father's wavy hair and big ears. Circa 1950.

moving to Chicago to work for the Illinois Central railroad, first as a Pullman porter and later as an engineer shoveling coal into the locomotive's hungry engine. As a little boy my Dad would wait for his father to come home after a sixteen-hour shift, his pecan-colored skin covered from head to toe in soot. Sitting on the sink in the blood-red bathroom they shared with six other families, Chippy would watch his father wring out a washcloth wiping down his body inch by inch, clearing off the soot. Often, just as his Dad was finishing cleaning up, he would get a call ordering him to report right back to the rail yard.

At Dolly's house in the great Smoky Mountains, August 2015.

As a Valentine's Day gift when I was ten, my father introduced me to my second love, Dolly Rebecca Parton. Dolly and her eight siblings grew up in a two-room cabin without electricity and running water deep in the Smoky Mountains. Her songs about her hardscrabble youth and eventual success pulled at my heart. Dolly proved to me there was a way out—that my childhood sufferings were only temporary.

Crouched low in the basement crawlspace with my Walkman's headphone snug against my ears, over and over I listened to *"In the Good Old Days, When Times Were Bad."*[4]

> *I've seen daddy's hands break open and bleed*
> *And I've seen him work 'til he's stiff as a board*
> *An' I've seen momma layin' in suffer and sickness*
> *In need of a doctor we couldn't afford*
> *Anything at all was more than we had*
> *In the good old days when times were bad*
>
> *No amount of money could buy from me*
> *The memories that I have of then*
> *No amount of money could pay me*
> *To go back and live through it again*
> *In the good old days when times were bad*

At age ten, I knew I was going through my bad days and they would end; that one day I would be able to look back and be grateful. Because Dolly survived, I would survive.

That's what Dolly gave me.

That's what my Dad gave me.

Day 2
December 18, 2010
Temple, TX

So, so cold.

Groggily, my eyes opened seeing my breath in front of me and scanned my Dad's bed.

Beep. Beep. Beep.

Yep, there he was. Both his heart rate and breathing were strong and regular.

The air had a heavy feeling—like when you walk into a room and realize you stepped into the middle of a fight.

Who had closed the door to the hallway?

What was that at the end of the bed? There was a large depression on the mattress and a looming dark shape. It looked like. . . . . .

Deep, cold terror washed over me, turning me into a frozen statue.

"Go back to sleep" a stern but not unkind voice commanded.

Immediately, my eyes obeyed while I remained still inside. Mercifully, I soon dropped back into sleep still buried under a mountain of blankets.

25 NOVEMBER 2015
QUEENS, NEW YORK CITY, NEW YORK

Over a meal in LaGuardia I am pumping my mother for details about my Dad's family for a class paper. As this is the first time we've seen each other in six months, we have not yet pissed each other off and are in high spirits.

"Did Grandmother Irene have any special objects—knick-knacks from her childhood or jewelry?"

"No. You see, Lindsey, I didn't know your grandmother like that. I was... the little brown girl your Dad brought around. No, she didn't even see me. And it was me—*me*—who took you guys to see her at [the nursing home] 77th and Stoney. Your Dad got so mad at me when he found out—he forbid me to take you there anymore."

I smile and look her in the eye, silently pleading for this conversation not to devolve into her all-too-familiar onslaught about the craziness of the Cameron Clan.

"But, I knew your Dad's father."

My ears perk up. Mentally I scan the family tree. My father's father had died eight years before I was born and three years before my parents met.

"How did you know him?"

"He came to me in a dream right after me and your Dad got married. He said that he was glad I was marrying Jake. That I was the right woman for him. I used to always tell your Dad that I knew his father." She shrugged her shoulders, a sheepish look on her face, her brown eyes soft. " I always felt like I knew him. And your Dad believed me."

If there ever was a non-believer, it was my Dad. For Christmas we watched David Attleboro's *Life on Earth*. A staunch atheist, the military and police work had eaten away my father's boyhood Catholic faith. What on earth did my mother say that turned my father into a believer?

ACT II

Day 3
December 19, 2010
Temple, Texas

Beep. Beep. Beep.

It was becoming obvious that my father wasn't going to die anytime soon, so he was to be transferred out of the ICU.

Late in the day a team of orderlies arrive, run a white sheet under him, and lift him onto a gurney. My Dad lays there grunting, eyes squeezed shut, while the orderlies push him away. I am to meet him in his new room.

Ten minutes later I hobble out of the elevator on crutches and, like a new mother attuned to her baby's cries, I hear my Dad's choked moans down the hall. Deep, dark groans in rapid staccato. I rush toward him. He's in agony, cold garlicky sweat oozing from his skin drenching the sheets making sounds like a wild animal's final death cry.

I jab the call button.
    Nurse comes.
        Morphine released.
            Muffled screams continue.

Jab button.
    Nurse comes.
        Morphine released.
            Muffled screams continue.

Jab button.
    Nurse comes.
        Morphine released.
            Muffled screams continue.

Jab button.
    No one comes.
        Muffled screams continue.

Listening to my father's cries I feel helpless. And guilty.

He is in pain.
    I am in pain.
        This must stop.
            What have I done?

Fevered, I rush into the hallway hopping on my good leg,
    "Morphine!
        Morphine!!
            I need morphine now!!!"

Nurse comes.

"He's had all the morphine he is allowed to at this time—three doses per four hours."

WHAT THE FUCK?

How can there be limits on the morphine a dying man can receive?

I go into _hysterics_, barely withholding myself from attacking the small, white nurse. _I scream. I cry._ I threaten to call her boss, to sue. _Christine,_ from hospice support staff, hears my anguish. She calls the doctor and requests permission to dispense more morphine.

The moaning stops.

CHRISTMAS 2011
CHICAGO, IL

My Aunt Carole is indulging me in one of my favorite pastimes, looking at old photo albums. In one photo, my Dad has his arm wrapped around a brown-skinned little girl with two long ponytails streaming down her back.

"Who's that?" I ask.

Carol takes a moment to answer, reaching deep into memory.

"That's. . . Beverly, I think. Your Dad dated her before your Mom. He loved that little girl. I remember all that hair."

We flip to the next page. My Dad is in his police uniform and hoisted on my Dad's hip is a young white

My father and lil' Trac, 1980s.

Playing with my dad and brother. The playfulness of my father reminds me of the tenderness he showed Beverley. Circa 1988.

baby no more than a year old. The child is mugging widely at the camera while my Dad is staring lovingly at the child.

"Who's that?" I ask, thinking this might be my half-sister, Veronica. We never talked about Veronica, but I remember Veronica's mother was white.

"That's your Dad's partner's son, lil' Trac. Tommie was killed while on the job. Your Dad was just crazy about lil Trac."

"Oh" I say, ignoring the plight of Tommie and lil' Trac, feeling a bit disappointed this is not a photo of the long-lost Veronica. "I thought this was my sister Veronica."

"No, no. But, I think I have a picture of Veronica at your grandmother Irene's house."

My mind scans through the family history. My father told me the Veronica story and this does not fit. In his version, after his first wife poisoned him, my Dad moved to Florida where he went to college by day and worked on the police force at night. He met a young white woman who had a baby to try and trap him into marriage. He refused, the small Southern police force turned against him, and he returned to Chicago alone.

My Aunt Carole gives me another version.

After the woman got pregnant and realized your Dad was not going to marry her, she threatened to have an abortion. She only decided to keep the baby after your father promised to take full custody. Your Dad returned to Chicago with baby Veronica and lived with me and your grandmother. We were going to help him raise the baby. Six months later, there was a custody battle, and the women's grandparents won custody. They were white.

I mention to my Aunt Carole this is a different version than I heard from my Dad.

"Oh, honey," she replied, "He didn't talk about it, but he was broke up when that baby left. I should know, I was living with him. He couldn't sleep for months and was chain-smoking. He had ulcers for months after."

The picture of Veronica in my grandmother Irene's house in Chicago lends more support to my Aunt's version.

I had always imagined my father coldly and cruelly abandoning his children—indeed he threatened to "shit can" me like his older two children each time I didn't do whatever he wanted. But perhaps he felt helpless after losing Beverly, lil Trac's Dad, and Veronica. Maybe it wasn't not caring that led him to abandon his children. Maybe it was being unable to stand the pain of caring too much.

Day 5
December 22, 2010
Temple, Texas

Beep. Beep. Beep

"I saw your father last night," I say to my Aunt Peggy. "He came to visit my Dad." I tell her about the cold, the dark shape, and the stern instructions. She believes me.

"He was always so close with our father."

I pick up my phone launching into another round of amends calls. My Dad had unflinchingly and hurt so many people in his life without remorse and I am determined he make amends before he dies. Aunt Peggy had been a victim of his wrath. Enraged that she was getting a root canal, as opposed to pulling the tooth, my Dad verbally attacked her in her own kitchen and had to be dragged away. (Yes, you read that right. My Dad attacked his sister because she was getting and paying for her own root canal, because he thought it would be more economical to pull the tooth).

Doggedly I call around and around the family tree begging my family to say a kind word to my Dad.

Everyone would say:

"Nice to hear from you Lindsey. Sorry to hear that Jake's in the hospital."

I'd ask for them to speak to my Dad. They would all reply.

"No ill-will against the dying—but I got nothing to say to him."

Then the wheedling would start.

"You wouldn't want [insert some incident where my Dad had mistreated this person] to be the way you remember him. He can't even talk back—say whatever you need to say to make your peace. And for him to find peace."

Then I would start the tears and, if needed, racking sobs.

"Please, please, please. If not for him, do it for me. Please so he can make amends and die easy. He's still here because he's waiting for something. He's waiting for you."

Beep. Beep. Beep

One by one, they fell like dominoes. I held my phone against my Dad's ear as they murmured their last goodbyes, their tinny sobs bouncing throbbing through the speakers. When we said our goodbyes, they said:

"That's my baby brother, Chippy. May he go in peace now."

"I hadn't talked to Uncle Chippy in so long. Thank you."

"Bless you, Lindsey, for doing. May you rest in peace, Cousin Chippy."

Beep. Beep. Beep

After each call, his face lost some of the tightness around the brow. With each call I breathed a bit easier crossing off one more person on my long list.

He was atoning. I was atoning.

DECEMBER 20, 2015
CHICAGO, IL

My Dad and his sisters only spoke about their father in the most reverent tones. As if he was holy.

"I don't know how he put up with our mother. He was such a quiet, gentle soul" my Aunt Carol said.

"He was such a kind man. Such a good, good man. I can never say anything bad about my father" my Aunt Peggy says as we're driving to her home after dinner at Olive Garden.

"He always asked me to make him pancakes. And I never wanted to."

She twisted around in the passenger's seat to look into my eyes.

"I would cut off both my arms," she continues wrapping her hands around the opposite elbow, "to make him pancakes."

My Dad had his own special way of asking for pancakes:

> *"You better help me take apart this carburetor!*
> *You better help me build this shed!*
> *You better help me rebuild this computer!*
> *You better help me prune the rose bushes!*
> ***Else, when I'm dead you'll regret it!!"***

And it worked. I could take apart a carbonator, build a shed, rebuild a computer, and prune rose bushes. Until the day I went to college, at age fifteen, I jumped.

Perhaps my Dad regretted things he hadn't done with his father and he wanted to make sure I didn't have regrets. But what if I did everything he wanted and still had regrets? Now what?

Day 8
December 25, 2010
Temple, Texas

Beep. Beep. Beep.

"He's fighting Death. Fighting to hang on. . . There is something he's waiting for," says Christine, the hospice nurse, in her Texan drawl as she leans over the bed to shine a light into my Dad's eyes. The pupils constrict.

Since yesterday he has been actively resisting death. His hands were frozen claws, clutching the sheets. Gulping and belching, his breath rattled in his chest like a slow-moving locomotive. And his vitals were as strong as ever.

Twice a day Christine visits us. She gives him sponge baths, seemingly unphased by the stench of a decomposing body. She increases my Dad's morphine allotment. (In response to the morphine incident. "That's just plain wrong. They should have known better, they should have given him the morphine before they moved him.") She reminds me I am doing my best. My absolute best. Even my own husband has left me. I have never felt so grateful for another human's presence.

Later that day my sister visits. I say, "Maybe Dad's doing his life review. And he doesn't like what he's seeing. That's why he's dying so hard."

I don't tell anyone about my prayer. How I've brought this suffering onto him. And me. I haven't left the hospital in eight days.

What is he waiting for?

What am I waiting for?

I grasp his hand, sweaty and clammy with stink.

"I can't do anything else. I'm sorry. I called everyone I can to make amends. There's no one else to call. No one else who wants to speak to us. I can't do any more. Please, please go in peace."

Though Christine has prepared me, the death rattle breath still sets my nerves on end. I twist and turn every night on the couch, haunted by its sick and wet melody. For months after his death it was the first sound I heard every morning.

Still his heart remains strong.

Beep. Beep. Beep.

It's Christmas Day. My father's greatest gift to me would be to die today.

DECEMBER 21, 2015
CHICAGO, IL

As I got older, I heard more and more tales about my Dad's unflinching stance toward death.

The first story he told me himself. Driving eighteen hours straight from Florida to Chicago, he calmly went into his father's sickroom and told him he had less than three months to live. Lung cancer from a life shoveling coal into the locomotive's belly.

"He was glad to know," my Dad claimed. "My mother, my sisters—Carol and Peggy—were too scared to tell him and kept bullshitting. A man gotta face death."

Three days later my Dad returned to Florida, never to see his father again. Three months later he was dead.

My mother's brother, my Uncle George, tells a similar story. More than twenty years later after the death of his father, my Dad walked into his father-in-law's sickroom and told him he was dying of complications from diabetes.

"I really, *really* hate that he told my Dad that," Uncle George said. "We didn't want to talk about it. You know what your Dad said? That the old man knew he was dying. That someone needed to look him in the eye and tell it to him straight."

As my Dad's dad was losing his battle with cancer, he spun my sister's wonderful tales about how they would travel to the Grand Canyon and Florida once he got better.

"Dad doesn't know how sick he is," my sisters would call me nervously, unsure of how to navigate these conversations.

His confidante, his friend, the only woman who understood him (as he so often claimed)—I would report back to him.

"I need to protect the sweetheart girls [my two younger sisters]. I don't want to scare them. I tell them I'm going to take them to the Grand Canyon when I get better."

At the time, I believed my father. But, after a nasty fall where he was left unattended on the bathroom floor for hours and his subsequent refusal to get a medical alert bracelet—"I can't accept I'm that bad off yet"—I wondered should I believe him?

My personal denial was just as acute. Living in the Middle East, tethered to a job I loved for all the wrong reasons, I crossed the Atlantic on a monthly basis but was openly relieved when my sister-in-law offered to take on the role of nursemaid. It never crossed my mind for an instant to take a leave of absence until it was much too late.

Maybe he was ready for his death and I wasn't. Maybe I was ready for his death and he wasn't.

Maybe neither of us was ready.

Just one more day.

ACT III

Day 9
December 26, 2010
Temple, Texas

Beep. Beep. Beep.

Death rattle.

Beep. Beep. Beep.

Death rattle.

I have been at the hospital so long, I am learning the staff routines. Today a new nurse takes Christine's place.

"Where is Christine?" I ask, trying to sound calm, but knowing I sound desperate

"It's her day off. She deserved a day off," the new nurse retorts. I later find out Christine is gone for the next ten days.

I'm not to begrudge Christine a day off but why didn't she tell me? How could we have our twice a day visit and she not mention she'll be gone the following day? There is no time to adjust. I'll never see her again. No way to tell her how much she means to me.

I remember my last conversation with her.

"Maybe your Dad doesn't want to die while you're here. You're here all the time." She gives a pointed look at my folded blankets on the edge of the couch. "Maybe you should take a break. You do have a life to live, you know, he would want you to live your life."

Yes, he would want me to live my life. He was so proud of my education. There was actually a billboard in our front yard, for five years, announcing my Harvard matriculation—and my career in the intelligence community—evidenced by a hanging flag and bumper sticker. There's no way he would have let me take a leave of absence from work; he had already refused for my sister to take a semester off college. But, I had *already* put my career on priority the past eighteen months while he drove himself alone to chemo. (While my sister-in-law volunteered to care for him, within two weeks he had cursed her out calling her a "Goddamn Mexican witch." She's Venezuelan.) And now I was here. Too late. On crutches, sleeping on a two-seater couch in a room full of strange sights, sounds, and smells.

Emboldened by Christine's last words, I sit beside him taking his hand again.

"I'm strong enough to be here if you want me here when you pass. The others, I'm not sure if they are strong enough, but I am. But, if you'd rather die alone that is fine, too. Just let me know."

To drown out the death rattle, I put on one of our family's anthem Alabama's "Roll On (Eighteen Wheeler)."[5] We listened to it all the time—long car trips, BBQ's, working in the garage. In the song, a driver's truck jack-knifes and the authorities can't do a search for him due to bad weather. His family prays that he would be found and, in a few hours, he calls.

Well, it's Wednesday evening, momma's waitin' by the phone
It rings but it's not his voice
Seems the highway patrol has found a jack-knifed rig
In a snow bank in Illinois
But the driver was missin'
And the search had been abandoned.
'Cause the weather had everything stalled

And they had checked all the houses and the local motels
When they had some more news they'd call
And she told them when they found him
To tell him that she loved him
And she hung up the phone singin'.

[Chorus:]
Roll on highway, roll on along
Roll on daddy till ya get back home
Roll on family, roll on crew
Roll on momma like I asked you to do
And roll on eighteen–wheeler roll on.

Momma and the children will be waiting up all night long
Thinkin' nothing but the worst is comin'
With the ringin' of the telephone
Oh, but the man upstairs was listening
When momma asked him to bring daddy home
And when the call came in it was daddy on the other end
Askin' her if she had been singin' the song, . . .

"Here's our song, Dad," I say as I place one earbud in his ear and the other in mine.

And I sing along.

NOVEMBER 2015
TEMPLE, TEXAS

Like all kids, I thought my Dad was immortal. My Dad was extra-special—every evening he put on his police uniform and every morning he returned safe after spending all night fighting bad guys. Like Superman.

I'm not sure why I had so much faith. Maybe it was our family anthem, "Eighteen Wheeler." Maybe it was his massive size. At the oddest times, he would shout, "I'm a two-hundred and twenty pounder" while pounding his chest like Tarzan. He relished in eating raw eggs and chugging fresh eggnog and would effortlessly pick us up, moving us up and down in an overhead press motion, while we squealed in mock protest. Maybe it was the way I saw him exert his will into the minute details of our lives. He had a desperate need to control others.

Cops are a special breed. Cynical and suspicious, they are continually exposed to humanity's worst.[6] Indeed, many officers see themselves as the only defense against social chaos. My father was no different. My mother, me, the streets of Chicago—these were all things to be controlled for their own good.

I've struggled to find out more about his life on the Force. He didn't like to talk about it. In a dark mood, he told me about finding a baby in a trashcan. A naïve twelve-year old, I asked if it was still alive. A look answered that question. One day when I pressed too hard, wanting to know more about the corruption in Chicago, he said,

"Look, I can't answer any more questions. You're supposed to trust the police. You need to trust the police. I can't tell you anymore."

Subject closed. No more would leave his lips.

Digging through old records, I find a story where my Dad was interviewing a man on 95th and Halsted. Casually a car drives by, shooting the man my Dad was talking to point-blank. The blood must have splattered on my Dad's uniform. What happened next? Did my Dad run and take cover? Draw his weapon taking aim at the killer? Or did he hold the man in his arms as he took his dying breath?

Don't worry. I'll hold you. I promise.

Day 10
December 27, 2010
Temple, Texas

Death of a heartbeat.

With my parents and siblings at my brother's West Point graduation. My father, who was undergoing chemo, bravely traveled up for the graduation. He said it was the proudest day of his life. Silently, I seethed because he missed my Harvard graduation five years before because I invited my mother. Circa May 2010.

Jake Bertrand CAMERON, Jr.

Birth: Mar. 22, 1945

Death: Dec. 27, 2010

U.S. Veteran

Born in Chicago, Illinois
Mr. Cameron was a U. S. Air Force Veteran, and a retired Lieutenant for the Chicago Police Department.

A private time of remembering and the scattering of his ashes will take place at the Grand Canyon at a later date.

West–Hurtt Funeral Home

Our days were numbered.

Ten in all.

TODAY
ANN ARBOR, MI

For more than two years after his death, I called his answering machine to hear his voice.

"This is Jake B. Cameron. I don't check this often, but when I do I'll give you a call back."

Beep.

I don't know why I kept calling. Scrolling through my phone one day, my husband joked I needed to see a therapist based on the number of calls. Perhaps I was hoping that one day I would get a call back. But, one day, the number was disconnected.

> *"We're sorry but you have reached a number that is disconnected or no longer in service. If you feel you have reached this number in error please check the number and try your call again."*

Still, I wait.
I am no stranger to miracles.

Yellow.

Color all my days yellow.

For hope springs eternal.

ENDNOTES

1 Translation into English: O God, Praised and Holy! O God, Merciful and Kind! Remove us from difficulties by Thy grace and favor. Verily, Thou art Merciful and Kind. Hear the song here: https://www.youtube.com/watch?v=Iv8HPAdaM78

2 In the 1950s, families who could not afford larger TV's purchased smaller sets that came with accompanying magnifier lenses.

3 Ford, Tennessee Ernie. "Sixteen Tons." *Sixteen Tons,* Capitol Records, 1955.

4 Parton, Dolly. "In the Good Old Days (When Times were Bad)." *In the Good Old Days (When Times were Bad),* RCA Victor, 1969.

5 Loggins, Dave and Alabama. "Roll On (Eighteen Wheeler)." *Roll On,* RCA, 1984

6 Balch, Robert. The Police Personality: Fact or Fiction. *Journal of Criminal Law and Criminology.* 1972. http://scholarlycommons.law.northwestern.edu/cgi/viewcontent.cgi?article=5774&context=jclc

Lindsey Cameron has been a historical re-enactor, professional bellydancer, janitor, intelligence analyst (aka spy), and professor. At thirty-four countries (and counting!), she has traveled across both the U.S. and Siberia alone, lived in the Sahara with nomads, and gotten guidance from the same oracle as Alexander the Great. Lindsey is notorious among her friends as being "always ready" for an existential conversation, her extensive collective of food for the apoca-

lypse, and organizing her bookshelves by color. She recently finished a two-volume book on her paternal lineage and is currently conducting research for the book on her maternal lineage. When not writing, Lindsey enjoys feasting on her adorable niblings—Riley, Rory, Declan, and Cameron.

Learn more at: **thespiritwalker.me**

Special Gift

I offer spirit guide and ancestral lineage readings.
For spirit guide readings, provide a list of questions that I will directly ask on your behalf.
For ancestral readings, I provide insights about the blessings and challenges from your maternal and paternal bloodlines.
Regardless of which reading you choose, I provide clear, direct messages and practical next-step guidance.

If interested, email me at **ldcameron@gmail.com** or visit my website at **thespiritwalker.me**

May you be well!

She—A Call To Surrender

BY COCO OYA CIENNA-REY

✤

Do you hear her calling?
Softly, oh so sweetly, edging you home

Away from fears and doubts of being
Of knowing your true worth
SHE, the divine river of truth that flows through life
I...... Can...... See......

SHE, who masquerades as another,
Know her intoxicating whispers as she caresses your soul

Feel her grace-filled essence, her majestic tones
She softens your edges, Sheds outdated skins—
Exposed and open to the elements
I...... feel...... Bare......

Break free from limitations
Expand into her loving embrace
Know you will never falter with her
I...... can...... breathe......

Lungs now and filled with divine presence
Capable of walking through life surrendered
With every step,
Love and illumination flow
Feel Her light guiding you home

This wasn't the story I wanted to write. I wanted to write of my recovery from trauma and ancestral healing, a specific tale of my mother and I and how her death catapulted me into the longest dark night of the soul and spiritual awakening and a journey of seeking truth.

On the day of submission, I lost what I had written. I never saved it, and it was unable to be retrieved. In that moment I had to make a choice to spiral out and lose my mind, or drop into the void and allow the truth of why to emerge. I had a deep sense that this was meant to happen, that it wasn't yet time to share our story. I needed to get out of the way and let the truth of the moment emerge.

This is the story I was asked to write by She who is, the Deep Dark Feminine essence that has been calling me to her for many years. She was asking me to write in a different way; to be present with what is, to clear the patterns and blocks that were limiting my full self-expression. With each line I wrote, I could feel the unraveling of eons of unexpressed creative truths of the women in my ancestral line who never got to follow their callings, to live their magic, and to listen to the internal voice calling us home.

I never set out to be a writer, but my soul and the universe had other ideas. I told myself it must be a cosmic joke; I had struggled with writing all of my life. At age 21 when I pursued my dream to go into higher education, I found out I was dyslexic. This shattered open the story that I had been told in school that I was lacking in intelligence and the fear I carried from reading books. My father would blow his top if he found any in the house, called them stupid things, his own insecurities forced upon me due to his inability to read well. Sometimes the thing we find the hardest is the very thing that we are called to do to break down the false belief that has been placed upon us by others and that we have carried. For me, putting words on the page is more than just pen on paper; each mark is a ritual in reclamation as I dive deeper into my truth, percolating and incubating the wisdom that wants to arise. It is an embodiment practice of reconnection. To understand that each moment is an initiation into the deeper part of being embodied and centred.

As a child, I kept a journal. I created my own words and writing code, a magical language just for me. Even then I was creating and making spells long before I realised it. Yet, the thought of being a writer never entered my mind. Later in my life during a shamanic session, I saw the wound I was carrying as the ancestral wounding of slaves being punished for reading or writing. These forbidden skills were hidden under the threat of death. I felt those echoes of the past seeping down the family line, and now I see why I was given the task to break that. This is my soul's call. Being a writer is soaked in my bones. This is a legacy to give voice to the voiceless, of clearing ancestral karma regarding claiming one's heartsong. So much alignment and many opportunities have arisen from heeding the call. Writing has shown me how to go within. To listen to my inner guidance and wisdom. To learn to trust that all things happen in divine timing. Even in the case of this piece, as I allow what is true to arise.

She who is will always send the whispers on the wind inviting you to own your power. I was sent many whispers along the path and I am only now recognising that she has been calling me to her all my life. I hadn't fully understood how to surrender until now. The feminine calls all beings who are ready to hear. Writing this chapter has deepened the art of surrender as I allow what wants to call me into service to move through. We draw our deepest desire through our longing. To open fully to this requires a higher level of vulnerability so we can open in the deepest way. The world is hungry for us—for our voices to come out in full chorus.

We still move through the world carrying the witch wounds and the wounds of colonialism that told us to hide and vilify our own magic, a magic that resides in our bones and hearts. It is part of who we are encoded in our bodies, as we face the plight of what we allowed ourselves to forget. As we hold the grief we carry of our own demise, where we were told we were too much, too loud, too dark or just too much damn woman. We can turn towards our despair or towards our deepest longing individually and collectively, knowing that something new is coming as we prepare the fertile soil of our bodies ready to receive Her full transmission. We are creating space, making room with clearer devotion and commitment, and moving out of our own way.

The Divine Mother is cutting though everything, to bring her message on a mass scale. She is calling to the feminine within us to rise, to awaken to the wisdoms shrouded in mystery until now. It is an alchemy of being, a process of life, an organic process of becoming, that is forever reshaping you into new forms to embrace life from the soul. We each have a fundamental journey to travel in life—a spell we need to break to reveal the magic that we are. We are building the bridge between the magical and the mundane, and between the seen and the unseen worlds. This is the reclamation. Our desire is a powerful force that attracts to us that which will fulfill our longing here on earth. We must move into the body to live fully to connect to the realm of our creative darkness. I lived a life for so many years only accepting a glimpse of my magical self, a reflection of my own mother who would always get great insights of things to come and could feel the earth's changes in the whispers of the wind. Yet, she would push away any mention of the magical realm.

I had also been afraid to tap into the magic that I knew; it felt too complex for my human eyes, too miraculous for my human heart. I carried all of the stories my mother had told me about Obeah being a sin to practice, and these stories blocked my ability to surrender to it. This is the wound of the oracle. A wound that was centuries old. Yet it wasn't until my encounter with the dark side of the feminine that I realised it was safe to open my heart to it. To take up space as Obeah Woman and claim my inherited magic. She allowed me to sink into the depths of my being to show me how to deep dive into life, into the pain in my heart and finally begin to digest the mass of emotions that I had been unwilling to feel. The support began to come in. We cannot do this alone. Teachers came to help me find my writing voice to help alchemise the fear I had to self-express. Even though the plight of Black women wasn't spoken of in my home, it was made clear that we were deemed second class, that we had to work harder to be recognised as worthy.

The Deep Dark feminine is part of this puzzle; she is the original, the creator of all life. She is the voice of the divine that calls the depth of your power forth. Yet, her voice is also feared. For once awakened, her roar will shake the foundations of all existence. The Primordial Mother can be very messy and really doesn't colour inside the lines. She often does the opposite to what human beings want her to do just to get our attention. She has been excluded from the norm, accused of sorcery, her supernatural tendencies, her sacred feminine arts punishable in the past by death. Her reawakening is cracking open this world. When we shed light on Her story, we heal the wounds of the world and remember all that words can never communicate.

We were disconnected from our Mothers' native tongue, our native narrative and language lost. Our ways of being forced underground, waiting for the unearthing of our inherent truth. We morphed into mere shadows of ourselves and became copies of unnatural ways. We severely lost our way. We lost the connection to the land, to our souls. Obeah was a medicine of the land in which we spoke to the earth and worked close to the land and knew that we were part of the earth. We were told that our ways were primitive, savage, and uncivilised. Our alignment with God/Goddess turned into religion doctrines and were superimposed with a white god. The connections to the deities and Orisha that served us severed; they are now speaking loud through the veil, willing us to hear their songs.

As women, by design our bodies carry a direct ancestral line back to the Deep Feminine and Divine Mother. We are planting new seeds in our consciousness by talking about lineage, ancestors, and ancient blood-lines, which are separate from the connection to our immediate family. We are expanding into the conscious field that connects us to a direct line to She who created all life. This resets the natural nature of the matri-archal line, one older than time. Women have always been spell-casters. We have to remember how to attune to our own knowing even if that means going against everything we have ever been told. This wild power is worthy of our attention. Our lives are a conversation with the great mystery that breathed us into being. In the contraction and expansion of Her breath we create space for new life to form. We are changing the narrative of suffering to surrender, from slavery to sovereignty, from loss to love, from death to rebirth. We are being stripped bare, so we can stop grasping, and surrender to life and Her will.

She has been calling me for so long, and this piece was just another act of surrender to Her. I had to trust that what wanted to come through was enough. *Is* enough. To get out of the way, even when I couldn't see the reasons why. Even when it felt counterintuitive. There was always a knowing that all was as it should be as I took direction from the Divine Mother. Our destiny, no matter how hard we try to ignore it, is imprinted on our DNA. From a young age, I had the sight of premonition—the ability to know things before they happened. This gift has been dampened over the years as I tended to my trauma wound. But a gift that we are born with will never leave; it will wait dormant until the time is right to come through. As a child, I daydreamed as a way of escaping the chaos at home. Yet, daydreaming now plays a role in being able to connect with the unseen world, the imagination a gift to bringing the unseen to life. The imagination is our core gift to being consciously creative and is our connection to the flowing realms of creation.

By reclaiming our gifts, we are bringing things back into natural order, handing back that which is no longer ours to carry. We are resurrecting our lack of self-expression, reclaiming the expansion of Her in our bodies. We are taking up the space we were designed to take up. We belong to the cosmic womb. We are de-armouring eons of falsehoods though our bodies. This is Beyond technique. This is a maturing into the soul, an energetic frequency that we transmit that can't easily be defined. It is a visceral feeling that emanates through the body. The body is an important piece of the puzzle as we feel the pains and pleasures that may have been handed down the line. We are learning to differentiate what belongs to us and what does not, that we have carried nonetheless. We are unearthing the stories marinating in our bones. This is a time in human history when, if we have done our internal work, our magic is revealed. We move away from the oppression of the outdated systems and break free into true alignment.

Our DNA is connected to Her, the Deep Primordial Mother. She is like the roots of a tree and its branches, we are the fruits that spring forth from Her. The more women who claim their stories and speak their power out into the world, the more Her codes of awakening are activated. This piece in its simplicity has taught me how life flows through from a greater source and how to get out of the way to receive Her. It has demonstrated that purpose unfolds as you take each step. It is not all revealed at once. It has shown me that the biggest challenges often turn out to be our soul's reclamation, which can lead to untold possibilities. It has reminded me to stand firm in my own truths and to honour my wisdom. That working with the field means what is right in one moment may not be in the next.

There is divine timing to all things. Nothing comes with ease until I put Her at the forefront of all that I do. Her pull to create is the strongest magnetic pull I have ever known. She will stop at nothing to illuminate and enliven me to live my fullest life. To unite with Her is to unite with life. Her will—not my will—be done. Her love knows no limits and has no bounds; it is timeless. She may be seen as Dark and at times so Deep she feels unreachable. Yet, She is the light of the world we are longing for. Our devotion to one another is mutual; She flows through me as I flow through Her and this is Her call to all women. She teaches every day how to surrender and let go of that which no longer serves. I am on a path of Remembrance. Leaning back into the arms of the Great Mother to receive her nourishment. Remembering the mystery as I offer up my devotion to the Her. The power of the feminine is to choose surrender.

Coco Oya Cienna-Rey is a UK-based creative, poet, soul guide, and writer published in several anthologies. Her creativity is informed by her journey as a devotee of the Tantric path (an embodied path of self-liberation) and her experience within the field of trauma. She has always felt a call to channel the Voice of the  Divine Feminine. Often thought-provoking yet always heartfelt, her work speaks of the sacred wisdom stored in the body, the non-linear nature of trauma and the embodiment of soul. She believes that our innate connection to the natural world can heal humanity and admires the human capacity to take the pains and chaos of life and transmute them into purpose, passion, and beauty.

Deeply sensitive and highly empathic, through guidance from the seen and unseen world, her passion is to share her journey to inspire and assist those that are ready to reclaim their authentic voice. Coco's gift as an intuitive and collective collaborator affords her the ability to understand the root of a given situation, and she is able to bring core issues to light for release and healing. Her growing body of work called Feminine Fundamentals speaks to the current evolutionary shift as we collectively balance the masculine and feminine principles within and without for both men and women. Her work also explores the concepts of relationships, intimacy, and connection as spiritual practice, all of which are the fundamental building blocks of life. Feminine Fundamentals aims to bring together like-minded souls who are ready to embrace their soul gifts.

Learn more at: **creativelycoco.com**

Special Gift

Feminine Fundamentals—8 Pillars to Unearthing the True You

This inspiring PDF introduces the '8 Pillars' which are the foundational principles for working with the Deep Feminine the 'Feminine Fundamentals' way. A way of living and being that puts Tantric philosophy at its forefront. The guide also outlines how working with the 'Elements of Nature' provides the bedrock upon which the Pillars stand. It offers tips and practices on connecting to the voice of your heart and igniting your desires.

Get access here: **creativelycoco.com/gift**

Remembrance

BY SHARDAY FOX

FAMILY

I was nineteen when Jhmil's life was taken. He had just graduated from college that spring. The following Monday, he was set to open the doors to his graphic arts business. His long locs and bright smile were part of his signature look. My mother and father played very active roles in our lives. They were both deeply devoted to helping us cultivate our passions at a young age. I gravitated towards recreational sports, and Jhmil gravitated to the arts.

Jhmil and I were opposites in many ways, yet very similar the older I got. Sadly, we weren't very close. Our six-year age difference played a big part. Jhmil was very family-oriented, and I on the other hand, was extremely self-absorbed as a child, and making friends took precedence over my home life. Many times Jhmil would do his best to help open my eyes about the importance of family and being selfless, but I was unwilling to listen to anything he had to say.

At some point during college, my brother started evolving. Knowing what I know now, he was beginning to remember his Divinity. His awakening made me extremely uncomfortable and resistant towards him and I didn't understand why. It's ironic how the light I resented in him was the light I ended up recognizing within myself sixteen years later.

That light was the Divine.

Months before Jhmil departed, both my grandparents transitioned due to age and health complications. Amidst Jhmil's passing, our parents were dealing with the grief of losing their parents less than a year prior. I was naive at the amount of grief we were collectively coping with. The three of us grieved and processed things in our own way since seeking professional help was never discussed. My parents opted to sell the house and move away for a fresh start. Sure, I could have gone with them, but selfishly I stayed in Jersey, scapegoating all that had just happened to our family.

Indoctrination had conditioned me to take the "safe" path in life: play small, follow the rules, get good grades, graduate college, work a 9–5, get married, start a family.

There's no such thing as one size fits all.

With neither healthy communication skills nor a framework for processing the trauma of Jhmil's departure, I went down a winding road of broken relationships. My trauma began with Jhmil's death. That fragmented little girl kept showing up in every friendship and intimate encounter, producing the same outcome. I didn't understand why I was unable to sustain a healthy relationship with a man. For years I blamed my father for my romantic shortcomings since passing the blame was easier to do. The resentment I carried towards him for not being emotionally available kept showing up in my relationships with men. It was selfish of me to harbor animosity towards my father when he, too, was going through his own unprocessed trauma.

Love is a trifecta:
acceptance, appreciation, and compassion.

SISTERHOOD

> ". . . I'm the master of my fate.
> I'm the captain of my soul."
> —*WILLIAM ERNEST HENLEY*

Joining a sorority a few years after Jhmil's passing wasn't the wisest decision. I was still traumatized and hadn't properly given myself time to grieve, let alone explore who I was at twenty-one. Nevertheless, a sorority was where I chose to plant myself in the spring of 2007. I saw sorority life as an opportunity to explore sisterhood, something I had longed for as a child. Admittedly it was a selfish and impulsive decision considering I'd just gone through the most traumatizing experience of my life. The work within the organization combined with community service initiatives, partying, binge drinking, road trips, step shows, homecomings, and Greek picnics; my college experience served as the perfect escape from my sad reality. This world took up so much of my energy that I didn't have time to expose myself to things outside of Greek life. Without knowing who I was, I was lost in a sea of emotions, barely staying afloat.

In this attraction-based universe, we attract who we are. This community was more of a container of wounded energies and unhealed trauma, and it was what I identified with for over a decade. Time and time again, I disregarded my feelings by ignoring microaggressions, projections, and blatant disrespect for the sake of sisterhood. Hurt people hurt people, and my active participation in breaking people left me feeling broken inside. I felt like I needed to guard myself around these women, so I took on a mean-girl persona to protect myself. It was the armor I needed so that no one could see how weak and wounded I felt within.

> "We wear the mask that grins and lies,
> It hides our cheeks and shades our eyes. . ."
> —*PAUL LAURENCE DUNBAR*

Authenticity was a concept I knew nothing of, so superficiality became the mask I wore for well over a decade. The thought of being my authentic self hadn't crossed my mind! I'd gotten so used to shape-shifting into different versions of myself to appease others that I had no idea who Sharday was. I was in such a deep sleep that I had zero concept of discernment or self-awareness. Pointing the finger elsewhere was much easier than having to look at myself in the mirror. My emotions ran rampant as anger consumed me, and lashing out became the norm. I felt dead on the inside, but with anger, I was able to express my pain.

I was angry at life.

I was angry at the people who took my brother's life.

I was angry at my parents for moving.

I was angry at myself for continuously making terrible decisions and having to deal with the consequences later on.

I was angry at being called crazy.

I was angry for being misunderstood.

I was angry at the irony of joining a sorority yet still feeling deeply alone.

I was angry at God.

With grief, I felt so powerless, so I chose anger instead. The magnitude of despair I was carrying around had me considering suicide on a few occasions. I desperately wanted someone—*anyone*—to see me. I needed help but didn't know where to turn, so I chose to act out to gain attention. My parents were grieving and processing in their own ways, and the last thing I wanted was to let them know how much I was struggling. I often felt alone. In my eyes, if I took my life, I would at least be seen and acknowledged, even if it were for a moment. Yes, that's selfish. But, in my defense, I was immersed in a toxic environment navigating life as a wounded little girl who hadn't properly grieved.

How can I be of service to all mankind?
Radical self-responsibility

Fast forward eleven years after initiating into the sorority, life humbled me and gave me the reality check I needed. I experienced domestic abuse from a partner in a fraternity and received little to no support amongst my peers. I was suffering alone in murky waters, where that darkness shined a bright light revealing the fractured points of this community I worked so hard to be part of. The discomfort I felt within was so strong that I couldn't ignore it anymore. The reality was that I was surrounded by women who were experiencing domestic abuse within their own relationships.

I felt stagnant, realizing that this environment I planted myself in at twenty-one had served its purpose and no longer aligned with my destiny. Consumed by external validation and material acquisition, I finally needed space to bud, blossom, and be. I was ready to experience every emotion necessary on the road towards healing and finally explore divine female embodiment practices. The time had come for me to leave shallow waters and dive deep into the depths of my soul, alone.

Walking away from relationships is not always easy, but often crucial. My desperation to shed all the layers of toxicity I had acquired over the years, plus having a man lay his hands on me without remorse, was what fueled my decision to officially renounce my Greek letter affiliation. Sometimes the only way to detox toxic environments is by walking away and detoxing the parts of you that resonated with it in the first place.

Every encounter and experience we have serves a Higher purpose. In hindsight, my time in the sorority served as a thirteen-year cycle that was necessary for my soul's expansion. I've learned that the willingness to change is the precursor to radical transformation.

> "When we are no longer able to
> change a situation, we are challenged
> to change ourselves".
> —*VIKTOR FRANKL*

WOMBMAN RISE TOGETHER

Every day my relationship with my Inner Being continues to deepen as I affirm it's okay to be my authentic self and that happiness is a choice. Our wombs are sacred portals to ancient feminine wisdom that, when tapped into, can create and heal worlds. However, those portals get blocked the more we give our bodies away to toxic people. Womb healing is not only beneficial, it's vital for the health of our future generations to come.

As I look back, I'm able to clearly see that every contrasting experience was there to serve my Highest good. For that, I have such reverence for that period of my life and for the moments that are etched in my heart forever. Life has a way of isolating you to the point where you have no other choice but to turn within. My sorority experience laid the foundation for my desired expansion. Needless to say, I had to experience what extreme loneliness felt like to appreciate what solitude provided; clarity and connection to my Higher Self.

I am my sister's keeper.

DISTORTED LOVE

> "Important encounters are planned
> by the souls long before the bodies
> see each other."
>
> —*PAULO COELHO*

"I need to call the police" was what immediately came to mind as I found myself sitting on the floor of my studio apartment, heart racing, covered in dirt and bruises, sobbing uncontrollably in disbelief, and frozen in fear.

Why is this happening to me?
Is this my karma?

That experience brought me to the lowest point in my life. What almost broke me was the karmic lesson I was meant to experience during this reincarnation, forcing me to get to the root cause of how I got here in the first place.

> "You don't attract what you want;
> you attract who you are."
>
> —*DR. WAYNE DYER*

I had put my total trust in this individual and relinquished my power by doing so. It took being physically assaulted for me to finally wake up, to embrace my inner power, and begin the process of course-correcting my life.

How did I get here?

As I started peeling back the layers of cultural conditioning and limiting beliefs I had adopted over the years, I began to notice my faulty foundation was due to my moral ambiguity. In 2014 a partner at the time broke up with me, which left me devastated. I was very unconscious and verbally abusive. Instead of taking time to focus on myself, I repeated old patterns: deny, deflect, and move on to the next relationship, which I did.

Past lessons repeat until you pass and complete.

Little did I know that a new seven-year cycle was getting ready to commence. I had accumulated a lot of negative karma throughout my 20's so it was a matter of time before it caught up with me. We met in the spring of 2015 at a "Meet the Greeks." The red flags were there, yet I chose to ignore the uneasy feeling I felt during our initial encounter. That unease was my Inner being forewarning me, but I wasn't spiritually-minded enough to recognize. My apprehension grew stronger as time passed while continuing to deny, ignore, and suppress my feelings towards him. We attracted one another through our vibration—there was a reason Spirit brought the two of us together. It took years for me to realize that this karmic relationship was what I needed in order to see how I was continuously showing up in the world.

I was unaware of how deep my wounds were until I attracted a wounded masculine as a partner. I lived life on autopilot, disassociating by numbing myself with alcohol and drugs throughout the relationship, especially during intimate moments. Disconnecting from my body was a form of protection. I had no business being in relation with anyone since I had no relation with myself. Over time, fear began creeping in.

I feared there was no way out.

I feared being alone.

I feared starting over again in my thirties.

I was in a perpetual state of powerlessness where I was constantly gaslighted when I would mention my unhappiness. The relationship was draining my life force slowly, and I had no outlet to express my pain. This wasn't love; this was possession.

> "Caged birds sing of freedom,
> free birds fly."
>
> —DR. MAYA ANGELOU

At thirty-two years old, I found myself starting to give in to societal dogma: give up and accept the hand I was dealt. However, Spirit had another plan for me. I ignored the clear signs of infidelity early on in the relationship. Once confronted, he begged for forgiveness and promised never to cheat again. Forgiving his behavior was one thing, but accepting him back magnified my insecurities and unworthiness.

Fast forward a year later; my life radically changed the night he tackled me to the ground after confronting him about resurfaced news of his ongoing infidelity. The same man who publicly speaks of women as Queens was the same person who violently held me pinned to the ground. The symbolism of being tossed to the ground felt like Spirit had taken me by the arms and shouted, "WAKE UP SHARDAY, REMEMBER WHO YOU ARE!"

*Ignoring signs will lead you
away from your destiny.*

SELF LOVE

At this point, I was still forming a new relationship with my Inner Being and went against my better sense of judgment by reopening Pandora's box—picking up the phone to offer forgiveness. My intention was to listen and leave things on amicable terms with him since we shared the same circle. The thought of us possibly working things out did cross my mind, but a year had passed, and the distance gave me clarity and strengthened my discernment. Shortly after reconciling, I expressed I no longer felt the same. Intuitively I knew he was still the same person, wearing a false mask. I felt strongly, and there was no way I would ignore my feelings this time, even if I were repeatedly gaslighted by friends. This was me honoring my boundaries and taking back my power.

Discernment is a light of protection from those who can't feel the darkness.

As uncomfortable as it was telling him I couldn't see us getting back together, it was necessary. There was no way I would turn back. The red flags I missed before were now glaringly obvious. He didn't take no for an answer. Instead, he chose manipulation and stalking as a means to wean his way back into my life. Catfishing was one of the main forms of manipulation. It became unquestionable that he was actively pursuing the same hobbies as me, tracking down coworkers and other people I knew conveniently trying to work his way back into my life. I felt like my life was being photocopied—as if that were something I would actually want from a partner! Still operating from a victim mentality, I couldn't wrap my head around why this was still happening after I made it crystal clear to him that I wanted to be left alone for good.

On my thirty-fourth birthday, I walked outside, got into my truck, and noticed the dashboard lights all on. I was confused and assumed it was just time to have my vehicle checked. So I had it towed to my mechanic. The next day I received a call, "Did you get into a fight with anyone?" my mechanic asked. Taken aback, my immediate response was no. Still, I hadn't put two and two together. "Are you sure? Because it seems as if someone crawled under your truck and cut the wires to your brakes!" she said. My heart sank, and I immediately knew. It took me a while to comprehend the severity of what had been done. At that point, it wasn't about revenge but total surrender.

As above, so below. As within, so without.

I created such unnecessary internal suffering by resisting what was right in front of my eyes. I had to take full accountability for having attracted this individual into my world. I was at such a loss trying to understand why this was all happening to me. The more I resisted my reality, the more his nefarious actions persisted. I finally sat down and asked my Inner Being, "What is all of this trying to show me?"

> "Emotional abuse can take many different forms. In an effort to control and manipulate you, the abuser might constantly monitor your whereabouts, insult you, threaten you, isolate you from family and friends."
>
> —*NATIONAL DOMESTIC ABUSE HOTLINE*

I felt deep betrayal watching friends, coworkers, and associates within the Greek letter community remain in support of him in spite of knowing what he had done. It seemed as if the more people I shared my story with, the more they normalized the situation and brushed it under the rug. I refused to continue living life as a victim, allowing external events to keep me low vibrationally. Thoughts create reality, and the reality I desired did not involve him, his affiliates, or any toxicity he was bringing my way. No longer was I vibrating with that wounded energy. Every time I'd get triggered by his behavior, the more I turned within to see what I still needed to work on within myself that identified with those toxic traits.

Once again, I found myself in an unhealthy relationship with a man, but this time it involved physical assault. It turned out that relationship revealed a core wound I was unable to see prior. It was the wake-up call I desperately needed. That experience allowed me time to reflect on how often I chased after men who were emotionally unavailable and detached. Rather than approaching relationships as they actually were, I continuously perceived them as dreams rather than reality. I was so busy putting relationships on a pedestal for nearly two decades rather than taking time to grow on my own and connect with Source.

Nothing is ever worth chasing after, especially if it means losing yourself in the process. I ran from myself for so long in search of a soulmate that I neglected to be the mate to my own soul first. Time and space were what I desperately needed to grow in love, by myself, with myself. How could I expect someone to give me love when I had never given it to myself?

The more you find yourself,
the more people you lose along the way.

FORGIVENESS

While everything was happening, my guardians of light worked overtime by sending me signs and angels to assist and protect. Even if no one else could see what was happening, I keenly knew what was up, and that was enough for me. No longer did I feel the need to share my experiences with anyone because suppressed trauma sometimes looks like normalizing and/ or ignoring abusive behavior.

Bridges built on half-truths will crumble.

For a long time, I lived in a constant state of fear, constantly peering over my shoulder. However, the more I surrendered to the Divine, the more I kept hearing "trust." A restraining order was something I should have pursued, but I was frozen in fear from all that was happening around me. Instead, I began spending time alone, taking my spiritual health more seriously, taking time every day multiple times a day to just sit with myself in quiet stillness. It was in those moments of solitude where I discovered my innate power and strength. His manipulative tactics no longer worked because I was able to see right through his illusion. It became clear as day. In hindsight, the e-motions (energy in motion) that I experienced throughout that relationship were vibrational indicators of my misalignment.

SPEAKING OUT

Abuse of any kind is detrimental to the human soul. Albeit there were several other situations that transpired, I share these specific events to make people aware of the darkness that exists in each of us. I am a mere microcosm of the macrocosm of wounded men and women experiencing life through unhealed trauma swiping from one person to the next in order to avoid having to sit with themselves.

I am not the only person to experience domestic abuse within the Greek community. I had peers who admired me because of the allure of how my relationship appeared from the outside. Little did they know what was really going on behind closed doors.

> "Domestic violence is a serious issue for
> all women at all socio-economic levels;
> however the issue is a heightened
> matter of life and death in
> African-American communities."
> —VIOLENCE POLICY CENTER

My intention is for my story to ignite individual healing journeys within the Greek letter community and beyond. Healing is a very personal, non-linear process which involves sitting with your spine aligned, eyes closed or softly gazing. Here is where you begin quieting the outside voices by focusing on your inhales and exhales. Over time you become accustomed to hearing your own voice within—the core essence of who you are. It's our willingness to take accountability for how we are individually showing up and potentially adding to collective volatility.

In this attraction-based universe, we're constantly attracting people who reflect back to us who we are. People enter and leave our lives based on what frequencies we're giving out. It took a while before I could think of that relationship as a blessing. But sometimes blessings are hidden in the darkest experiences, for light can only be understood from the wisdom of darkness. That karmic relationship showed me who I was and how I was showing up in the world and for that I am forever grateful. Sometimes experiencing what you don't want brings clarity around what you do want, since clarity is the language that the universe understands.

Forgiveness isn't always easy, but it's absolutely essential for our souls' evolution. Forgiveness, however, does not mean reconciliation. Reconciliation is free will of choice. Protecting yourself from people or situations that once hurt you is spiritually wise. Not everyone is willing to let go, but it's the willingness to let go which provides freedom. In order to move past that karmic cycle and bring it to a close for good, I had to seek help from my Higher Self to release the hate I held in my heart towards him. In time my heart became light again once I decided to cut the energetic cord that once connected us. That soul contract officially came to an end, and for the first time, I felt free.

> *Forgive others not because they deserve it*
> *but because you deserve peace.*

EMBRACING THE UNKNOWN

Sometimes from our limited perspective, we can't see what does and doesn't serve us until we look back and connect the dots. The Universe is always conspiring in our favor, believe it or not. As a result of that karmic experience, my edges have softened as I continue to embrace the highly sensitive being that I am. I give myself full permission to feel, sense, and listen to what emotions arise within me. As I commit to leaning deeper into my heart space, I'm better equipped at processing my feelings while holding a compassionate space for others.

I desired radical transformation. However, first I needed to become a vibrational match to what I was asking for. This meant letting go of what no longer served me while rebuilding the relationship with my younger self, forgiving her, offering her compassion, and trusting that my inner guidance would direct me from here on out. I stopped dwelling on the past and the many ways I could have done better because if I had known better I would have done just that. Those contrasting experiences crystallized what I truly desire in life: **to be surrounded by spiritually-minded relationships.**

ALCHEMY

We all possess the ability to change, and that change begins with willingness. Free will is our birthright. We are free to choose what we want, but we aren't free from the consequences of those choices. Sometimes those choices end up hurting us in the long run the more we continue to harbor hatred and animosity from the past. In the present moment, there is only creation, and it's dependent on where you direct your attention.

I was carrying around so much pain, anger, grief, and a heavy weight of other downward spiraling emotions. I made the choice to let them all go. This is where my father and I differ. Between Jhmil's passing coupled with his own childhood trauma, my father chose fear and anger as his armor. Part of my healing process has been reminding myself that beyond the label, my father is a sovereign being and possesses the same free will to do as he wishes as I do. This is his life, and he has his own path to walk and lessons to learn in this lifetime.

Through his unconscious behavior, my father continues to show me the importance of forgiveness and compassion. He's not only strengthening me spiritually, but he is also teaching me what it means to love unconditionally. It's not about abandoning him at his lowest point or resenting him for not being present in my life as an adult but releasing judgment and actively forgiving him.

We're on this earthly plane—our learning ground—for 100 years at best. We're all operating at different levels of consciousness, doing the best we can with our level of understanding. You never know what silent battles people are facing and what they have endured. It's about learning how to see past our ego and from the lens of kindness and compassion. Looking at life from this perspective could help us be more forgiving towards ourselves and one another. After all, we are sharing this human experience.

I'm Sorry
Please Forgive Me
I Love You
Thank You
—*HO'OPONOPONO PRAYER*

STRENGTH RETURNS

Everything we see, do, and experience in our physical reality originates in the mental realm. Thoughts turn to things that manifest reality. Once I grasped this immutable universal truth, I began paying closer attention to my thoughts by releasing old narratives that were steeped in unworthiness. I began speaking new life into me rooted in love and acceptance.

The ending of that chapter gave me time to do the one thing I'd neglected for so long—soul work. I found happiness, acceptance, and validation within myself and stopped searching externally. In retrospect, I see how these past seventeen years were what my soul needed to experience to get me to the place I am now.

Contrast refines vision.

METAMORPHOSIS

Perhaps the people who anger, disturb, or hurt us are meant to serve as our greatest spiritual teachers to assist us in healing and self-actualization. I reflect and give thanks for all the experiences and people I've met along my journey so far. I'm most grateful to those soul contracts who profoundly impacted and helped shape my life, leading me to this point of co-creation with the Universe. I've learned that adversities are an essential part of our soul's expansion. Life ebbs and flows in cycles. Healing isn't linear; there will be detours and roadblocks, and yet somehow, the Universe still manages to put you right where you're meant to be.

> *A tree can't grow to heaven*
> *unless its roots reach down to hell.*

The longer you pretend to be someone you aren't, the longer it will take to get back on your unique path. When you learn to follow your bliss, you begin drawing in the right people and situations into your life that help to propel you forward. Relationships become richer, life becomes fuller, and your soul begins to expand. It took seventeen years for me to finally get back on my unique path. Just as the caterpillar undergoes a period of gestation before fully morphing into a butterfly, so do you. Living in the past and stressing over the future will have you missing the divine presence that dwells within you right now in this present moment.

The more you continue to heal, the more you awaken from this collective amnesia of separateness and recognize the Oneness in all things. By stepping out of the matrix programming and into the heart of nature, the more you begin to remember your Divinity. We are here to learn, to expand, to experience, to create, and above all things, to love.

> *Remember that you are a quintessential piece of*
> *Divine revelation.*

Sharday Fox Johnson is an author, alchemist, wellness, and movement practitioner. Sharday began her journey in the wellness industry nearly a decade ago as a licensed massage therapist and bodyworker, where she first began falling in love with the human body. Sharday is also an integrative nutrition health coach, yoga instructor, and movement practitioner. Her passion is discovering human potential and expressing it artistically. She speaks two languages fluently: Energy and English. On her path of healing Sharday explores movement while openly sharing her story in hopes that it will awaken and influence people to discover their power.

Learn more at: **shardayfox.com**

If you or someone you know is experiencing Domestic Violence, please visit **thehotline.org** *to get immediate help and/or* **ncadv.org** *for community support. You don't have to suffer alone.*

Moment in a Hurricane:
How I Turned Disaster into Deliverance
BY LATOYA O. GARRETT

The moment I thought I would go to jail for the rest of my life, is the moment my world started to change. It's funny how you start thinking about your life when you're threatened with losing it. Here's my story.

In the fall of 2002, my cousin, who I saw as a motherly figure, died while incarcerated. She had been in jail for a couple of weeks—for something minor—and was scheduled to make bond in a few days. According to the guards and inmates, she was standing in the breakfast line to get her food when she suddenly collapsed onto the floor. They later discovered that it was a heart attack.

It's as if she somehow knew her time was up, since the week before she died, her mother had received a letter from my cousin saying how much she loved her and that she didn't want her worrying too much.

Losing my cousin was devastating because she was like a mother to me. As a kid, I was always around her and people would constantly ask, "Is that your daughter?" She'd smile and say, "Yeah, something like that."

Trying to process my cousin's death was one of the hardest things I thought I would have to deal with until I received some news that altered my entire existence. I never thought in a million years something like this would touch my life but when two of my daughters told me that a close family member had been molesting them for two years, my world changed forever.

Is history destined to repeat itself? Just a few months ago, my cousin was here in this hell hole and now I'm in the place I never thought I'd be. This space is too small, the food is horrible and it's too many people in one room. I'm afraid to show any signs of weakness or they'll try and take advantage of me. And this crazy girl has already been threatening to rape me and turn me out. I'm glad I have some fight in me because at 4'11", I need to make sure I can protect my short self from these Amazon giants in this jail cell. I can't believe I allowed myself to get into this situation but now that I'm here, I have to deal with it. Nevertheless, I miss my kids soooo much and I want to go home.

Going to jail for committing a crime versus not paying tickets are definitely different experiences. When I went to jail for speeding tickets, they had me in a holding cell for two days and I cried the whole time and didn't eat. Now I'm locked up with murderers, rapists, and robbers for God knows how long, so I have to eat the slop they're serving me and I can't cry. . . at least not without anyone seeing me and trying to punk me.

When I found out this close family member physically and mentally abused my children, life no longer mattered to me because I felt like I failed my kids. I put them in harm's way of a predator.

My world stopped turning and, for a moment, I went temporarily insane. So when a so-called friend came to me with a ridiculous proposition, I accepted. Hell, I figured, "What did I have to lose? I've already let my kids down and lost my cousin so what's the point in trying to live right?"

Adrian wanted me to help him recover some money from a former friend and my role in the scenario was supposed to be really simple. He said nobody would get hurt because he knew me well enough to know that I didn't have the heart to seriously harm someone, even if I was hurting and didn't give a damn about life at the moment.

At that point, I had known my friend for almost three years but hadn't gotten into his personal life too much. I knew he had a lot of women and because they knew me as his platonic friend, they'd always call me looking for him. I'd have to call him (usually when he was out with another woman) to tell him, "Girlfriend #3 just called me so make sure to call her." That was the extent of our relationship but over time, we became pretty cool—or so I thought.

He'd told me about a guy he used to do business with back in the day who had stolen from him and owed him some money. Because he had been dodging my friend, the plan was to get the guy to meet him somewhere and make him repay the money.

He decided the best place to have the guy meet was at my house since it was neutral ground. I figured it wasn't a bad idea and didn't see any harm in that until. . .

The moment Adrian pulled out that gun is the exact moment I realized that I'd made a terrible mistake.

Things went left real fast.

Adrian demanded that I tie the guy up so now I'm scared. "Tie him up with what?"

He put his backpack on my dining room chair, pulled some rope out of his bag, and tossed the rope to me. "Use this," he said, "And hurry up!"

My mind was racing a thousand miles a minute. I didn't sign up for this. I thought this was supposed to be a conversation. Sure, it may have gotten a little heated but no ropes and guns were supposed to be involved.

I tried my best to tie his hands behind his back but, hell, I didn't know what I was doing. Of course, my so-called friend got frustrated and pushed me out of the way to finish the job. Once he secured the knot, he put the guy in my closet under the stairs and blindfolded him.

"Keep an eye on him until I get back. I need to go grab something from the store".

"Wait, you're leaving me here with him by myself? Hell, no. I'm not doing this!"

"He's secure. He won't get loose."

He walks out and I'm pacing back and forth trying to think clearly.

"There's a man tied up in my closet and it ain't role-playing either. What am I supposed to do? If I leave him tied up and Adrian comes back, there's no telling what he will do to him. And if I let him go, this guy might try to hurt me. Or my friend may get pissed off at me for letting him go. Think think think."

The closet door creaked a little as I was opening it, "Listen, I don't know what's going on but I can't be part of this."

I loosened the knot a smidgen and hauled ass outta there. Yes, I left my own house.

I was scared, worried, and furious all at the same time. *"You just got me caught up in an armed robbery situation. And this shit happened at my damn house."* My thoughts were racing.

I hope he got away.

I decided to stay with my mom for a while because my home didn't feel the same after that. Plus, Adrian has been showing up unannounced, calling my phone all the time, and stalking the hell out of me. He's been asking me who I've talked to, where I'm going, or what I've said. I really don't trust who he is or what he's capable of at this point.

When Adrian finally got arrested, I was very relieved but little did I know that it was just the beginning.

My so-called friend got arrested and then my family member went to jail for molesting my children. Less than a month later, I was picked up on aggravated robbery charges.

Well, at least now I know for sure he got away.

My bond was originally set at $100k and of course I didn't have that kind of money. I also couldn't afford a decent lawyer so the court appointed me one. He turned out to be my guardian angel. The lawyer went back and forth with the judge and DA to get my bond reduced. He had a good argument since I'd never been to jail for anything more than traffic tickets. The first attempt got the bond reduced to $50k and I remained in jail because I still couldn't pay that amount.

I sat in jail for 3½ months before my lawyer was able to get my bond dropped to $2,500, which is unheard of for an aggravated case. I'm really feeling hopeful because all I need is for someone to take $250 to the bail bondsman so I can get home to my kids. They've already been through enough and they need their mother.

The day my mother went to post my bond, she had a massive stroke that put her in a wheelchair. And my kids were put into foster care. I thought life was bad before, but now, the system has my kids and I'm still in jail. Plus, I have a felony case pending.

All I could think about was never seeing my kids again.

Even though I had been bonded out, it took a week for me to be released. They wanted to put a monitor on my leg to keep track of me until my trial date.

My mom's house feels so empty and I'm all alone because she was admitted into a nursing home after being discharged from the hospital. My kids are living with strangers and I have no job, no car and I've lost my home. This leg monitor is ridiculous. How do they expect me to get anything done when I can only go outside for a few hours, four days a week?

What now? I needed to find a way to see my kids and I hope they didn't split them up.

I was able to speak with the caseworker handling my CPS case and she made arrangements for me to see my children. After the first visit with my children, I knew I had to figure out how to get them home. I wasn't concerned about the robbery case, how much time I would get, or what would happen in court, I just wanted my kids.

Even though there were no guarantees, I sat down with the caseworker and made a plan.

Parenting classes. Counseling. Job search. Transportation issues. Looking for a place to live. Community service. And only one hour a week with my kids? How could I get all this done in such a short time and a couple of hours a day?

They gave me an impossible task to accomplish and are probably praying that I fail because they don't want me to get my kids anyway. But I have to prove them wrong. I have to turn this around.

I struggled but little by little, one class completed. One job lead. One counseling session finished. One hour of community service turned in.

This went on for months until one day, I was offered Section 8 housing to get a place to live. I found a job and got a car. And then the best thing that could have happened to me was being told that my kids were coming home three days before Christmas.

Life was looking brighter but the eye of the hurricane had really just begun.

Now it was time to heal. I had to celebrate my kids coming home while learning how to communicate about sexual abuse and have the "It's not your fault" conversation with them. I had to explain to them why it took me eight months to get them back home and why I had been in jail. And I had to learn how to forgive someone who had taken the most precious thing from me. . . my kids' innocence.

I wore the monitor for nine months until the courts decided I wasn't a flight risk but had to wait two years to go to court for my robbery charges.

During the time it took me to get my kids back and go to court, I needed something to keep me sane during all this madness.

I was working at a tax office when I got the idea to host a community event and in 2004, I got my taste of the entrepreneurial life. I was putting together an event called Dance Explosion, which featured a series of competitions, performances, and giveaways. The event had to be put on hold because things were happening in my life and I didn't feel ready.

By the time I started back working on the event, Hurricane Katrina hit Louisiana and a lot of the survivors ended up in my city, Dallas, Texas. Whoa! I needed to do something.

All I could think about at this point was, "How can I impact these people's lives with what I know? How can I help them to see the light during a time such as this?"

I didn't quite know what I was being called to assist with, but I knew I had to help. So I got on the phone, called the radio station (not hoping for much), and got through. I told them I was hosting an event and would like to make an announcement inviting anyone to drop off donations of toiletries, blankets, and household items to help these survivors. Then I contacted the Dallas Independent School District and asked if they would be willing to donate a bus for the day to transport fifty families to my event and back so they could have some kind of relief from the tragedy that just hit. They agreed.

When I got to the venue where I was hosting the event I was floored. There were overflowing boxes everywhere! People had heard me on the radio and dropped things off for these families. And then the survivors showed up. Everyone had a good time and even though I had my own trials to deal with, none of it mattered at that moment. Seeing those people smile through the pain was all that I needed to keep going.

DAY OF THE TRIAL

I am sweating bullets. I don't know what to expect but prison time. How will my kids react when they see their mother being dragged away from them forever? My heart couldn't take it. I thought about ending it before it started. If I take my own life right now then I wouldn't have to see the hurt in my kids' eyes or hear them say "Mom, you weren't there for us. Again." But something inside told me to keep going. You've come this far, this ain't the time to give up.

And then it happened. The judge said, "Approach the bench." Butterflies in my stomach. I felt like I was about to crap myself. I looked around, asking myself "Where's the jury and when does the trial start?"

One year probation. No need to report to an officer. No community service. All your charges have been reduced to misdemeanors. No trial.

"What did you say?" I didn't hear that correctly. "I have what?"

The district attorney called me into his office.

"Latoya, you're not like these criminals I see coming in this courtroom day in and day out. You're not a bad person, just someone who got caught up in a bad situation because you were hurting. But I see a light at the end of your tunnel. It's something about you. Stop hurting people and do good with what you have. And If I ever see you in my courtroom or any other courtroom, I will make sure they throw the book at you. Now get out of here and go live your life."

It turns out that my lawyer, the judge, and the DA were all good friends.

Before walking into the courtroom that day and after contemplating ending everything right then, I told myself and God, "If I get out of this situation, I will use everything I know and have learned to inspire others."

And guess what? I was given the opportunity to do just that.

Latoya Garrett, is an award-winning storyteller, community builder and the original Storiologist. She helps rising thought leaders, entrepreneurs and visionaries strengthen their personal and professional relationships through conversational storytelling.

Latoya's passion for connecting people to the right resources and opportunities stemmed from a desire to bring like-minded individuals together for stimulating conversations, interactive events and transformative experiences.

Her work managing, producing, and advising on over 1,000 events and projects since 2004, has positioned her as a community influencer. Her work has been featured in local news articles and valued by top nonprofits and large organizations. Latoya uses her relationship-building and networking skills to teach others how to partner with the right people, establish valuable connections and expand their network.

When she's not developing thoughts into words or creating stories out of conversations, you can find her taking millions of personality quizzes, looking for community events to attend or developing fresh engaging stories to tell.

Learn more at: **latoyagarrett.com**

Special Gift

A 5 minute breath-focused meditation
to help you face your fears and step back into
the present moment.

**drive.google.com/file/d/1ceReQ
RN-LmsElOeuSb2TapGVPQqG6iph/view?ts=61239257**

YeMamaYa, Cleansing the Heart of the Hurts from the Mother Wound

BY JOCELYN GORDON

I stood, and I waited—the wild jungle behind me, the beckoning ocean before. I always gave reverence to the sea. And despite identifying as a Water Baby, I was tentative.

The ocean giveth and she taketh away.

Stepping forward, alone and timeless, it appears I had the beach to myself. Even more to consider in terms of safety, and yet it was clear that the moment was sacred.

Familiar yet foreign, this beach was new to me—brown sand rather than white or pink; rocks making mosaics, driftwood accenting the terrain.

Stepping forward and stepping over, I heard howler monkeys and my own thoughts.

A Queen of Cups, I arrived at the cusp of land and sea and contemplated my origin. I felt a desire to conjure my future.

Entering the ocean sea—tipa tipa, step by step—I proceeded, grounded yet compliant like bamboo. This was my home. I was familiar with fierce love.

Called forward, I walked with the water draping my legs like a long bridal train. I waded and waited, not knowing for what. . .

Is it safe, am I safe? What am I doing here?

"Come closer," She said.

Observing the ocean and the light, the foam and gentle roar, I complied.

"Come closer."

I immersed myself, head underwater. Silence ensued. Standing out was nothing yet everything. And in the space between the words and the worlds, She appeared in my heart.

THE MOTHER OF THE WATERS

This was 2010 in Puntarenas, Dominical on my first trip to Costa Rica. I had entered new territory in my professional and creative life, working more deeply with women, movement, and embodiment. The retreat center, where I would be guiding and teaching more than twenty women, was a short walk away. It was also the beginning of a new relationship with my mother and the pain we had caused each other.

For as long as I can remember, I've been a disruptor in my family lineage. I entered the family constellation clear that the mother-daughter distortion and betrayal ended with me—and that I would not carry it forward. I remember feeling this as a young child without even knowing the "story" that wove its way between my great-grandmother and my grandmother, my grandmother and my mother, and now, between my mom and me. I could feel the ripples of concentric circles that extended beyond those I knew.

In my work as a somatic educator, pre-conception doula, and conscious conception coach, I have noticed that the patterns of pain experienced in one's own life have origins in the lives of those who came before—our ancestors. If looked upon closely yet from a higher perspective (attained through frequency shifting, or entering a space of consciousness alternative to the default mind), the patterns of addiction, betrayal, and abuse can be seen and acknowledged through the lens of love. For many, this pattern is eased; for some, it is fully transformed into power. In preparation for bringing a soul to the earth, this conscious journey makes the energetic environment more clear and open for the descendant coming forward. You can also embrace this approach as a way to rebirth yourself.

As I write this, I remember standing in the bathroom as a child, near the age of five, and feeling into my matrilineal timeline. I now realize a thread that weaves me backward and forward to the ocean on the day She revealed herself to me.

MOTHER WHOSE CHILDREN ARE THE FISH

Yemaya—the Yoruba and Afro-Caribbean Mother of Mothers, Goddess of the Ocean—revealed herself to me not in form, but in spirit through the bridge between my heart and my eyes.

Protector of women, conception, pregnancy, and childbirth, Yemaya is a water spirit and orisha, patron of the ocean, rivers, and waterways. She resides in the upper depths of the water—the spaces that the sun penetrates. Her husband is the god of soil and their daughter, the goddess of wind.

She is deeply loving and nurturing, protective and strong, caring for her children—humanity—with gentility, and when necessary, destruction and fierce love.

Yemaya—in long-form, *Yeye Omo Eja,* which means "Mother Whose Children are the Fish"—is often called upon after conception for protection of the gestating child, during childbirth for ease, and to heal matters of the heart by cleansing sorrow. As the ultimate mother, the consummate matriarch, Yemaya embodies the full characteristics of nurturance and love.

THE GODDESS WHO MADE ME

My mom—a goddess in form, six foot two, gorgeous and glowing, uber-successful in business, dedicated and obliged to the commitments that come with family, enjoyed and admired by a strong community of friends, has her own secrets and womanly sorrows.

My mother and her sister were raised to be perfect. A matter of survival. Black people couldn't survive by being *good enough;* they had to be excellent. This higher standard brings much to celebrate and also comes with an intensity that can affect the inner spirit and health of a person.

My mother was born after the Great Depression to rather progressive parents who paved uncharted territory for black people. Her mother, Corrynne, was raised in the Bronx, attended Brooklyn College, worked for the U.S. government as a mathematician during World War II, and opened a gyrotonic fitness center in New Jersey in 1964. She traveled extensively. Russia, Afghanistan, Turkey, and more—rather unheard for a woman of her color and in her time. She was very involved in her community, a member of the Alpha Kappa Alpha Sorority, and a contributor to scholarships for students in need.

My paternal grandfather was born poor and black in Smithfield, Virginia. He was able to go to school—a one-room schoolhouse—because *his* grandfather paid the teacher in room and board. Immediately after high school, my grandfather made his way north. He met my grandmother in 1945 after his journey as a Tuskegee Airman serving within the air tower command center. He later attended Rutgers University, became an internationally-regarded electrical engineer, received a Congressional Gold Medal, and was an esteemed guest at the initial inauguration of President Obama.

While Corrynne nurtured her budding career, her daughter—my mother—spent a lot of time with her grandmother, known as Nana. There was a current of tension between the two women, as Corrynne both needed the help and probably felt some jealousy and resentment of being crowded out of the usual mother-daughter bond. By the time Corrynne had her second daughter twelve years after my mother, her career was firmly established, and the second daughter was raised differently. My mother, in her adult years, reconciled what she gained: the depth of love she had with Nana.

ISLAND BABY

I was conceived and born in Bermuda, a beautiful landscape surrounded by blue water and bordered by pink-and-white sand. My beautiful mother and I were close. She said I was loving and feisty.

From the lens of my innocence, my mom's first fall from grace happened when I was five as my parents were divorcing. This shifted her attention from me to her professional pursuits (or at least it felt that way to me at that age). Unlike her a generation earlier, I didn't have a Nana at home to fill in the gaps. In my innocence and deep loss, I decided that I didn't want to be like her, my mother. I projected onto my mother my sadness from not having my dad around. When she later married a man who I didn't like, much less love, I felt betrayed and alone.

In my early adolescence, I was molested by a family friend, and I felt like my mother didn't protect me. For decades, intense arguments ensued, and it took years for me to articulate my rage.

My mom and I have been each other's agitator—and each other's ally. We have encouraged the other to let go of control. Mom has journeyed with me through my own solo parenting journeys as the bookend parent of two young queens—one who is entering young adulthood (Jordan), and the other in her early single digits (Sienna). Mom was a huge support with my eldest daughter—financially and physically—and offered her blessing as Jordan and I moved to Bali in 2014 to become global citizens, build my online school, and anticipate meeting the father of my youngest (a true story which includes a ten-year conscious conception journey, a story I share in my book *Make Space For Baby*).

During the early years of my eldest's life, I still shadow-danced with my own unprocessed grief and rage. Fiercely protective, I created a lifestyle of close proximity. But some of that time included me in a frozen pattern with my own trauma. At times I was close but not always present. I awakened to the reality that, though my mother somehow made single motherhood look glamorous, it is not.

Even as a lineage disruptor, I've made some parenting mistakes. Shocking, right? I've been unavailable at times, forced to make challenging decisions (as is a norm in this life) and during my time in Bali, married a man that my eldest didn't like (as a rule, I feel it is important to partner with people your children admire, respect, and appreciate, but I say this having hindsight).

And yet, through divine providence, conscious effort, and being in the prayers of our ancestors, my daughters and I are emotionally close. My eldest loves to tell me how I could have done things better in those former days of our karmic journey. I listen.

Trauma-informed embodiment practice, presence with nature, motherhood, time, and love have been my healing balms. With personal growth, I began to soften and grow in gratitude for the structures that my mother's professional success afforded. As I simultaneously claimed my own unique life path, I realized that I was the dream of my ancestors. I embraced being generationally blessed with unprecedented freedom. This permission to roam brought us—my mom, my daughters, and me—transformative immersions in culture and nature-rich landscapes around the world. As such, I am currently parenting my youngest differently than my first.

> "Mother is the word for God in the lips and
> hearts of little children."
> —WILLIAM MAKEPEACE THACKERY

As I emerged to the top of the water, a realization washed over me—a child deifies the mother, regarding the mother as a god, perfect and holy. This is natural and necessary for survival, as symbolically and literally, the mother is the giver of life, sustainer, and affirmer. However, looking up to the mother, the child places her on a pedestal of perfection—a throne that is also a tall and precarious ladder. The fall is steep.

Apotheosis, the elevation of a human to god status, makes the fall back to earth so very painful for both mother and child. Can anyone hurt a child more than its mother?

At some point, for our own peace, we must make peace with our mother's wounds and womanhood, accepting her journey as an epic with plot twists, mishaps, victories, and challenges, just as within our own lives. We must grieve the fantasy and separate the woman from the goddess archetype. In this way, we can embrace authenticity rather than perfection, acceptance over approval, and allow the full spectrum of our own being.

As we grow into womanhood and become mothers ourselves, we accumulate our own triumphs and tragedies. With maturity, our podium ascends and we meet our mother, no longer seeing her on a pedestal.

> "The mother-child relationship can be seen
> as the first relationship violated
> by patriarchy."
> —ADRIENNE RICH

It would be remiss to discuss the Mother Wound without acknowledging the dominating culture of patriarchy, which amplifies the illusion of perfection and separates the Earth, the body, and the feminine from the divinity of life.

With power being the dominating drive and influence within patriarchy, the Mother Wound is a struggle with and for empowerment. Affecting self-esteem and sense of self, the wound disrupts the development of authentic confidence.

Look around and within and you will see women and daughters using dysfunctional coping methods to deal with pervasive feelings of shame ("something is wrong with me") and unworthiness ("I'm not good enough") and to suppress a vague yet enduring sense of loss. The influence of the pain of what was denied and not received, mixed with a struggle to reach one's full potential, can manifest as self-sabotage, control, depression, addiction, anxiety, and the generational perpetuation of pain. All this is amplified by the separation of self from nature, a denial of the Earth as us and She as we.

A commitment to address the Mother Wound is essential for unraveling the influences of patriarchy. Explicating the pain and seeking healing around the foundational relationship in life and with life— Mother—is essential for true well-being. What awaits is a reconnection with the full spectrum of life and a renewed ability to live true and truly empowered. Healing the Mother Wound is a contribution to lineage healing, helping women liberate themselves, accept their sacred humanity, and grow in love.

STEPS TOWARD RECONCILING THE MOTHER WOUND

Here are some ways that you can align with Self, Spirit, and Nature to help you alchemize the Mother Wound:

Make a Sacred Declaration and Ally with Spirit

Reconnect with the Elements and Ally with Nature

Create an Altar

Cast a Wide Net of Compassion

Grieve the Mothering You Didn't Receive

Nurture Yourself

Seek Support

MAKE A SACRED DECLARATION AND ALLY WITH SPIRIT

A declaration is an announcement, explicit and clear, of your desire—your desire to live unhindered by the resentment, grudges, guilt, and density of the pain from the Mother Wound. This statement should be seasoned with willingness, watered with sincerity, and peppered by an open heart. It should be informed by what you want and what you are ready to release and receive. It should allow space for personal and divine intervention.

Declarations are also a statement of faith and belief in the good things coming.

On this healing journey, to declare—to make clear—is a first step and one you can embrace in the many moments that you will revisit this sacred topic. Your declaration can be a reminder, a compass, and a soothing balm. Return to it when you feel doubtful or find yourself complaining or complacent. Expect this powerful statement to create a shift in your psyche, your heart, and your life. Allow your declaration to transform over time as you receive blessings of enlightenment.

Here are some tips to help you cultivate your sacred declaration:

- Grab a journal and pen and find a comfortable space (you may wish to have a timer present for a forthcoming step).

- Get quiet and center in your heart.

- Focus on the rise and fall of your breath as you imagine and feel yourself in a natural space by the water.

- Bring into your heart the relationship with mother, motherhood, and mothering—feel the feels as you tune into the tides of this emotional energy.

- While in this feeling state, journal and free-write without stopping for ten minutes or more. Return to your heart and create an intention or series of intentions with clear "I AM _____" statements established in the present such as "I am successful, I forgive. I am forgiven," or "I am supported, I am free." You may feel called to a more specific statement such as "I release the burdens of the past and embrace the joy of the moment."

- Consider expanding your declaration by turning it/them into a poem, prayer, or song.

- Call in your connection with Spirit, Great Mystery, God, your higher self, and or ancestors as you sing, speak, shout, or whisper your sacred declaration. Repeat it over and over.

- For example: "Great Spirit, I decree and declare that I am successful. Waves of compassion wash through me. I release the burdens of the past and embrace the joy of the moment. My heart is uplifted and my life is supported. I forgive and I am forgiven. I am free! And so it is. Ashe. Aho. Amen."

- You may wish to explore one or all of the following journal prompts:

  > How has the mother relationship influenced your life, relationships, and decisions?

  > What resentments, wishes, or grudges might you be holding against the mother figures in your life?

  > What guilt, grudges, and resentment do you hold around your own mothering?

  > What are you learning in your life right now?

> › What are you releasing?

> › What do you want—what do you really, *really* want?

> › Write a fulfilling unfolding: How would you like to feel about your mother, mothering, and motherhood?

> › Write a letter (a letter you will not send) to your mother, inner child, children, or Creator: What is your wish and desire for healing and forgiveness?

RECONNECT WITH THE ELEMENTS AND ALLY WITH NATURE

The spirit of our planet is often referred to as "Great Mother" or Gaia. We are made of the elements that make her—earth, water, air, fire, and spirit—and will return to the elements upon death. Her elements connect us with all of creation; they whisper the stories of the past, reveal insight that will heal the present, and express the medicine that will nourish the future.

Mama Gaia, or Nature, calls you back to yourself—out of the head and into the body, back from the techno craze and into her sacred rhythms. She is a powerful healer. When out of sync with her rhythms, the effects are witnessed individually as anxiety, depression, and chronic pain—and collectively as ecological injustice.

Yemaya revealed herself to me in the ocean. She helped to cleanse my sorrows. The ocean waves as her grace refreshed me with compassion and allowed me to move forward, accepting of my own womanhood and my mother's.

Your time with nature is about listening, realizing, harmonizing, and allowing. Trust in the power of presence allied with nature. Allow Mother Nature to transform density (i.e., crap) into the fertile soil that permits the brilliance of your lotus heart to emerge and grow.

Make a commitment to ally with the Earth, a natural healer:

Spend time in the sun, at the ocean, or near waterfalls. Bathe yourself in her waters. The negative ions released as UV rays meet dynamically moving water, can charge and create shifts in your physiology and energy. Evidence shows that exposure to negative ions can reduce symptoms of depression, improve your mood, boost immunity, and help your body fight disease.

Find a cathedral of trees to call your own. *Forest Bathing* is a Japanese concept that emerged in 1982 when citizens were urged to explore wooden areas as a form of therapy. Evidence shows that time with the trees can decrease stress hormones and regulate heart rate and blood pressure, all of which support trauma remediation. Create time each week (or each day if you can!) to Forest Bathe; lean on trees, sit on a rock, and meditate or journal, dance, breathe and move as a way to heal from within, speak with the ancestors, connect with God, and receive wisdom.

Place your feet and body on the Earth. Skin-to-earth contact, knowing as "Earthing," brings you in direct contact with the Earth's rhythms. Experiments with Earthing show improvements in sleep, reduction of chronic pain, and increase of vitality.

All pain and dis-ease are said to start on the energetic and emotional levels. Walk barefoot, garden, place your body on the sand, and harmonize with the earth in support of your energetic, emotional, and physiological healing.

CREATE AN ALTAR

An altar is a physical representation of your inner intention and sacred declaration. Altars have been used for centuries and across cultures as shrines for special occasions or as ongoing, evolving representations of a person or culture's connection with Spirit.

Your altar or altars represent sacred space and can become your marked space for prayer, reflection, conscious movement, meditation, or contemplation. Your altar can remind you of your purpose and power. As you collect each altar item, place them on the altar and then visit the altar each day, you bring your attention to your intention, you focus on what truly matters, and you call forth the insight, energy, and divine guidance that will help you heal, release, and receive.

I find the most potent altars have items representing each of the elements:

Earth: flowers, crystals, fruits, and vegetables

Water: a bowl or glass of water, seashells, river rocks, sea glass

Air: feathers and or smudging elements such as sweetgrass, cedar, or mugwort

Fire: candles (flamed or battery-powered)

Spirit: pictures or symbols representing ancestors, your deity of focus, or spiritual guide/s

Gathering Your Items. Keep your declaration in your heart as you gather the items for your altar. Get creative and stay open to the perfect items arriving in the most serendipitous ways. You may also wish to pay attention to your dreams noticing images, words, or songs that you may wish to write, find, and place on your altar.

Creating Your Altar. When setting up your altar, create a mood with music, movement, and meditation. Place each item with intention and move things around until the placement feels right. Release perfectionism and have fun.

Maintaining Your Altar. Be sure to keep the energy at your altar fresh and alive. You can do this by lighting a candle each day, smudging the area and your home throughout the day, setting fresh flowers, or sitting or standing at the altar with your hands at your heart.

Re-Creating Your Altar. You will know when it is time to redo your altar. Some people create new altars with each new or full moon; others re-create altars in flow with their menstrual cycle. Perhaps you wish to create an altar on your mother's birthday. You will know when the energy has shifted and when the altar needs to be renewed to represent what is most potent for you and your life.

Altar In Writing

My youngest daughter and I recreate our altar every four to six weeks. We created an altar for the writing of this piece. I wanted it to represent Yemaya, my mother, my daughters, the intention for this piece, and my forthcoming book *Make Space For Baby: A Preconception Guidebook Preparing Your Heart, Home & Body For Sacred Parenthood*. Yemaya resides in the ocean, and her colors are blue and white, so I purchased blue fabric, a soft burlap weave cloth to represent netting fisher-people use, and white candles. At a farmers' market, I found a beautiful and sizable conch shell. At the local craft store, I purchased pearl-like trims and string lights with an outside casing of Himalayan salt. We live by the ocean and have a lot of shells, so my daughter placed some delicately on the altar. She also positioned photos and enjoyed helping me with the flower decorations. I light the main candle in the morning and smudge the area a few times a day, which is centering for me. I renew the saltwater bowl every other day. We don't have a television so my main altar is in the living room at the wall where a TV might be. Above it is a profile drawing of my mom and I taken from years ago on one of her visits to see me in college. The image was drawn twenty-six years ago. I was twenty, an emerging woman, and my mom was forty-six, the same chronological age I am at the time of this writing.

CAST A WIDE NET OF COMPASSION

Years ago in meditation, this definition of compassion came to me: "Compassion is the container that holds all things." This definition of compassion—not to be mistaken for complacency or having none to poor boundaries—allows you to honor the full spectrum of your personhood and that of another. To be clear, it does not mean condoning abuse, violence, or neglect. It does include easing your own suffering, forgiving yourself, and seeking to do the same toward others. Compassion is the balm that can soothe rigidity and shame and can fuel the courage to establish healthy boundaries as you become a guardian of your peace.

Can you hold a wide container of compassion for yourself?

This is deep work so please be patient and gentle.

GRIEVE THE MOTHERING YOU DID NOT RECEIVE

In my moment with Yemaya, I began the process of grieving the mother I did not have and, more so, the shame-infused fantasy of motherhood perfection projected by society. Sorting my story of *mother* allowed me to receive, accept, and celebrate the sacred woman who nurtured my life. In turn, I can reclaim and accept myself.

Use the invitations here to create space in your day and life for grief and grieving.

NURTURE YOURSELF

Self-care is essential, both to tend to your earth body and to fill your cup so you have the emotional energy to show up for this process. In a society that does not esteem the feminine (as evidenced by first world maternal and infant care, among many other examples) and disparages the Earth rather than nurturing and protecting it, cleansing the hurts of the Mother Wound is both an individual process of healing and a form of activism. This is a process of unraveling the negative imprints of patriarchy, including a forced and unrealistic idea of productivity, and the lies we tell ourselves and have been told. This includes understanding patterns of neglect, acknowledging the decisions you've been forced to make to be productive, renegotiating your relationship with your body (and rest!), and reestablishing alignment with your natural rhythms.

The invitations in this section are all forms of self-care. Quiet, contemplative, and sometimes wild moments will reveal to you the ways you can more deeply love, nurture, and empower yourself.

SEEK SUPPORT

You may be reparenting yourself. You may be seeking to show up for your child or children in renewed ways. You may be navigating an addiction or focused on trauma remediation. Whether or not your Mother Wound is directly related to your mother or stimulated by a breach in connection with the earth or Spirit, community and support are essential. I encourage you to find a therapist that allies with the body, not just the mind. Cultivate a village and web of support that includes a coach, allies, trusted childcare providers, and support groups. Essentially, this is inner-child work and ancestral healing.

> "Children begin by loving their parents;
> as they grow older they judge them;
> sometimes, they forgive them."
>
> *—OSCAR WILDE*

We all have to make practical and sometimes heartbreaking decisions. We are living within an oppressive system while simultaneously crafting solutions that cultivate surviving and thriving. Women have to walk the tightrope of parenting and profession, providing and nurturing, self-care and selflessness, no matter the presence of communal support. But we are resilient. We are powerful.

As I write this, I again feel into my mother's humanity and her personal journey. I accept her womanhood and celebrate her unique path. I forgive and allow. There is love here.

With love, I accept my own motherhood travails and celebrate my growth. I forgive and allow. There is love here.

Looking forward, I embrace the sacred journey of my daughters. I ask for their forgiveness and celebrate their sacred autonomy. There is love here.

I give thanks to Yemaya for her graces shared that day in Dominical.

An agent of nature and spirit, Yemaya represents water, flow, empowerment, and a lineage of strength.

Her invitation:

Be soft enough to yield and fierce enough to disrupt.

Dive in. It is time.

Called a "Yoga Rebel" by Yoga Journal Magazine, **Jocelyn Gordon** is known for her joyful integrations of dance, yoga and meditation— HoopYogini™ and Bhakti Boogie Yoga.

She has toured nationally with Wanderlust, is a six time presenter at the Bali Spirit Festival, has worked with Academy Award winning actresses Halle Berry and Marisa Tomei, and was recently featured on Apple News as the Meditation Guide for the *Essence Magazine* Virtual Wellness House.

Jocelyn is a mother of two young queens and is currently writing *Make Space For Baby: A Preconception Guidebook Preparing Your Heart, Home & Body For Sacred Parenthood.* As a Conscious Conception Coach and Rebirth Guide, she supports people considering parenting by helping them up-level their health and vibration before pregnancy. As The Course Doula, Jocelyn helps healers create their first online course and coaching offerings. Jocelyn's offerings support women with fertility, embodiment and leadership.

Learn more at: **HoopYogini.com/connect, JocelynGordon.com**

Special Gift

The Inner Circle
**A monthly self-care membership for conscious leaders.
Find your center and fill your cup.**

The Inner Circle is a Membership Portal *for Space Holders,
Educators and Conscious Leaders with weekly live classes,
monthly online retreats, resources, and community activations to
keep your cup overflowing as you serve the world.*
**Jocelyn Gordon delivers time-proven practices that help you
connect, center, and circulate your energy.**

Access The Inner Circle for free! This link for *Ancient-Future
Unity* readers extends a 14-day FREE trial:
bit.ly/TIC14DAYS

How I Freed My Voice as a Black Woman

BY JACKIE GRAVES

I am laughing—and flying.

Salt spray splashes my face, and I taste freedom. I'm riding a boat out to swim with the dolphins in Hawaii.

"Sit anywhere you like," our guide says, and I straddle the edge, one leg dangling in the water, one leg in the boat.

My thighs grip the inflated tube like I'm riding a horse or even a whale. I spread my arms wide. My full body YES feels like open wings.

I arch back, heart lifting to the sky.

I used to believe I had to work hard for everything. To push my body beyond its limits and struggle through life in constant pain to get what I wanted. That was my reality for a long time.

But this is a journey about surrender.

To write my memoir, I had to surrender to the divine spark that drove me.

I was writing the deepest secrets of my childhood, the deepest shames of my adult life, the deepest grief. The grief, pain, and shame stories echoed in my head so long until they were all I could hear—not good enough, not worthy, not white enough, not Black enough, not lovable.

To keep putting down one word after another was an immense act of faith.

It was all too much for anyone else to deal with—or so I told myself. I kept the stories inside for so long, with a smile on my face, so no one could see the pain.

I wish I could say it happened in a flash, a brilliant, beautiful awakening, like a shooting star across the sky. But awakening takes time for many of us.

In my dreams, I see Atlas.

He towers over me, his thighs chiseled, bulky things. Smooth sockets of stone stare at me where his eyes should be, and I stifle a shudder.

My Mom, my sisters, and I passed this statue every day on the way to the Donnell Library or Central Park.

In my dreams, I stand stock-still, so he won't see me. Atlas hoists the world on his back, straining under its weight, rage on his face. I know I cannot make a sound, or he will kill me.

I swallow the fear, but a primal sound escapes my throat, a moan, my terror.

Atlas turns and glares at me with eyes that aren't there.

Skyscrapers etch a jagged scar in the blue above his head. Fear pounds my chest.

Atlas sneers and rears back. The world is heavy—and he is sick of it, sick of it all. Sick of holding it, sick of looking at me. He hurls the world like a comet—and I am too small to make him stop. I am powerless to save the world.

Atlas with eyes like Daddy.

I silenced my voice as a young child.

My angry, scary father could be triggered by anything at any time— the wind closing a door, a too-loud peal of laughter. When Daddy was home, an invisible hand clamped over my mouth and strangled my throat.

FACTS.

I am 52 years old, an educator of 30 years. I am the second of four daughters, a middle child from the time I was fourteen months. I am a sister. I have no biological children.

I identify as Black. I also identify as mixed race, born of parents who inhabited very different-colored bodies and who walked very different life paths, from each other and from me.

Growing up, when people asked me what I was, existential anguish gripped my soul. In 1970s New York City, we didn't have a language for mixedness. I knew I was different, something "other" and indefinable. Sometimes "special." Most of the time "wrong." I wanted to fix myself, to fit in, to be one with all.

I knew from a young age that I was a writer—I kept "Books," as I called them (rather than "journals")—where I recorded my thoughts, overheard scraps of conversations, attempts at poems that I never shared with anyone.

Growing up, I struggled with identity. My Black father hit and silenced me; my white mother was carted away to a mental hospital. I was not Black enough, not white enough. What the hell was I anyway?

I knew a truth deep inside my soul—We are all One. One love. One heart—and yet separation was my reality. My white and Black worlds never met, never overlapped, inhabited different spaces. I kept my groups of friends separate.

While I was in grad school getting my Master's in Creative Writing, I had visions of my book. I was coming to voice, workshopping stories and poems, and teaching writing to bright-eyed youth.

I loved my students; I loved to write; I loved to inspire. I was good at it—everybody told me. But I couldn't feel their praise. My heart hardened against myself. Not good enough, not worthy. My father's angry, critical voice from childhood, internalized and omnipresent.

To free my voice as a Black woman required many choices and mini-miracles. Finding my *yes* in a world that spoke *no after no.*

I wrote myself into becoming, unlocking my secrets as the stories unwound onto the page.

I swim over the coral reef, becoming one with the fishies. The bright yellow tang, the long, pale-blue needle-nosed fish, the white-and-black striped Moorish idol. Their magnificent shapes and brilliant colors dance with the waves.

I see light streaming through my hands.

I am in an underwater world of magic and bliss.

Gliding effortlessly through the water, my body undulates with the mysteries of the ocean. My heart swells as the tide surges, yanking me this way and that. I hold my hands out in front of me, palms catching fragments of illumination. Light filters from the surface, transforms into prisms that splay from my fingers, out and down to the coral reef below.

I am that; I am all; I am one.

Waves of pleasure run through me, and I laugh. I breathe an *mmmmmm* into my pleasure center, and a song of satisfaction escapes my snorkel. I am joy; I am ecstasy, body bobbing with each breath, sensual as seaweed, pulled with the ocean.

That's when the dolphins come to me.

It's as if I am slipping into dreamtime. Synchronized sleek skin gliding above and below. Beside me. Smiling with the innocence of a baby in its sleep. Something loosens in my shoulders—fear, grief, sadness, loss—as my heart opens, safe in the embrace of the pod.

Surrender.
I feel the joy, let it activate and permeate every cell of my being.
I give myself permission to receive this ocean blessing.
My birthright of pleasure and abundance and liberation.
Feels so good. Feels so good.

I am a writer, teacher, healer, a lightworker shamanista priestess. It's taken me 52 years to discover and declare this identity.

Years of conditioning from society, family, religion, and education have layered shame and fear over my expression of truth.

If I speak my truth, those around me will die.

It is a work of faith and trust to open myself to a deeper truth: I will die if I do not speak.

I learn to drop my grounding roots deep into the earth, to burrow down and connect with the center of Mother Earth, to allow myself to be held and nurtured by the Great Mother. It takes becoming completely broken until I am willing to surrender the ego identity that has sustained me all these years. I realize that her identity is only a tiny part of the grandeur and magnificence of who I am and who I came to be. I have to let her go. I have to let parts of myself that no longer serve me die.

I cut myself free from the rape matrix. If I make a sound, I will be raped again and again and again. Primal terror cages my heart. Fear of the dark, fear of the unknown, fear of opening my mouth to speak out.

The fear comes not only from this lifetime but from past lives—many, many past lives. I am an old soul, a brave soul, who chose to incarnate into this experience of density in order to bring through liberation codes. When I free myself, I free many people. My liberation is the liberation of us all.

As I free myself, I free my ancestors—back and back into the past—forward and forward into future generations. I free future versions of myself. I close off timelines of rape and enslavement. As I heal myself, I bring an end to personal, collective, and ancestral suffering.

Chills rise on my arms and little hairs stand up. The truth has been written. I have been witnessed by my ancestors and celebrated and cheered. My ancestors are singing.

I source safety. Spirit has my back. Ancestors walk with me. Angels guide me. There is nothing to fear. I flow with ease and grace and joy.

I sing underwater, a song of joy and love, running energy through my body with every breath thru my snorkel. A wave of pleasure courses through me, and I exhale a pleasure song:

mmmmmmm
aaaaaaaahhhhh

The dolphins move up and down through the water like alpha waves. Their rhythmic motions entrancing the ocean around me. I feel suspended in their energy. Light radiates through my hands making magic pyramids, while I, moving like a mermaid, sense the dolphins next to me. I could reach out and touch them. Their joyful smiles.

A softening of stiffness and stuckness where my back has held burden, unworthiness, exhaustion, resentment—releasing like a butterfly fish, flying underwater.

I choose surrender.

I surrender to the call of my heart. I surrender to the path of joy, bliss, and pleasure.

It was hard to decide to allow myself this trip to Hawaii—to spend money at this difficult time, when everyone in my family is struggling, when I don't have money to spare. Who am I to experience something so decadent, so exhilarating, and wonderful?

And yet, it is exactly what I want. What my heart wanted. What my soul yearned for.

Limiting beliefs had kept me paralyzed for so long, afraid of speaking up and speaking out. By making this trip, I choose to step into a new reality—to step out of old patterns and oppressive cycles that keep me stuck in an infinite loop. With choice after choice, I create a new way of being, one that is more authentic, more aligned, kinder, less critical. Why deny the call of your soul?

An ancient part of me screams: *You're so selfish! You don't get to put yourself first. To give yourself pleasure and joy and fun when others are suffering.*

My rebirthed Self responds: *Oh, but you must. Choose joy, love, and freedom! Choose abundance! Your ancestors struggled so you wouldn't have to. To deny your liberation is to deny your ancestors. You're here to break the cycles. Claim your freedom now!*

My ancestors are with me now. I feel their presence, their celebration, their support.

For too long, I'd identified with legacies of oppression, poverty, and enslavement in my Black experience. To claim my joy as a Black woman is a revolutionary act. To declare my freedom is to dismantle, decolonize, and denounce that which has bound and gagged me.

I am here to rise, to liberate my voice, and to lead other women into liberating their voices. Our greatest pain will become our purpose. When we face the pain—feel it, dance with it, release it—we come out the other side transformed, transmuted, and glowingly in our power.

Trust me when I say: No matter how shameful they may feel, our stories are our strength.

And it's safe to hold our power. We don't have to give it away to anyone anymore—or cut ourselves into little pieces so everyone can get a slice. We get to gift ourselves loving self-care. To make time for ourselves, our needs, our wants, wishes, and desires. To give to others from a full heart—not from obligation, overgiving, codependence, or duty, which only leaves us feeling under-appreciated, under-valued, depleted.

We get to free ourselves.

I close my eyes.
I see myself radiant and free.
I claim back all parts of me—the abandoned, neglected, abused, and traumatized. I greet them like long-lost precious children.
I claim back all my victories—my awards, achievements, accomplishments; the never-fully acknowledged, denied, deflected; the celebrations I didn't think I deserved.
I claim them all.
I see the Oneness within myself.

I see the Oneness of all.
I vision a world of abundance where we each
are blessed to be in perfect harmony with our soul gifts,
the earth, and each other.

I can't stop looking at my hands underwater.
Light spills from my palms.
I am a magical creator being spinning webs of light.
The dolphins are swimming next to me.
And we are free.

Jackie Graves is a High Priestess of the new Golden Age, a writer, teacher, and healer. She has taught writing for over thirty years and is a tenured faculty member in the English Department at Laney College. She loves to write—short stories, poems, personal essays, plays, and most recently memoir. She believes in the transformative  power of the written and spoken word, and has been blessed to witness many of her students change their lives through finding their voices in writing.

Jackie's spiritual journey began after her sister suffered a massive stroke at the age of 38, four days after the birth of her sister's first child. Despite the doctor's dire predictions, after 7 days in a coma, her sister miraculously woke up. Jackie was initiated into divine feminine ways and wisdom while caring for her newborn niece and sister in the initial months following this trauma. Jackie's path led to a dark decade of the soul and her subsequent rebirth as a lightworker shamanista priestess. Jackie chronicles this story in her upcoming memoir, *Why We Wake Up: A Story of Stroke, Survival, and the Seven Keys of Self Realization.*

Jackie's unique brilliance is activating, awakening, and embodying light. Through her light, Jackie helps others to transmute shadow aspects, limiting beliefs, old stories, and conditioning that no longer serve. As a mixed-race woman, who has healed many ancestral wounds and integrated her white and Black lineages through her own embodiment, she carries the codes of peace and oneness. She helps other women leaders to liberate their voices in order to be the change the world needs today.

Learn more at: **jackiegraves.com**

Special Gift

Activate Your Voice Meditation

What do you yearn to express?
What soul gift do you wish to bring out?
Do you desire to bring healing to a relationship in your life
through an expression of your soul truth?
What is true for you?

Bring a journal and something to write with, as this Activate Your Voice Meditation brings you into an expanded state where you are empowered to speak (and write) your soul truth in order to heal your voice, love yourself more deeply, create new visions, and lead your life from a space of liberation.

Access here: **jackiegraves.com/gift**

Wisdom of the Green Nations

BY KIYOKO GUILLORY-GONZALEZ

I recall a time deep within me when I knew the Earth better than I do now. It was an unbroken chain of divine wisdom, seeded and encoded with records from the dawn of time. The seasons, whispers of magical rites of ash, wind, dirt, fire, and holy water initiations within my village were all just glimpses of memories connected within the multidimensional timeline.

The current times have caused many of us to be pulled out of ourselves, forced to assess how we want to live and which choices we can make to live a self-governing and joyful existence steeped in wellness. My dreams, day and night, have given me clear glimpses of my true soul's liberation and the path towards my ancestors' freedom dance. I have spoken to countless others in my community about how they also feel the call towards the reclamation and remembrance of their union with divine power and unconditional love. Our eyes and hearts are seeing past the veils. The winds of change are clearing the fog for those who are in right relationship with the Earth—those who aspire to cultivate true love.

As a Community Herbalist, you set on an endless road gleaning hidden Earth love wisdom. Although nowadays for herbalists, naturalist or not, the times have beckoned us to pay attention to the insight toward self-healing, the environment, and enhancing our servitude toward our communities. My path steered me from one herb school to another, often finding myself the only Black woman or person of color seeking to deepen my wisdom with the Green Nations, a name given for our kindred plant kingdom.

I always found it to be the biggest joke that there were very few melanated people in the many classes where I had to share myself and my innate ancestral wisdom in a community where my life experience and struggles were foreign to the primarily white attendants. At times I felt strings pulling at my aura, a feeling of being consumed, a vessel being sipped through a straw. I had to learn better boundaries and how to be mindful about asking for protection.

The herbal world can attract some of the most unhealed and surprisingly rigid people—many of whom are searching to heal their sense of emptiness and disconnection. I recall feeling drained and irritated, running into inquisitive succubus-like people. I had to call upon daily prayers, mantras, and meditations to prevent myself from falling into a state of cyclical blaming and name-calling.

I was in a place where I did not want to be. I deserved to feel empowered in my domain of self, not yielding to or entertaining lower vibrations. I realized that an infiltration was happening, and I was giving away my power by pleasing people simply to avoid any confrontation that would leave a scarring resonance. The exchange of energy rarely felt warm or welcoming; rather, it was competitive and inquisitive. Conversations in class somehow kept turning toward our differences.

The path of a Black Herbalist, a Rootworker, has been one of igniting an inner blue flame that continues to burn as bright and hot as possible, a flame that many of my enslaved ancestors struggled to keep lit. But somehow, they did and turned it into a glorious bonfire that emitted sparks of inspiration and invincibility rising into the ether. With each step I take on the ascension ladder of perseverance, faith, and grace, it feels like I am the oxygen adding strength to each of my ancestors' soul flames. It has been a path of liberation to openly practice and be what my forebears could not be—tracking encrypted knowledge within the smell of the soil.

When I channel into village life and the many layers of spirits within a village, I sense the full encompassing support that many of our ancestors had before being enslaved. In a close-knit community, the group's success depends on trust and unity in conjunction with those around you, so people-pleasing comes from an innate first reaction to trust one another. However, once the ancestors were enslaved and torn apart from family, colonizers used the best parts of our spirits against us. Ultimate trust and loving kindness turned into fear, shame, and ridicule.

The autopilot reaction to people-pleasing comes from two sides of a spectrum: one side is true soul recognition, love and gratitude for others, and the remembrance of village life: camaraderie. The opposite side is our relationship to fear as well as living a substantial part of our lives in an ego-dominant survival mindset and/or in fight or flight.

Even as days were lived through a scaling system of constant traumas, we are now called to heal by any means necessary, release stored trauma, and bring higher discernment and clarity to the forefront.

I have experienced alarming moments of autopilot reactions of diminishment when passing a white man or woman. Often, I can sense the tension in the air before the encounter even occurs—as a thickening in the air or slight friction in my body temple that feels detectable as stored ancestral trauma. My initial feeling about this reaction was self-shaming until I shined light into myself. I fixed my gaze intentionally in a direction that I felt to be energetically oppressive and allowed my eyes to remain impervious. I had to develop a self-worshipping ethic to cleanse my mind, body, and spirit from this toxic collective memory. It is incredible, all the complexity in the decision to make someone else feel more comfortable, in place of your own. Those occurrences had to be transmuted and dispelled. Indeed they have!

Deactivating this automatic response takes focus and attention on presence—so love up on yourself and call on the ancestors for support in grounding into the Earth where you can access the love. The biggest lie of our time is that the infinite source of love and divine power within us all is unreachable or outside of ourselves. Standing firm in our human light essence and reclaiming our sovereignty is our right and our path toward loving ourselves, each other, and the Earth.

This is a global mandate.

Spirit has had quite an agenda over the past five years, directing me to healing circles, women's gatherings, sweat lodges, and communities where, at the time, I perceived maligned intentions and predation due to this country's unhealed roots in White Supremacy.

I give thanks to the most high for being blessed in having the voice to call out this injustice in the moments that I saw it. These expressions came from an empowered place, confrontational in the healthiest way I could imagine. I felt my senses heightened—my ancestors have been keen on showing me how to get to the root of any place by exposing true colors, and by any means necessary.

When I hear people say, "they see no color, " I feel triggered, as well as when I hear others use the words "We," "All One," and even "One Love." Although this reality is a vigilant prayer I hold and believe in.

I felt my powers of intuition heightened in the places where people convene in the name of healing. It is a spiritual big business of the privileged Whiteness to undermine the power of Black people, take from it, commodify it, and repackage it as if they were the originating source of wisdom. This has been the pattern throughout our history—but now, it's the place where evolved beings and allies who identify as White can set the standard and do the work to break those patterns, starting with ownership of privilege and recognizing how the illness within that mindset has caused suffering to other people's ancestors.

Attending an event reminded me of how uneasy I felt about teaching at this forest convention, but I was intrigued when I heard there would be POC-only classes and circles. Apprehensively, I decided to give it a go around and send prayers that some substance would come out of it and honor myself to share my heart's work.

I knew that there was foul play involved when a white woman asked if I could give a Xhosa African Dream Root (Silene capensis) ceremony as if that was the only thing she was interested in. I assumed she had seen pictures from social media. She did not inquire about my lineage and work leading up to my practice with this sacred dream medicine, which is used to connect with the ancestors and as ceremonial medicine for rites of passage. The hosts of the gathering did not inquire about the Xhosa African Dream Root prior to the event; it was seemingly unimportant to them. However this sacred root is revered by Xhosa, Zulu, and Bantu tribes in the Eastern Cape of South Africa. A libation of the root is poured or rubbed on a cow as well as the chosen individual coming of age. Traditionally, the cow is later sacrificed as an offering to the ancestors. I let this woman know that I had no intention of sharing the medicine in a "spiritually casual" way. This can lead to toxic, predatory behaviors involving sacred indigenous medicine as we have seen with Ayahuasca and so many others.

There were many red flags going into this event, but my vow to offer a class share superseded the notes that my intuition was collecting along the way.

When I finally arrived on the land in a very discreet location in Northern California, I was greeted by an elder Black woman who I was thrilled to have present at the gathering. The time came to all circle up and introduce ourselves. One by one, we all took turns sharing our lineages, why we came, what we hoped to glean from the circle and each other, and lastly, what classes we planned on offering. After the initial meeting, I was able to locate all the other melanated sisters who came—a breath of fresh air.

Wordless understanding and acceptance is a divine gift. We connected on the reasons we decided to come to this particular gathering. We commented on the need to work to slow down, reconnect with a green natural environment, empower our prayers through the use of our hands while crafting, and unanimously share and be witnessed in our power. A day passed. (If you have ever gone to gatherings, you know that just a few days can feel like many, as time tends to bend and warp in spaces where circles are formed.)

The true blessing that I brought back into my everyday life was the understanding and witnessing that every connection with a human being is an opportunity to enter into our heart portal.

I gave a share about how we can deepen our humanity by intention-alizing the use of our hearts and initiating them daily to be unbridled, open, and liberated (as difficult as the revolving doors into our internal voids may be.) I believe the heart is where we all source our relationship with Grace—interactions that stem from deep-rooted hearts immersed in the birthing place of true love in all forms.

This is humanity's cyclical way of giving back to the Earth and hon-oring the great mystery that never fails us. Unfortunately, our disconnect from this source of spirit and the turnover to and an unbalanced ego gives rise to fear, separation, and avarice.

Transformative rituals can offer support to any heart warrior who is in the midst of unpacking and unblocking from all of the deliberate attacks made on the body temple, while reversing the ripples of ancestral trauma. The process requires daily attention to grace and is constant work as one digs deeper into connection with Spirit that grants us access to deep, latent spaces that need attention in order to resurface for clearing.

Two days into the gathering, there was an Elders' circle scheduled. We gave offerings to four directions, honored the elements, and gave reverence to the ancestors. Finally, there came a time when the gathering elders had time to talk about their lineage and ancestral family. Since there was only one elder I thought to identify as Black, it took me for a loop when she said that her lineage was Cree and Blackfoot and she completely left out African American. Later, in another circle, she said that we all have suffered and that she saw no color lines.

Something within me had to call to her attention that although that is the utopian place that rainbow bringers see as a vigilant prayer to the end, we cannot move forward until we recognize the illness within us and around us—the inner oppression and our relationship to ignoring the layers of healing injustice that must be brought to the surface.

I was looking up to her as a grandmother; I felt hurt and let down that her life circumstances had led her to spiritual bypassing and what I was interpreting at the time as people-pleasing and self-denial. I was confused by how a Black elder from the South chose to overlook her blackness as a source of power as well as choosing not to acknowledge the pain of the clear separation that was exemplified at that gathering.

Another time, I was asked to support a sister's spiritual rite of passage at a peyote ceremony and sweat lodge in the middle of nowhere, California. There were about ten people in total; four were people of color, and two were of Native American ancestry. One sister of Native descent asked the White elder hosting the ceremony to describe her particular relationship and connection to the land and the indigenous territory we were on, but the question was continually avoided. We asked in many ways for her to respect the indigenous ancestors—to no avail.

It is imperative to come correct as possible in spiritual circles and give respect to the ancestors of a given territory and to bring clarity to those who are not from that land the honor of getting to know the land by speaking the name of the tribe that once occupied that territory. There is power in the name of a People, especially when spoken in their homeland.

I have witnessed a lot of predatory behavior and cultural appropriation within spiritual communities. I think people of color see this more often than not. There are so many factors at play dismantling the way a person identifies, spiritually and culturally.

Dispelling a colonizer/colonization mindset takes an incredible amount of intentionality. It's rooted wiring spanning over a great amount of time can be overwhelming and exhausting. Despite all this I empower myself by loving on the melanated skin. Black women were the beginning, mama Earth and if we initiated humanity then we can also be the leaders and bridge-gappers to healing this distortion.

In all attempts to reclaim what has been lost through erasure, being severed, or put seemingly out of reach, the global mandate as it appears, is gleaning back the bits of soul that were left scattered. Those lost pieces have already become whole in so many forms. It's time to follow the same trails that our ancestors tracked for spiritual invincibility.

The habit of people-pleasing and other means of contrived and calculated soul mutilation has dug a large hole in the Earth that we have to climb out of, but this has also given us time to get to know how to use our spiritual tools that were hidden in the Earth by our guides, angels, and ancestors. The journey is our power!

I remember when my eyes were attuned to the green. As this verdant landscape was all I ever knew. The feeling is ever so present every time my feet meet the ground or my hands move around soil, silt, clay, and sand. It's all there. There is an inner awareness of the embodied presence of the creek, streams, and tributaries leading to the oceans of Yemaya. I am clear that my ancestors came from a place where the heart lotus beckoned all of us to express equanimous love for all living things.

When I sit with all that is remembered within me, I realize my divinity in reclaiming my roots was through life's moment-to-moment rituals. Awakening the ritual inside of everything is the work and due-diligence at hand.

Trauma is stored in our collective memory and stems from internalized fear, mistreatment and mutilation stored in our DNA. Epigenetics is fairly recent in the world of science, and brings awareness around claiming our personal power to support us moving past these limiting and reactionary fear-based patterns. Research has highlighted that although our genomes are fixed phenotypes, the expression of our genes can show the more favorable aspects of our DNA through incorporating a regimen of self-care practices. Our environment, quality of air, stress, amount of exercise and diet have an immense effect on which phenotypes become predominant in expression.

We can choose to make healthful changes to our environment to liberate ourselves. There is so much more to dismantle but our environment, what we put into our body temples and self-worship can initiate us into higher times and ways of being.

Anointing oneself can be the greatest way to send a message to the body temple that it is loved and appreciated, as well as dispel excess fire within the heart chakra. Ritualizing oils and charging my hands through prayerful intentions has shifted many moments of despair in my life. I imagine a surge of source energy shooting through my eyes rooted in complete support for my entire lineage in the past and in the future to grow and heal.

Another thing that I find helpful is to write a short list of affirmations such as "I release this feeling of lack now and forever, for I am powerful in every imaginable way," or "I am exalted in love by my ancestors and my magic runs deep."

Each time I remind myself that I am loved, I free my ancestral line from the exhaustive pains of toxic spatial maintenance. The power of love rituals and prayers in all forms will birth Agape ripples that will put us on the path towards greatness in grace.

Divine love, go forth and make smooth your way!

Kiyoko Guillory-Gonzalez is a community herbalist/numerologist, urban farmer,
educator, mother, wife and Cancerian. She
holds a BA in Sociology from University of
California, Los Angeles and now resides
in Costa Rica on the Caribbean coast living in harmony with the land on a 40-acre
farm and retreat center called Finca Phoenix (fincaphoenix.com). She believes her
path as herbalist and healer is the culmi-
nation of many lifetimes of work merging
into this life. She holds great importance

on creating and living in higher vibrational timelines to create bridges
for those who need support integrating greater timelines. She runs
a home practice and herbal apothecary called Eudaimonia Botan-
ica, (**eudaimoniabotanica.com**) that is currently transitioning into
rainforest medicine from the local bush. Her initiation into herbalism
began in a small pueblo in Jalisco, Mexico called Rancho Viejo. She
learned about traditional plant medicine from the elders of the village that would often walk the hillsides and gather wild herbs for tea
and liniments and many other herbal preparations. Since then she has
attended four schools of traditional herbalism. She defines herself as
an Earth prayer medicine maker and elemental sorceress who focuses
on initiating hearts to raise the vibration of this planet in order to create the paradigm shift needed to sustain ourselves and generations
to come.

Kiyoko's Creole paternal lineage has multiple generations from
Louisiana and her maternal lineage is Creole, Chocktaw and Japanese
heritage. The details of her ancestors only goes back a few generations. However, she has been able to trace the Earth rituals, magical
rites and superstition from stories of the elders in her family. This way
of moving in the world was commonplace among her ancestors. Once
we commit to tracking our heritage, the imagery and jewels of the past
emerge. Kiyoko's maternal grandmother, Toshiko, was a war bride from

Kumamoto, Japan. She was a transplant folk herbalist. Foraging for herbs and mushrooms on forested mountainsides was one of her favorite pastimes. Kiyoko, like her grandmother, focuses on enlivening the wisdom of ancestral and akashic healing through the teachings of plant spirits, creating community centered in sustainable farming, and inspiring children to immerse themselves in Earth-loving practices. Kiyoko's vocations and life paths have all pointed to retracing the tracks that her ancestors and guides have left behind. Her belief is that the Earth is mandating our spirits to be in contact with the Earth devas and to work with them in harmony. She finds the deepest importance in living in close connection and right relationship with seeds, soil, the seasons, and dancing with the timing in all things.

Learn more at: **fincaphoenix.com** Launching soon **eudaimoniabotanica.com**

Special Gift

Flower Guardian Meditation

My gift to the spirits reading this book is a guided meditation to meet the Flower Wisdom Guardians. This initiation expands our practice of enhancing our colors and spiritual healing work by opening ourselves to the flower realm and the elementals that facilitate our pathway to ascension.

drive.google.com/file/ d/1Z9BrtpXB4YhlOOuRwwlZFXDk7ON-Kpjl/view?usp=sharing

---

The Power of Art as a Form of Ancestral Retrospection

BY KATIA HERRERA

Art has been part of my life since I can remember, my connection with nature, with life has always driven me to create different and innovative things from the most magical and esoteric point of view. I was always interested in magic and the galaxy, and was visually attracted to the strangest and most unique colors and art forms. Throughout my life I have struggled to be understood—the mind of an artist sometimes goes so far back and thinks so differently that it is difficult for other people to reach that level of understanding.

I grew up in the Dominican Republic where Eurocentric culture prevails despite being a country of the mixture of three cultures: Taino, African, and Spanish. Despite racial diversity, there is still racism toward people who have a dark skin color, and acceptance and more admiration for white prevails.

Being a Dominican all my life, with Dominican parents and grandparents, I suffered rejection from other countrymen assuming that I was Haitian (a national of our neighboring country). As a girl, I did not understand why being of another nationality was an insult, until in my adolescence I understood that it was because of the great rejection that Dominicans generally have of blacks.

As I was growing up I realized that I hated my afro hair, and of course this was thanks to all those prejudices that we have about blackness. I remember that it was a horror for me to spend weeks without straightening my hair or having it really straight, until Knowledge gave me power and freedom. It gave me the ability to love myself and my roots and connect to my ancestral past. Little by little, I learned more about my roots. The more information I acquired about my ancestors, the more I fell in love with their beautiful essence, who I really was, and where I was going.

After accepting my true identity and starting the beautiful connection with my blackness, I began to admire my ancestors, our history, and how strong and powerful we have been—and are—throughout history. I have had a strong connection with art throughout my life and experienced many forms of it: drawing, photography, painting, crafts. . . But none of them filled me or gave me enough motivation until I started doing digital art. Here, I found a strong enough purpose for my art to continue creating, a purpose that would make my soul happy and also carry a positive message to people. This is how creativepowerr was born.

I began to make art with the purpose of portraying black in a powerful, strong, independent way, but at the same time mixing it with fruity fantasy and magic since very few blacks are represented in this way. Usually, black is associated with poverty, slavery, weakness. With my art, my purpose is to eradicate all the negative connotations associated and instead represent ourselves as gods, kings, and deities—beyond a mythological or fantasy aspect so that each person feels the power of the images within and can connect with that ancient magic.

When I started making art, from day one I proposed that all art I made would include black people as a way to pay honor and homage to my African ancestors, their power, and all their beautiful heritage for us. Now, why mix the ancestral with futurism and magic? I think that the past is closely related to the future, the past gives us the necessary tools to build a better future. As a person from generation Z, despite the fact that I love the ancestral, traditions, and magic. I also love technology and am attracted to the idea of futurism and life in other galaxies and planets. For this reason, I create Afrofuturist art because it unites those two parts of my being.

For me, art has been a form of ancestral retrospection because it has allowed me to know my inner self through creation. Through the connection with my ancestors, I am able to access my creativity every day and transmit the power that they transmit to me. This work is extremely magical and I believe that each person should give themselves the opportunity to take the journey inward and travel into the future.

Katia Herrera is a 21-year-old digital visual artist from the noisy city of Santo Domingo in the Dominican Republic. Despite Herrera being a self-proclaimed introvert, her artwork is remarkably loud in a world trying to quiet black voices. With titles like *Black Woman, You Own the Moon, Earth Goddess, Forever,* and *Universe Protector,* Herrera's legacy will be marked by her passion for highlighting the endurance and perseverance of black folks of old and present to contrast the narrative that black skin should only be associated with slavery.

One of her most lovely and vivaciously titled works, *Universe Protector,* portrays the black soul as a divine entity full of strength, power, and greatness. In her youth, her love of graphic design was stimulated by her parents' artistry and the Photoshop her father had downloaded onto his computer for his professional photography.

Herrera worked with brands like Facebook for the "Black History Month" campaign in 2021 and Adobe Photoshop for the Photoshop swipe tutorial in 2021 with the theme "mystical." Katia has been featured in magazines like Bitch media "fantasy" issue and 5th edition *of CosEffect* magazine. Herrera has also worked with many merging artists of the time such as Jamaican artists Leno Banton and blvk h3ro. Katia is the creator of the cover art of *Ancient-Future Unity.*

Learn more at: **IG: @Creativepowerr; FB: Creativepowerr**

Written on Fire

BY LIBRA MAYO

You witnessed my birth
Bright and glowing
Shooting through the sky
A tail of light
From the dark matter womb I entered
Ancient songs from Sirius etched on emeralds
placed in my heart by God herself
I was born on fire
My chakras made of gold from the sun
Plasma, passion, purpose
like lightning through the ionosphere
I landed on Gaia
Baptized in a lapis temple
in a pool of oudh and blue lotus
Golden beings wrapped me in their wings
Held me 'til time was my friend
Freedom came like a butterfly from a chrysalis
My breath is a dancer

My hair a zephyr breeze

My first cry a prayer that broke the veil

My melanin contains the antidote you seek

past and present

Malachite and azurite mimic its charge

Ancestors rejoiced of my coming

On the sands of Timbuktu they watched me in the night sky

Sheet music with compositions in sacred geometry

appear in my dreams

Galactic guides whisper the melody

I Am fire

Forgiving centuries of transgressions upon my people

past and present

It is fuel

Turning inside out and outside in

Activating light language

that pours from my lips like honey

Is it a spell or medicine?

I heal dimensions

Mountains on Andromeda pulse in my presence

Oceans on Arcturus rise to greet me

Within seconds I travel from one life to the next

All existing at once

Before the Great Pyramid in Egypt I stand

surrounded by colonizers

oppressors with privilege

past and present

I fall into a trance
My mission downloaded
Feel my fire
Palms raised and vibrating
Flames shoot out
Transmuting all that is not of the light
Clearing the sight and heart
of those who believe we are not one
My ancestors whisper
"She has come."

Libra Mayo was born and raised in Washington, D.C. She attended New York University's Tisch School of the Arts and studied filmmaking. She has lived in New York City, Boston and Los Angeles and longs to travel and meditate at every sacred site around the world. Libra is inspired by the cosmos, the elements, music, and love. She is a mom, Starseed, Sci-fi/fantasy writer, photographer, and abstract painter. Libra also loves songwriting and is working on a documentary film project. She is currently training as  a yoga teacher with the goal of helping women and children who have been victimized or survived human trafficking heal trauma.

Learn more at: **facebook.com/lib.mayo; instagram.com/electricraw; electricraw@yahoo.com.**

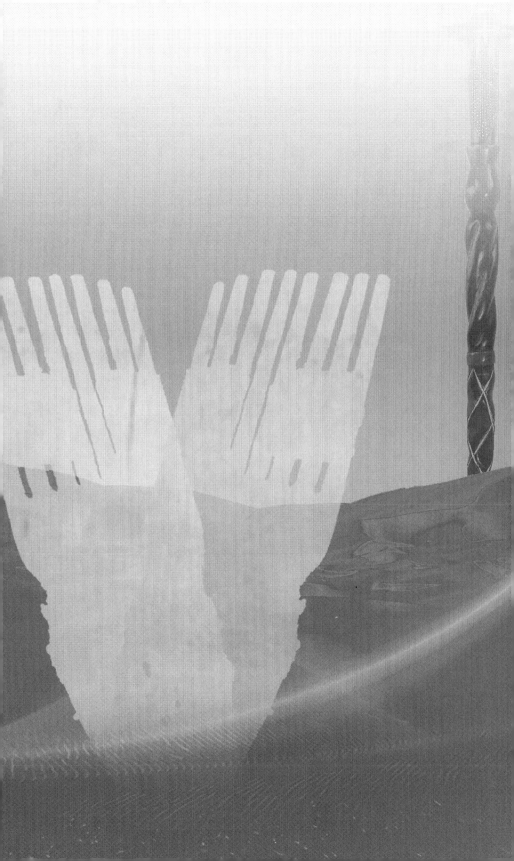

Look At Me

A Reflection Forward

BY STACÈ MIDDLEBROOKS

I was alone splashing water on my face in a dark, candle-lit bathroom in a beautiful retreat home in Hawaii when I first saw her. Her skin was bronze and glowed like embers reflecting the smoldering flames inside. Her eyes held coppery fire in their gaze. Her hair flowed like thick, long lush waves of lava; curls slowly meandering where they willed. She wore lion's fur over the bust of a deep turquoise garment that draped behind her like a billowing cloud. A sword was anchored in her belt, and it felt familiar. I was in awe of this warrioress, this wise queen in front of me.

How did I get here? That was a question I asked myself almost incessantly in my corporate career. How did I become a corporate girl? How was I in these meetings all day talking about things that did not move me? How was I conforming to what the corporate machine was telling me I needed to be. . . to compete, to be accepted and approved of, to be good enough?

The corporate life. . . It was fascinating how it was everything I saw in movies. I witnessed the secrets, betrayals, desperation, greed, and learned how to survive. I learned that surviving meant living and breathing this corporate life. I believed I had to "out-corporate" people to succeed. It is what women more senior than I shared would keep me "safe." It was exhausting to pretend to care about business while ensuring the safety of my femininity and my Blackness at the same time. Exhausting and heavy. . .

I didn't come from a corporate family or money and didn't have many of the experiences my colleagues had growing up. I was different. I wanted to feel safe in this place where I felt like such a stranger, where I feared they would one day find out I didn't belong, that I was different—didn't care about the bottom line, or that I wanted to fully express my femininity and my Blackness and not be held back for it. What if they found out I wasn't committed and I would rather spend all my time singing, dancing, studying Egyptology and other African spiritual concepts? It was the truth—the truth I felt I needed to hide in order to feel safe. So, I played the corporate girl part. I walked it, talked it, dressed it, and lived it like those who "made it" advised. It was my uniform I put on each day wishing I could wear something else. I liked the money, the promotions, traveling, and dining at exquisite restaurants. Who am I fooling. . . I loved that part! BUT. . . The deepest part of me knew I was separating myself from myself to do it, to be it, and it was suffocating me.

It feels like I held my breath for over twenty years playing my part in the corporate movie. . . I often wondered which character I was playing at any given moment. That is exactly what I did. I played a series of characters. . . for years. . . I was performing and moving farther away from being who I longed to express and fulfill.

At heart, I was never the corporate type. I did it well because I watched my mother do it in the 70s and 80s as one of the few Black women in leadership at her job in a male-dominated industry. I was a quick study on navigating corporate politics because I had my mother as my secret weapon. Who else was going to tell a young, Black woman how to move in corporate spaces and not get scathed each day? No one but another Black woman who had lived it and done it. . .

I continued to advance and get promoted. With each promotion I thought, "Whew, I made it through that hurdle," not "Wow, I am proud of myself. I deserve this." It was always just something to get through. I was happy about the promotions, but it felt odd to be happy about getting to the next level and simultaneously feeling more of myself fading away. I was happy about more money but knew I was only promoted because I conformed to their idea of what I should be. I would ask myself, "Do they know who I really am?" Did I? I learned how to perform safely in the corporate world, but I did not realize how unsafe I was to my own beingness... for decades.

I was at war with myself. I was dispossessed of my beingness, and my intuition knew. I would not allow her in because... that didn't seem safe. How was I supposed to integrate who I had learned to become with who I knew I had always been? I am not sure I knew integration was an option.

I was a creative, intuitive soul meant to bring light and joy, but I was masquerading around like the stoic, corporate girl. I did not believe I could be both. I longed to see who I really could be but feared what would happen, what people would say... and what if my fully integrated and embodied being made me walk away from everything I knew and had built? Would I be letting people down, letting myself down? That did not feel safe, but I still longed to see clearly into myself, my purpose, my beingness. I longed to see.

Her wrists, adorned with brass and gold, flickered in the darkness as she moved closer—prowling toward me. "Look at me," she whispered; then a second time, "Look at me," she spoke with conviction. Her call was like ocean waves inviting me in.

Already prayed up and protected, I took a deep breath and slowly moved closer to the image in the mirror, just then noticing the African décor accenting the room. I noticed the baskets and the artwork as I got closer to the mirror. "Look. . . at. . . me," she dared, and it

resounded in my head like a slow thunder roll, but as safe as I have
ever felt. So, I looked at her and I saw into her. . . clearly.

I was always an intuitive being. As a child, I remember knowing things I could not explain, seeing visions of different lives I could not explain. Looking into my intuition was like looking into a kaleidoscope—bright, vivid, clear, and beautiful, but it did not seem normal or safe. So, I shut down those gifts. After a while, I could not see through my intuition anymore, or maybe I stopped trusting my kaleidoscope. Either way, I lived disconnected and untethered to it, knowing it was always there, longing for me to come home to it.

I was always a creative being. I loved musicals—Fame, Bubbling Brown Sugar, Dreamgirls, and, yes, Grease. As a child, I danced, sang, wrote plays, and anyone who found themselves in my room was a captive audience—friends, family, neighbors. It didn't matter as long as I could express my true self and experience them enjoying that expression. Even into my early 30s, I wrote songs, poems, and stories. I sang and discovered Middle Eastern dance, where I felt at home with myself. Artistic creativity lit me up, set me ablaze. I found so much courage, confidence, and joy in self-expression. It was the kind of joy I could not seem to maintain while "corporating" and I was taught that was the priority; to create a secure future for myself, not living a dream. After feeling so disconnected for so long, I struggled to dance, sing, or write. I slowly, undecidedly, abandoned it all. My creative nature took a back seat to what the world and scarcity-thinking told me was important and safe. I didn't believe I could have it all. I was either going to be in my full expression or have a secure future. Was it possible to have it all?

There I was, at a crossroads, already having left corporate to start my own company and still feeling unfulfilled. Something kept nagging at me, waking me at 3 AM for hours, drawing me back to writing, singing, and dancing. However, it didn't feel familiar anymore. I felt like a stranger to my own creativity.

How did I get here? Where was my voice? I was not sure I would know it if I heard it. That scared me. Where was my movement, my flow? I wasn't sure my body would feel it again. And that scared me. Where was my vision? I wasn't sure I would see clearly, intuitively again. . . and that really scared me.

I saw her clearly. Eye to eye, pressing my face into the mirror. I felt her energy, her soul, her being, coursing through my veins, sending light through my body. I felt her ecstatic joy erupt. And, suddenly, droves of the ancestors behind her came into view. They fit into the African décor surrounding me, and I somehow was in the same scene with them. I saw the sun making its exit from the sky, and I could see the stars just start to sparkle—almost like they were waiting for this moment. I could feel the evening breeze on my skin, floating all around me. I could hear the nocturnal creatures coming alive with activity. I could smell the grass and the dirt, and it all felt so familiar, natural, even safe.

For so long, I hid the essence of myself from the world, sharing only with those closest to me. Outside of that, I intentionally separated my social groups. Each group knew certain aspects of me and reflected a part of me. They would likely be shocked at the other aspects they didn't know. I had love for all but believed all would not have love for the other. Interpreted, that meant I believed each group would not have love for the other aspects of me. So, there I was, turning fifty, still living a compartmentalized life. Disjointed, disembodied, disconnected from my whole self.

It became clear how I got here, and I needed to know how to undo it all. I felt stuck in the life I created, saying "yes" when I was screaming "no" inside and saying "no" when I really wanted to say "yes." And it was all because of a need for safety that I had not created for myself. I let the world tell me what was safe, who I should be, and relinquished my power in doing so.

It felt like I had been holding my breath for decades, and I was suf-focating. I don't know if anyone outside of my inner circle knew because I had perfected performing. I was what I needed to be (to feel safe) when I needed to be it. I felt so at home with myself, with my husband, my parents, my closest friends... Could I really be at home with myself in public? Was that an option?

I did not realize I had abandoned my creativity and intuition for so long. I was deep into dispossessing my beingness and yearned to reclaim myself. As I walked into a new decade turning fifty, I decided I had to live more liberated. I wanted a life that was integrated and whole. I knew that is where my power would be—living wholly and in my essence in all the spaces of my life. I had to heal old traumas, release old beliefs, travel to the pit of my pain to excavate it all. I needed a purging, a cleansing to wash over me and carry me into this new decade free of performance, free of "should," free of fear of judgment—mine and other people's. I did not know how I would do it, but I knew I was tired of the war within myself. My inner warrior was ready to be freed. The essence of me longed to be free.

So, I embarked on a spiritual journey. I needed a spiritual retreat, but we were in the midst of the COVID pandemic. I was not comfortable traveling or interacting with anyone outside my household, even though I was fully vaccinated. How could I justify going to Hawaii on a retreat during the pandemic? I no longer had that corporate job to fly me for free and put me up in a fancy hotel. Was I really going to spend thou-sands of dollars to travel to Hawaii for a week?

Enter my scarcity thinking... "I do not have enough time and money. The other women who will be there are much more integrated and more embodied than I am—I won't belong. We are in a pandemic. I do not feel safe." That is what I told myself. I wore those thoughts like a shield, protecting me from all the "what ifs." What if this is a bad idea? What if I don't open myself fully and don't get what I need? (I was prone to doing that.) That scarcity-thinking shield felt heavy, like a lead vest. It was blocking my heart from receiving more abundance, more life, more liberty. It was all about not having enough and not being enough... just like my corporate career was driven by fear of not having enough. Even when I succeeded, I still thought I was not enough. What I had plenty of was fear. It was too scary, quite honestly, to imagine what I would see about myself and what it would be like to be free of fear, shame, and guilt. I also knew what those had already cost me.

She led them proudly toward me and they circled us. I found myself face to face with her in the middle of all the ancestors. The linen and cotton in my turquoise jumper swayed in the wind as if to move me into flow. I stood facing her, amazed and still. She began to sway and hum. It was a prelude to what came next. She. . . danced. . . and the ancestors danced behind her. She sang. . . and they echoed her. She roared. . .

. . . and they delighted in the power of her voice. She was in her essence and all was aligned within her.

She placed her hand on my heart. I felt eons of waiting, long-ing, and yearning for connection. . . dissipate. She moved fluidly—animating and inviting me to template her every move. She breathed in deeply with contentment, a long, deliberate breath sensing every-thing present. . . and breathed out a slow, euphoric breath. . . and I breathed with her. In. . . and. . . out. . . In. . . and out. . . I breathed a breath I didn't know I had—no more suffocating.

That was the release, the purging, the opening of my heart, the expansion of my belief in possibilities, the casting off of shadows, and the spark of embers inside that needed to ignite. Fear, shame, and guilt had been released in that breath and I was free. I felt compelled to sing, to dance because I saw she. . . was. . . me. . . and I was her.

I danced and they all danced with me. I sang, and they all sang with me. I opened my mouth, felt the power inside rise to my belly and my throat and I ROARED.

Silence. They watched as I fell to my knees, weeping, breathing deeply, hands clutching my heart, eyes closed. I felt her kneel beside me and hold me. Together, we breathed an integrated, whole breath. . . and. . . WE ROARED.

There it was. In that moment—the coming home to myself.

I roared as I stood up, taking my place in the center. Instantly, I was back in that dark, candle-lit bathroom accented with African décor. With all the ancestors behind me and her with me, being me, I took a deep breath. . . in. . . and out.

I roared as I opened the door and began to emerge from that dark room. . . and I delighted in the presence of my essence and in the power of my voice.

Stacè Middlebrooks is a lightworker, women's empowerment coach, and diversity, equity, and inclusion consultant with over twenty years of corporate experience. She has been a Chief Diversity Officer and a global leader in diversity, equity, and inclusion at Fortune 500 companies. After corporate life, Stacè created her own company, Purpose Powered Coaching + Consulting. She coaches women, especially women of color in leadership, using her gifts as a lightworker combined with her expertise in navigating corporate spaces to support women in  being their most authentic and aligned selves so they can live and lead with purpose and power.

Stacè is working on her dissertation for her Ph.D. in performance psychology. She holds a Master's degree (Georgia State University) and a Bachelor's degree (Spelman College) in sociology. She was certified as an authentic vocation coach gaining the title Professional Certified Career Coach and is a Certified Conscious Business Coach.

Stacè has been a Middle Eastern dance instructor and choreographer, singer, and writer. Her ability to bring her creativity and intuition to her work inspires her clients to go deeper, stretch farther, and elevate higher than they imagined.

Stacè's lightworker gifts, creative expression, corporate background, and coaching expertise have made her a sought-after coach and consultant.

Learn more at: **info@purposepoweredcc.com**

Special Gift

Authenticity Breakthroughs

Tips to Access Your Unique Powerful Presence©

Use the link below for a FREE insight into the VIEW Model©
to fine-tune your authenticity!
purposepoweredcc.com/afw-free-download

The Real Soul Food

Lightening karmic weight, breaking ancestral addictions, and healing your lineage, one bite at a time

BY IVEY MOORE

Lineage is a gift that we all share. A mother and father who birthed you, and the trails of mothers and fathers that came before both of them. To think that you were a seed inside of your mother as she was still growing in the womb of her mother is a miracle all on its own.

Whether your lineage brings up thoughts of joy and peace, or of shame, pain, and fear, your lineage is a precious gift. Why? Because you are the sacred living manifestation of it, and thus the current creator of its trajectory. You have the power to shape and mold it with your actions and intentions. . . or the lack thereof.

There are past, present, and future members of your lineage who are all existing on different timelines right now. Your actions, today, create a ripple effect, touching all those in your lineage.

More clearly stated:

As you heal yourself, you heal your ancestors. As you heal yourself, you bless the next generation with infinite potentialities that exceed the best of what you've been able to accomplish. You are rewiring the biological genes that you will pass to your descendants, which carry intergenerational trauma. Through this healing, you maintain the wisdom learned from the pain of your ancestors, but you clear the slate of the toxic patterns and emotional wounds that lingered along with that wisdom. The generations to come are freed from carrying that pain forth.

The great transition that is currently manifesting on Earth creates an ideal environment for a shift within your lineage. Thus, I call upon you to make the changes necessary to wake up old souls and revitalize their essence. To pivot trauma timelines with radical change and objective self-awareness. To command the power that has always been yours, while witnessing any attachment to victimhood until it dissipates into the ethers. And I ask you to do this with every bite you take.

The idea that healing your lineage through food is possible may sound trivial to some. However, if you correlate the understanding that trauma stems from pain with the truth that a large majority of black people suffer and die from food-based lifestyle diseases, you may begin to see where I'm coming from.

A word on pain. The pain in the collective African American lineage runs deep, and it is not rooted in food. The dehumanization, degradation, and segregation that our ancestors faced is inexcusable, preposterous, and a disgrace to all of humanity. It has created a mighty heavy load that most of us still carry today. Though often masked by seemingly current socio-economic issues, this load is rooted in pain that has been passed down within our genes. It plays out in every generation. It's heavy. The weight must be lifted, gradually at least, for the collective to rise.

Furthermore, our culture is LIT! Most would argue that we have the best dance moves, the hottest music, and (of course) our cooking skills are unmatched. Black culture is known for *soul food,* the most feel-good food of all time. We may even question your blackness if you've never caught the *"itis"* from one of your grandma's home-cooked meals.

Yet this part of our culture imposes a silent pain onto our lineage, increasing the weight of the load we bear. Soul food is a key African American genre of food and also the name of an iconic African American movie. One in which the loving grandmother of a large family was known for her nurturing home-cooked Sunday dinners that brought the whole family together. A true matriarch, she was. Slightly obese, and resistant to medical care, she dies from a food-based lifestyle disease. I think we know diabetes all too well. After dealing with familial issues and separation after her death, her descendants come back together, with love, cooking those same feel-good meals for Sunday dinner as the movie concludes.

See what happened there? Clinging to old patterns that stimulated a love response, they willingly opted into the lifestyle behaviors, disguised as tradition, that lead to the demise of their most recent ancestor. How can we truly live a legacy of love without accountability and change?

Are we justly loving ourselves, or clinging to the quickest dopamine fix in an effort to detach from the pain?

A deeper dive on pain. Food causes a whole world of trouble for humans. It's like a drug. So good to taste, and offers the comfort of a mother's hug. Yet that same nurturing meal can land us in a hospital bed, curled over in pain. Most often, the foods we reach for, to numb or silence the trials of life, cause some form of inflammation in the body. Stomach and digestive issues, skin erosions, joint pain, heart disease, diabetes, cancer. . . and the list goes on. Here's a key:

Inflammation = Agitation

When there's agitation in the body, there's agitation in the mind. When we don't feel our best, we don't act our best. *This opens the door for generational "curses" to thrive.* Bad habits like yelling, cursing, fighting, and abuse find comfort in an agitated environment. Agitated families don't stay together. Agitated communities don't thrive.

Likewise, when our eating habits are poor, so is the effort we put forth in our work. We settle for *good enough* instead of pushing our abilities to the highest potential. We maintain, at best, but we don't conquer. It's time for the black community to rise. Merely maintaining our current successes is neither acceptable nor comfortable. We must conquer. We must rise.

The battle to be won starts within.

More on pain. You are what you eat, and karma is a bitch! Open your mind a bit, and bear with me, as this section may confront your comfort zone.

A vast majority of the African diaspora was enslaved for a period of time. The painful weight of this reality has not been fully healed and is thus carried, in some form, by most. Today, there are millions of Earthlings being brutally enslaved, quietly behind closed doors, for our enjoyment. They are forced into gruesome close quarters for the extent of their short lives. They are sick, tired, and bred for business while mothers are immediately separated from their young after birth. Finally, they are killed in torturous ways. You guessed it. I'm referring to the meat industry. Your chicken wings, pork bellies, burgers, and turkey legs are pieces of beings that lived a torturous life and likely died in agony. But hey... out of sight, out of mind. Right? Once they're delivered to you, fried golden to perfection, you can't help but smile. And I'm not judging. I've been there and done that too.

Though plant-based for many years, I grew up eating delicious bacon, pork chops, chicken, and the likes. I never even considered the lives of the animals I ate, because we're all so detached from the process. Yes, humans have consumed animals for thousands of years. However, the current-day meat production practices create an energy that our ancestors didn't consume.

To be clear, I'm not here to force a vegan agenda on anyone. As a wellness coach, my motto is that everyone's body is different, and you must choose foods that cater to your body's needs. That may not always mean 100% vegan. However, I will address the energy of the factory farm animal.

Energy transfers. It never dies.

The weight of an enslaved soul is heavy. We don't need more of that. Atop the energetic density of meat, we face residuals of trauma when we consume factory-farmed animals. These are the animals that show up as meat products on the shelves of your favorite grocery chain.

For years, I've joked that most of the population has mad cow disease. Do you see the anger, fighting, and slaughtering humans do to each other? Even some of the highest-level politicians act as barbaric as an enslaved beast. But if you consider the journey of the beasts they eat, how can you blame them?

The journey of a down cow:

A life of agony she leads. Artificially inseminated, she squeals and screams as her womb is penetrated by a foreign contraption of her overlords. Afraid, she fights until she's tazed into submission. A tear drops from her eye. The only form of emotion she can't control amidst her fear-bound body.

For months, the pain of pregnancy, she bears. Upon birth, her heart is instantly attached to her young. To feel and feed him is her sole purpose on earth and she does it with pride. Days later, her infant is gone. She mourns. For days and days, the loss of her love and purpose binds her in depression.

The overlords attach her nipples to a machine and pump and pump. This is her new purpose. She mourns, chained to her milking stall for the rest of her functioning life.

Again, and again, this happens. Insemination, pregnancy, love, loss, depression, and pumping labor. This is her life year after year. More loss. More depression. More draining of every ounce of life within her.

One day she falls. The overlords shake her and lift her, urging her to cooperate. Consumed with exhaustion, she falls again. There's not one ounce of life-giving essence left to drain from her. Her energy is spent. Her heart is so heavy; it's the only load she has energy to carry. She's a down cow. Existing only for a short while until her fate is ended. Either by her heavy heart or her ankle. Her ankle, you question? Yes, they'll string her up by her ankle. Suspended in the air, they'll slit her throat and she'll quiver and shake until she drowns on her own blood.

Tragic, indeed. Forgive the raw truth, but this is a standard process in the cattle industry. No worries, though. She's still a viable meat product. She'll debut, perfectly packaged, at your favorite fast food joint.

McBurger with a side of depression and rage, anyone?
Cheers!

The weight we bear is enough. I urge you to lighten your load as you heal trauma within your lineage. Does this mean never eating a piece of meat again? No, it doesn't have to. For some it does, and I honor that. I also honor those who cannot imagine living without meat.

Here's what we can all do: lighten the loads we carry. Reduce meat consumption for the health of your physical and energetic bodies. When you do choose to consume meat, be conscious of the source. Seek local farmers with compassion and humane practices. Most importantly, transmute the energy of the meat you consume.

Ancient cultures had great respect for the animals they consumed for meat. People cared for the animals and supported their natural living environment. When they killed, they did so swiftly, with compassion. They thanked the animal for its service and offering. In respect of the sacrifice, they wasted no parts of the body.

When we tune into the energy of our food, we become more aware of our own mortal nature, and the connection we all share as spiritual, energetic beings. Be conscious of this relationship when consuming your energy.

Plants are true light energy. They are the Christ beings of the human diet. The truth, the light, and the way. *The real food for the soul.* Even in the first book of the Bible, God proclaims:

> *Behold, I have given you every **herb bearing seed**, which*
> *is upon the face of all the earth, and every tree, in which*
> *the **fruit** of the tree yielding **seed**; <u>to you it shall be for meat</u>.*

This is the way toward healing. Even as Hippocrates wrote,

> *"Let **food** be thy medicine, and let medicine be thy **food**."*

Healing your lineage is notably spiritual work. Yet, there are layers to spiritual healing. Shedding some density within the physical vessel allows prolonged and more clarified connections in higher realms. Plants offer this lightness. Spiritual ascension requires an activated body. The body is activated by fasting and plants.

The "soul food" that we are accustomed to is an expression of love that seeks to coddle pain. It is enduring and has its place in history. But now is time for healing. Healing requires discomfort and an upheaval of all the demons we don't want to face. We can't be coddled through healing. We must face the process head on. The real soul food elevates the consciousness, aligning the mind-body-soul connection. It supports the clarity that connects us to the truth of who we are.

We are vibrational beings. Every cell in your body is constantly moving to the tone of the organ, mass, or fluid it is a part of. Dense foods have a slow vibration. Think of density as foods that are harder to digest. Meat is one of the densest foods we can eat. Its digestion time is longer than most plants, and it is the flesh of an animal with its own karmic weight.

Processed foods, containing man-made chemical creations, are unnatural to the body and thus also yield heavier density as the body must exert excess energy to digest them. They often cause inflammation, which again is agitation.

Eating more fresh, living plants allows your body to vibrate at higher frequencies. They are lightweight and often made primarily of water, as are you. They contain sacred earth wisdom, which assists your body in functioning within the local climate and environmental conditions where the plant is grown. They are easy for the body to understand and quickly digest. They quicken your spiritual and emotional connection to the energetic world around you. As Earthlings of this unique time in history, we're being called—and dare I say, required—to take on a higher vibrating vessel to usher in the new ways of being. This work is for your lineage and the collective. This work is necessary to bring humanity forward.

WILL YOU ACCEPT THE CALL?

This is the part where you choose the red pill or the blue pill, Neophyte. As your Lady of Metamorphosis, here's what I'll offer: tips to bringing forth the lightness within yourself and subsequently, your lineage.

1. Breathe

The first food is breath. Before food, and even before water, the breath is what sustains you. Most modern humans totally suck at breathing, and the vast majority of us have never been taught exactly how vital it is. Proper breath work expands your consciousness, allowing space for the multifaceted healing that is needed at this time. Just as proper breathing supports our emotional and spiritual assimilation, it also helps our bodies better digest food.

Start by breathing deeply before each meal. You can take this time to give thanks for the food and acknowledge its journey to your plate. Then breathe deeply, again, upon finishing your meal. Practice deep belly breaths that expand the abdomen, not just the chest. Once comfortable with this daily practice, look into more advanced breathing techniques. Key terms to search: **Pranayama, Breath of Fire, breath work, William Hoff.**

2. Diagnose Your Triggers

Cravings typically correlate directly to deficiencies within the body. For instance, chocolate cravings usually signal a deficiency in magnesium, while salty cravings may signal an electrolyte imbalance.

Seeing the correlation between carvings and dietary needs can also help us understand how our emotional bad habits are closely related to ancestral triggers.

Understanding this helps us step out of clinging to dopamine fixes to provide our emotional body what it needs to thrive. What experiences and feelings most often lead you to eat the foods that you know you shouldn't? What foods do you reach for in celebration? What foods do you reach for during sorrow? Create an awareness practice on what emotions and experiences trigger your dietary choices.

3. Cleanse

No healing journey starts without a cleanse or detox. There are several modalities to cleanse and detox the body. The one you choose should be carefully tailored to your body's specific needs. Consulting a holistic wellness practitioner is the best place to start if you don't know where to begin. Some of my favorite cleansing modalities are as follows:

Fasting. Fasting has been used as a healing practice for thousands of years. It is the practice of limiting or eliminating the intake of food for a period of time. Once the digestive process stops, your body can allocate a significant amount of energy to self-healing. There are several types of fasts to consider, stemming from water-only fasts to juice fasting to just restricting the intake of certain types of foods from your diet. It is advised to gradually build your fasting practice over time. Though water fasting is by far one of the most healing practices, it is also very intense and can be harmful if done too long or without proper understanding of the refeeding process. Starting with a juice fast or intermittent fasting, then working your way up to water fasting is highly advised.

Colon Cleansing. The gut is the second brain. Because the health of our digestive system impacts our decisions, thoughts, and overall mood, it's important to focus on gut health during any healing journey. Herbal colon cleanses are easily accessible and very effective. The next step up would be visiting a professional colon hydro-therapist.

Raw Food Diet. If you yearn to feel fully alive and spiritually connected, a raw food diet will definitely support you. The vibrant energy and clarity received from consuming only raw, living plant food is unmatched. Because of the recent popularity of the raw vegan diet, there are many books and recipes to simplify the process and make it enjoyable. Mono meals, meals consisting of only one food, are optimal for digestion.

The goal, with any type of cleanse, is to remove the dense foods that saturate your diet and replace them with healing, cleansing whole foods from the earth. Reduce your intake of processed foods, such as cakes, breads, cereals, cookies, and pre-packaged food. Increase your intake of fruits and vegetables, from the farm (or the produce section) directly to your table, with little to no cooking in between.

4. Nourish

As you nourish your body, you nourish your soul. Bless your cells, and the genes you will pass forth, with living vibrant plant food. *Do this often in remembrance of your ancestors.* Remembering what they were not allotted while confined. Remembering what they could not afford when building foundation in a foreign land. Remembering what they were not taught they needed after years of receiving scraps. Remembering the comfort foods they clung to while enduring the pain of Jim Crow, segregation, protesting for your rights, and living in fear while witnessing their peers being lynched for existing. Nourish them. Nourish your cells with the light of a fresh, organic cucumber. Enrich your bloodline with a beet picked from a local farm. Warm up your genes with the spiciness of the supple leaves of watercress. Sweeten your spirit with a piece of ripe papaya. Lighten your load with plants.

5. Assess

Assess how you feel. As you cleanse and nourish your cells, determine what works and what doesn't work. Your body is unique, so you don't have to do something just because it's supposed to be good for you. This is an intuitive process. Keep a log of specific foods and how they make you feel after consuming them. What emotions come up after eating each food? Through your assessment, find your *light energy foods.* One of mine is grapes. I find that when I feast on just grapes, I get a feeling of joyful contentment. Nourished, mineralized, and satiated, my soul smiles. I'm at peace. Find the foods that offer you this feeling. In an effort to live a legacy of love, healing the physical body is vital as it increases your capacity to feel and share divine love.

Peace

I wish you the lightness of the sweetest fruit in your lineage-healing journey. It is a powerful act to take this responsibility seriously. Your work is needed, valid, and aligned. . . as you are the chosen creator.

Be well.

Ivey Moore is a wellness enthu-
siast, health coach, and liv-
ing testament to the power of
healing naturally with plants.
As a self-proclaimed wellness
junkie, her desire to learn about
different modalities of natural
healing not only lead to healing herself, but her insight and
guidance has also helped thousands on their natural wellness journey.

Ivey finds wonder in the uniqueness of life experiences around the world. Thus her passport stamp collection grows as quickly as her curiosity about foreign lands she has yet to discover. During her travels, Ivey loves to find the best vegan restaurants in each city she visits. Though a bit of a wellness snob, she lets her hair down to try the best vegan meals around the globe.

You can chat with Ivey on Instagram at **@WholisticVegan** or check out her videos on plant-based eating and natural wellness guidance on Youtube as **Wholistic Vegan**.

Special Gift

7-Day Vegan Meal Plan

Want a FREE copy of Ivey's 7-day Vegan Meal plan?
Grab yours at **eepurl.com/gkKd9b**

The Art of Elite Feminine Sovereignty

BY ASHLEY MUSE (ROBERTSON)

On June 13, 2016, I woke up at 3 AM to a phone call from the hospital. I woke up from my sleep wondering who would be calling me at that hour. When I picked up, it was the doctor telling me that my dad had passed away. I was lying in bed, and I remember the entire house feeling dark, cold, and empty. My heart sank into my chest with a feeling of sorrow that he was gone and yet relief that he was no longer in pain.

He had suffered from liver cancer the past year, and I knew that this day was coming. All of my fears began rushing to the surface. My mind started racing.

How am I going to live without my father?

But then I realized that I had been living without him for a long time. Physically he was always there, but due to his own internal wounds and struggles, he was mentally and emotionally distant.

The fact that he was now physically gone seemed to amplify that void that was always there within me.

As time moved on, the deep void within my soul didn't seem to go away. I started searching for something, but I didn't quite know what it was. All I knew was that I needed to go home.

But where was home?

I found myself testing out various things to see what could fill that emptiness that was aching within my soul.

I thought money would be the answer. So I found myself behind the bar at a local golf club. Creating luscious drinks and bantering with well-off older gentlemen was amusing and allowed me to temporarily hide from my problems. It was an easy job that allowed me to put on a pretty smile, flirt but yet still portray a facade that they couldn't quite figure out.

The men were enamored by this beautiful flirtatious goddess serving them. And the flattery sure was uplifting to my ego. Every day, I had handfuls of crisp cash tossed to me. And my eyes would light up the more I got to crinkle each bill between my fingertips. I was showered with gourmet chocolates, imported wines, gift cards to my favorite stores, and vibrant roses weekly—one would think I was living a dream!

I believed that one day, the cash and gifts would fill the void within my soul. So I began to work even more, picking up long shifts, staying after hours, hoping, wishing, and pining that one day this money would somehow save me from my heartbreak. Maybe the male attention would soothe it? But that never happened.

After some time, I realized the money and attention weren't the answer to my void. It gave me a temporary high, but yet at the end of the day, this emptiness came bursting back stronger than ever, calling out to me, yearning for something greater. . .

I was determined to finally figure out what my problem was. The journey began with a simple google search that resulted in me slogging through vast realms of the internet while being constantly bombarded with quick-fix Youtube videos and blogs full of cheesy tactics on "how to love yourself" and "how to be confident." I thought, "No, there is something more than this. I don't want to be a shallow woman. There is something deeper for me."

I encountered many pushy marketers and social media gurus on my timeline trying to persuade me into what felt like "selling myself out" because of their teachings that the key to power is our shiny appearance and sexual allure. Although those things can be helpful, I knew it wasn't the full answer.

You would think that being showered with gifts, money, and attention would be the pinnacle of power for a woman, but it wasn't. To make matters worse, the more I got lost in that facade, the worse I ended up feeling because all I was doing was running away from myself.

Where is the depth?! I kept asking myself. There was something else there for me. I didn't know what it was, but I was determined to find it.

One day, I was browsing through a spiritual community on Facebook and came across Nicole Gayle's inspiring words about Divine Feminine Energy.

When I heard her speak, I felt a deep resonance within my spirit, calling me to learn more from her. She felt like my long-lost aunt, channeling the divine messages I needed to hear. She had the uncanny ability to intuitively see through whatever problem I presented and delivered the most on-point, mind-bending, articulate answers.

I wasted a lot of time looking externally for the solution when it was within me the whole time. I already had the key to my sovereignty to unlock my cosmic treasures, and it was Nicole that helped me find it.

I spent some time on the fence about investing in her program. I kept it safe by using the free and low-cost information first, and although it gave me clarity, I knew I needed more.

$1,777 was steep for me and felt like a huge risk to take. "What if it doesn't work? Is she a scammer? Is she selling me a dream?" In August 2016, I sat on a sandy white beach in Newport, Rhode Island, soaking in the sunshine and feeling the fresh breeze brush against my skin as I contemplated this investment. I decided to go for it. What could I possibly lose?

I still remember my very first session with Nicole. I sat in my car, awaiting her invitation into our sacred meeting. All I could do was ponder on the questions she was going to ask me and the answers I would give. I felt nervous about opening up to her—I had never been so vulnerable with anyone before in my life. My throat was dry and my palms were moist, but I remained grounded and sipped on my chilled bottle of water, which helped me cool down and relax.

A few minutes into the phone call, she asked me some very penetrative questions.

"Do you realize you have been searching for your dad?" she asked me firmly.

"The void you feel. . . you are looking for his love."

My ego didn't want to hear what she was saying. The last thing I ever wanted to be was one of "those girls" with "daddy issues."

But I sat with her suggestions and allowed them to sink into my system, and I realized she was correct. The male attention and the money were simply my external attempt to fill the void within my heart.

I let my guard down and allowed Nicole to guide me into uncharted territory—new inner realms that I never even knew existed.

Over the following twelve weeks with Nicole, I experienced detailed spiritual healing practices that allowed me to face the deepest parts of myself that I had been unconsciously avoiding. She introduced me to my cosmic breath. This allowed me to expand my consciousness and transcend my daunting self-doubts so I could reconnect with God. Nicole instilled wisdom within me about my chakras, and one by one, we balanced them, leading to a deep feeling of groundedness. Together we chanted Buddhist mantras that were said to have been around for thousands of years, allowing me to tap into the ancient wisdom within my own body. The mantras soothed my nervous system and dissolved the nagging anxiousness that haunted me. Each week, I fell in love with myself even more as I uncovered various aspects of myself that were hidden below the surface of my awareness.

The most potent practice allowed me to meet my inner child for the first time. As it turns out, there was a little girl in me that was alone this whole time! She felt orphaned and abandoned not only by her family, but by *me*. The more I tried escaping her through those cheesy facades, cheap attention, and money, the more rageful and isolated she became.

That little girl within me was trying to call me home to my soul—the home I was yearning for.

By the end of the twelve weeks, I felt like a different person. I could finally breathe. The colors of life got more crisp and vibrant. That girl with daddy issues blossomed into a woman with a vision for her life, and I could finally feel my essence for the first time—now that I didn't have those filters and distortions in the way.

In one of our final calls, Nicole planted a seed in my mind. She said, "It's time to begin thinking about your mission. You need to share what you've learned so you can help others along this path."

What on earth was she thinking? I am no expert and I have no idea what I am doing. How am I going to teach any of this?

Then all my fears rushed to the surface. The thought of having an online business and sharing this journey felt terrifying. Having people challenge my content, the possibility of people misunderstanding what I say, the idea of putting videos of myself for thousands of people to critique, and sharing my wisdom really challenged the piece of me that preferred to hide and fly under the radar. I have often observed other mentors within the industry and wondered how they did it. How did they remain so grounded in their sense of self, even while having so many eyes on them?

I decided to go for it. What else could I lose? If I came this far, why not try?

I hired Nicole again for business mentoring and together, we created my brand from scratch. She taught me the ins and outs of online branding, and how to irresistibly write my words in a way that created arousal and intrigue in my audience. Slowly I began building my audience and had people sending me messages and leaving me comments about how inspiring I was. I thought to myself, "Are they talking about me?" And yes, they were. I still carried a lot of doubt along the way, but the feedback motivated me to keep going.

I also began to fall in love with writing. As a little girl, I would create stories in school using stickers. It felt good to be able to tap into that creative little girl within me on this journey. The process of using my words to move the spirit in people was fascinating to me, thus the reason why I chose the name Ashley *Muse*. A muse is a woman who inspires and moves you in an artistic way. I aspire to be a muse to ignite my soul and show you how to ignite yours, too.

When it came time to create the healing system to use with my clients, I knew I wanted to make it deep. I didn't want to teach "fluffy spirituality" because that approach had never gotten me anywhere in the past. It was only divine truth that allowed me to see real transformation.

February 2020 was the official launch of my website, and although it was a slow start, it began to pick up very rapidly throughout the year as I grew. I was committed to getting my face out there, even through all of my discomfort and anxiety.

As of now, I officially run three online programs. The theme of each is learning how to cultivate a deep relationship to who you are, and healing beyond the facade we usually attach to for safety.

I feel as though my healing methods are channeled from God. I wake up in the mornings with electricity bursting through my veins and new concepts to create every day. Every day I am channeling, testing, creating, and trying new things to be able to share with my clients.

My work is different from traditional talk therapy. In my domain, instead of just talking, we work with embodiment to transform from the inside out as we create new imprints within the energy field, dissolving the old blockages and patterns and resurrecting them into permanent sovereignty.

Embodiment is not just intellectually understanding concepts, but accessing the body to transmute blocks. We use sensations, visualizations, chanting, and vibrations of the soul as a holistic approach, providing results on all levels—mind, body, and spirit.

I've learned my nature as a woman isn't to be flat and one-dimensional. We are the cosmic universe, and we contain many layers, flavors, and textures on a spiritual level. When you learn how to tap into that, your life will change forever. You will see yourself become more grounded and filling your skin. You will clear your distortions and finally navigate the world embodied as the truth of who you are.

A woman is a masterpiece of art. She is here to be a divine temple with sacred messages exuding from her spirit that must be heard. That is why I am here—to show women the way of their infinite nature and how to embody the unique art of elite feminine sovereignty.

Ashley Muse is a divine feminine energy mentor and expert who has impacted thousands of women around the globe to heal the wounds within their hearts and awaken the irresistible magic within their souls—in record time.

She specializes in showing women how to fall madly in love with themselves beyond their wildest dreams, attract and sustain dream love with high-quality men, and cultivate deep fulfillment within their lives that lasts a lifetime.

She has impacted a wide range of women internationally, from successful entrepreneurs, models, lawyers, stay-at-home moms, and everyday modern women. She is the founder of The Art of Elite Feminine Sovereignty online program and a regular contributor to popular blogging websites.

Since Ashley's spiritual journey began in 2015, she has worked alongside many top industry experts, gathering knowledge on neuro-linguistic programming, relationship dynamics, spirituality, meditation, and emotional healing. Since then, she has created a signature healing system that is raved about by many women, allowing them to break free from their restrictions and awaken to their natural state of divine feminine energy.

Ashley is committed to being a muse for the entire world, inspiring others to find the most unique and authentic version of themselves so they can experience life beyond the wounded limitations and struggles that society burdens us with.

When she's not creating and inventing new projects, you can find her wandering barefoot through the park and soaking in the sunshine, enjoying sensual movement at her favorite pole-dancing studios, or getting lost in a stimulating podcast to expand her knowledge of personal development and human nature.

Visit Ashley's website to view her mentoring options and to sign up to get notified about upcoming program launches: **ashleymusecoaching.com.**

Special Gift

Elite Feminine Woman Masterclass

event.webinarjam.com/register/1/n7966h7

Spiritual Sight, Freedom, and Power

BY AYANNA NEFERTAARI

For most of us, the story goes a little like this:

We are born into a strange world—with parents, guardians, or whoever it is that raises us; and these guardians who look over us usually believe in limits.

In many cases, these parents had already lived a life where they had no control and no power over their circumstances (because of their past, that is what they believed in, a world where they had no control; thus that is what they created).

As a child, more than likely, as you watched these people live these lives, you picked up on the idea yourself. The idea that nothing was in your control.

The idea that you were powerless, and life was too wild for a human to relax in.

For me, it was losing my father. It was watching a divorce and physical assault. It was sexual abuse that left me questioning if I had any power in this world.

And for me, the initiation into my power started with my realization as an adult that I could let go of all the lies that life taught me as a child and a young adult. I could choose to live a new life where I was the one in control.

Through my story, I will show you how to take back your power too. I'll show you the key to embodying your co-creative will and creating the life of your choosing—even in a crazy world.

I'm one of the lucky ones.

For a few years, my life started off stable. I have memories of being a little girl running around a big ol' house that my mama and daddy lived in.

I remember the playground in the backyard. My sister and I would go back there, run around, slide down the slide, and swing on the swings. I have one memory of my father being out there with us.

The sun was loud—shining—and my father was smiling.

If only someone would have told me I was running out of time.

I don't remember much about the divorce; I was five, and I barely knew that it was happening. All I know is that one day we were in the big house with the playground, and the next my sister and I were in a small apartment with my mama.

The situation was complicated.

As my memory recalls, there were a few reasons for the divorce—the main one being my dad cheated on my mother with a woman he met in a strip club. (For a long time I had resistance against the power of sex work and sexuality because of this trauma, another conversation for another day, but know that sex work is also holy.)

After the divorce, my mom moved us into an apartment where we lived on the bottom floor.

The place felt small. There were ant houses growing out of the walls and mildew from flooding upstairs, but my mom made it livable. We had twin beds from thrift stores and comforters from Family Dollar.

Now, as a young adult myself, I don't know how she took care of all of us by herself. That's what I call strength.

From this time, I also have memories of Ms. Lameechee—the other woman.

Skinny and confident. She knew what she wanted. She had long straight hair.

And she was pregnant with my new little brother.

I didn't know whether to admire her—or to hate her like my mom did.

But she was a part of the story now. Love wasn't simple. People leave. People cheat. And I couldn't control that. . . at least that is what life was teaching me.

Another set-up. . . circumstances that led me to believe that I had no power in this world.

One day, my mother and father were peacefully married—the next day, they were not.

Have you, as a seven-year-old, ever watched your mother, talking to her best friend on the phone while eating dinner with you and your sister in a small apartment?

Have you ever watched that same mother chatting, and then out of nowhere, she falls off the chair, starts convulsing and bleeding from her mouth, and having a seizure?

I have. I was the oldest, but I froze when it happened. My little sister, two years younger, reminded me that our mama had left numbers on the fridge in case something scary happened to her.

So we called the numbers.

Our father didn't live with us then, but he came that night to check in, I suppose, and I left with him.

I was a daddy's girl.

And I have always felt guilty as an adult for leaving my mother that night. . .

Now, I realize, I just wanted things to be normal and calm again.

I wanted my daddy back. I wanted my family back.

I wanted to feel safe.

By now, I have only a few faint memories of my father left—the most interesting one being a memory after he and my mother were separated, and getting a divorce. I don't remember seeing him hitting her; I don't even specifically remember the cop who showed up. But

I remember knowing that the cops were there. And that he had done something bad.

My mom had already moved out with my sister and me into the tiny apartment where we lived on the bottom floor.

One day, I believe she was dropping us off to spend the weekend with him, and I guess they got into an argument because the next thing I remember is blue lights and a feeling of "something is wrong, why is something always wrong, nowadays?"

Something wasn't right—things were chaotic and crazy and I didn't understand what was going on.

This was another moment where I learned from the people around me that I had no power over my circumstances, and I would carry that lie into my future, into my business, and into my relationships until I realized that my past was not an accurate reflection of truth.

It started off good—him being a father/co-parent. . .

He would pick us up every weekend. We would get fish sandwiches off of the Mcdonald's menu. He'd wake up on Saturday mornings and cook us a large vegetarian breakfast while watching anime and listening to jazz music.

We would go outside and climb the rocks outside of his apartment and ride our bikes up the street.

Then I suppose this is when he got busy.

Our visits became once every other weekend. Then once a month.

Then it became—let me just take my kids to work with me in the office on occasion.

I have a memory of my sister and me in a conference room drawing all over a whiteboard with markers while our father worked somewhere else in the building. He told us not to leave the room, but when we had to use the restroom, we snuck out. I guess this particular bathroom was fancier than anything that we had seen before, because there were tampons in little blue boxes for free.

So quickly we visited our dad at his desk with the tampon box asking, "What is this, daddy?"

I remember him laughing.

I remember him alive then.

But now, that's all I remember.

I think that is the part about grief that stings—the fact that with time you forget the specifics, and all that is left is a feeling.

A moment.

An emotion.

For a while, he disappeared to Africa.

He was what the pre-teen version of myself would complain about to her friends as a deadbeat and absentee father.

But right before my father left for Africa, he stopped by to visit my sister and me.

It had been months since we had last heard from him.

My mother had moved into a house and met a new man.

The new man had sons who had moved with us into this new house.

One of the sons molested me.

I was ten years old.

I remember my dad pulling up a few months later. I was sitting in the car next to him as he told me he would be back in a few months from Africa. I guess I was too angry to tell him what happened. If you were here, I thought, you would know that I needed you.

So I didn't tell him.

I had no idea I would never get another chance.

I had no idea that in that moment I would train myself to hold onto my deepest secrets and pains alone. . . until I would realize later as an adult, with time and with healing, that I am never really alone.

A few years later, pops died in Africa in a car accident.

(I snuck in my mama's room as a teenager to read the death certificate and couldn't make it past the second sentence... apparently, he flew out of the car, hit a tree, and went into a coma for two days.)

He was already gone by the time we heard about it.

By that time, we were already angry with him. He was getting emails all the way in Africa from his pre-teen daughters who had a bone to pick with him that he wasn't there.

He was getting emails from the preteens who needed their father to talk them through their first few crushes in middle school.

And we were so angry that he was nowhere to be found.

I would have taken it more personally (him leaving) if he hadn't also left his new wife and their son, my little brother, too.

He chose himself; he chose his business. My uncle, his brother, swears he did it for us so that we would never have to worry about money. Apparently, that is why he went to Africa to grow his business. If this is true, I wish he would have asked me which one I would have preferred.

I still carry a bit of anger about it all, if I am honest. I have had to reprogram so much because he left. Because he chose something other than me.

But that's my healing journey.

At the funeral, I remember looking at him in the casket.

It looked like him, but something was off. I could tell they had to fix him. But I hadn't seen him in years and would barely have recognized him anyway.

The funeral was packed and sad. His mother wailed the entire time. I saw my favorite cousins for the first time in years, and I realized that life changes, a lot, with time. I realized that someone could be loved by many strangers and forget to tend to his own family.

And I realized, deeply, that I was mortal.

I remember wanting to cry but not really being able to—or maybe being afraid to in front of all the people. I hadn't even cried when I first heard the news. I did not break down. I walked away to my room and closed the door in shock.

But even though I wasn't crying, I was broken. I remember the drive on the way to the cemetery. I remember my father's parents riding in the limousine and my sister and I barely being a part of the funeral. . . I remember feeling so distant from a man who I wanted to be close to, even in his death.

As they lowered him into the ground, they never asked us kids if we wanted to say anything.

As they threw flowers at his casket and lowered it, I remember thinking: How do you say goodbye to someone as they are going into the ground? How do I say goodbye when I never got the chance?

It's impossible.

A couple of years later, we spent the summer with our grandmother. She showed us old pictures of our father and the staff he used to carry around.

She is an intense woman who would often break down in tears talking about it, but she keeps a box full of his things in a closet.

She told us the story of when he came back to the States for a visit before he died. He didn't come to see us. I don't think she realized how painful it was to hear that story.

I am still reprogramming the desire to be a priority.

After my dad died, the feeling of powerlessness turned into an anger toward life and God.

High school is a blur. If I am honest, I cut myself a few times. I wanted a pain I could control.

Losing my father was my rock bottom. Losing him as a teenager felt impossible to handle.

I know people have experienced tougher things, but I can't say that I have.

Death was my initiation. During high school, I lost not only my father but four other people. I was confronted with our mortality. We are, I knew, temporary.

And I was scared.

Fear and power cannot take up the same space. So my power was gone, I was far away from my soul. And it took about five years for me to find my way back.

He visited me a few times during high school in my dreams.

The dreams still feel sacred to me, so I do not share them often, but I will share one with you here today—the one that continues to rock my world and transform my spirituality.

In this dream, my mom and my sisters and I are cleaning out that old house we used to live in as a family. We are packing things up and moving—of course he is not there.

By the time I had this dream, we had not only moved out of that home, but in and out of several others. But, for some reason, this dream was set in the old childhood home with the swing set in the backyard.

We are cleaning up, packing the bags, putting pictures of us and him into boxes and then suddenly it's just me upstairs in the attic (an attic I did not know existed as a child; perhaps my dream state made it up).

But attics and heaven—you see how the subconscious communicates?

Anyway, I'm in the attic now, and there is an animal in a cage and, for some reason, I know that the animal is him. He is trapped in a cage. I know now that the cage is the skin of a human. It's our human covering.

But the animal is trying to get out of the cage. So I let it out and as soon as I do, it transforms before me into my father.

He looks at me, finally free, and smiles. His heart light.

He keeps the smile and waves goodbye to me, as he fades away into wherever he has gone.

All I knew is that he was finally free and happy.

High school was tough, but by senior year, I found my way back into a church, step one of me finding my way back to God and power (but also a big hindrance—we'll get more into that later).

What saved me from getting too caught up in the cult-like church for too long? The dreams I had of my father. I knew he wasn't in hell even though he wasn't a Christian.

I trusted this knowing in my soul, even when pastors would try to scare me into believing something different in order to believe in their God.

I went off to college, slowly finding my way back to myself, and eventually, I was led to meditate.

Meditation is the real initiation back into your power—power over your thoughts—though I didn't realize I was doing it at the time

I remember that the Zen Center was like a second home. My soul kept telling me that I needed to learn to meditate so I Googled the nearest center and was there by the next Sunday.

The smell of the priest's breath is still embedded into my memory. She would give me books about love and compassion and Hinduism, we would chant loving-kindness prayers, and eventually I left the church and found the God that lived within...

I remember being in the seventh grade, right before I was confronted with the trauma of losing my father, and when I first began to understand the concept of God. I remember going to this church a few times and carrying around a yellow folder.

I wrote "I love God" all over that folder and carried it around with me, along with the new testament like it was gold.

God had always been my lover; pain had made me forget.

Meditation and spirituality are what made me remember.

That Zen Buddhist center kept getting me back to my seventh-grade heart.

College was a time of rediscovering my relationship to spirituality. Before I could remember my power, I had to remember God.

As someone who had gone through trauma and had been saved by personal growth and spirituality, I wanted to help others do the same. I started my business while I was in college, though I didn't actually start making money until quite later.

I remember sitting next to an ex in my car after driving home from class one day and telling him, "I just want to talk about spirituality and write for a living."

So I built a website, I wrote a book.

But deep down I still felt powerless. So I quit that first business within some months.

A couple of years later I tried again, I would sign up for network marketing and build some of the dopest friendships; they would remind me to believe in my dreams, and I would believe so much that I would quit my job and dive full time into my business. . .

Bad idea, though.

Deep down, I still believed it when they said that life had to be hard. That things were not in my control.

Deep down I was still mad at God for taking my father from me, which reflected in what I was able to manifest.

So quitting my job was not what I should have done until I trusted God more.

I found myself homeless and living out of my car until eventually, I went back into the workforce.

I still carry around a *New York Times* article written about my dad.

He didn't have a chance to tell me before he passed, but apparently, he made over $100,000 his first year in business. While he was working in that office with the conference room, he was also fixing computers in his own business, and for a little while, it worked well for him.

My mom would tell me about how they would drive around and hang flyers about his business when they were in college.

I am realizing now that they hung the flyers together, but when he began to reach some of his goals, she was no longer a part of the story.

(We don't realize all the subtle things life can teach us, even lies like love and business cannot last together.)

For a while, I self-sabotaged my business because I was afraid to become the person who abandoned her family for a dream, like my father.

These things do affect us.

And this is the real healing, figuring out what lies you picked up and erasing them so that you can step into the success that is your birthright, before life and the stories try to stop you.

For the last couple of years, I have been full-time in my business—meaning that I have not worked for anyone else—and I have used my skills to help generate over 6 figures in the online space with my clients.

The trauma of losing my father is still there and still affects me on occasion. But I have healed enough to where I have been able to build a business that supports my right to feel emotions and grieve for a day if I need it. Just earlier this week I spent the day dancing to move some energy on a Monday.

But this level of my success, stepping into 5-figure months, only came with one very important revelation—the revelation that the truest power was faith in God.

No matter what happens.

For a long time, I blamed Source for things that had nothing to do with Source.

Humans make their own reality, including my dad, who would constantly say to my mom in their youth that he was going to die young like Jesus. And, so, in a way, perhaps he manifested his reality.

When did the shift happen for me? I found myself on my porch one day, talking to my coach, and realizing that I still needed to trust God more. That's when it shifted.

That is when my power came back to me.

I realized that I no longer had to hold the past against God—that if Source had its way, everyone, including my father, would know nothing but joy and abundance.

We've picked up so many stories, and because we are so powerful, we live and create from those stories. Even if they are no good for us.

That is when my freedom, which is power, came back to me.

When I realized that I am safe with God. And that anything that tries to convince me otherwise, is a part of the illusion.

The journey is back to God.

The journey is back to your remembering that you are connected, that all of us are connected to something sacred and powerful that gives breath to all life.

The journey is a personal relationship with Source that allows you to trust your dreams and desires as guides into your highest level of living. The journey is to not let your pain define you and make you, but to live beyond it.

I found myself saying to a client the other day, "I am not afraid of my feelings, not even the negative ones (most of the time). I feel things like depression and sadness—sometimes I journal on it, or sometimes my body just calls for me to rest and feel all the things for a few days (which may involve crying or yelling). Even so, I've learned that emotions are not who I am but energy that needs to be moved. So I stopped resisting emotions. Once you give them space to breathe, they typically tell you what you need to feel better."

In that moment, I realized that I am doing exactly what I told an ex in a car so long ago that I wanted I do with my life. I am writing and talking about spirituality for a living. I help people spiritually align with how they show up in their businesses. And there's power in that.

We are powerful. Whatever we say, goes (outside of the free will of everyone else, of course).

We are powerful.

And we can trust Source, God, the universe, to support us in our evolution.

Even when it looks a little crazy sometimes, never trust the illusions.

Trust your spiritual sight.

Ayanna Nefertaari is a business mentor for spiritual women in business, and she owns an online e-commerce spiritual shop where you can get all things crystals, elixrs, digital courses, and more.

Using spiritual wisdom, her understanding of the energetic nature of business, and feminine money, Ayanna has helped hundreds of women step deeper into their confidence, wealth, and impact.

She calls herself the Goddess Re-Awakener.

Learn more at: **spiritualgoddessmagic.com.**

Whole and Holy

BY NYAKUIY PUOY

Growing up between two cultures that are diametrically opposed to one another is not for the faint of heart. It's especially brutal, as an indigenous being, living within an imperialist-colonialist nation.

Not being firmly rooted in your own authentic culture, as you would be without the influence of the other, creates the space for cultural loss. Losing aspects of your cultural self disrupts your internal groundedness and brings about an internal war, one that leads to fragmentation. This fragmentation creates a split within the individual, wherein one is no longer whole, and it makes one feel un-holy.

This is erasure.

The first syllable of my name, *Nya*, doesn't start with a hard "n". . . like when I fix my mouth to say "no." Rather, it's a softer, full-bodied, tongue-caressing-the-roof-of-your-mouth kind of "n." It has flavor; it's sensual; it flows; it's not so. . . rigid. Nya is also a prefix for the word *nyal*, which means girl in my native language, *Thok Naath*.

Kuiy, the second syllable of my name, sounds like the word "queen" would sound without the "n" at the end. With an "eh" sound for the letter "a" and a slight decrescendo from the first syllable to the second, you have *Nya*kuiy.

I made my world debut in the fall of '92 in Addis Ababa. The first thing that came out of the doctor's mouth when I was born was ትንሽ or *tinishi*, which is the Amharic translation for the word small. I was definitely a small one at 5 pounds and 5 ounces. So I was named: *Nyakuiy.*

Yes, my name in *thok naath* literally translates into "little or small girl." In *Nuer* culture, names are sacred and significant. They are usually timestamps in history since we are traditionally an oral culture; a person's name can offer details about the circumstances surrounding their birth. Sometimes names foreshadow or map out an individual's life, like a blueprint. One thing for certain is that one's name is always going to remind them of who they are, where they're from, and why they are here.

Western imperialism and invasion, in addition to the already oppressive dictatorial force, which was the northern Sudan Arab governance, created ripe conditions for the displacement of many of my people from our native Nuer lands. This is how my family ended up in Addis Ababa.

By the time I was eighteen months old, my parents, with me in tow, had trekked across the mountainous borders of Ethiopia into Kenya on foot, and had lived in three different refugee camps before we were sponsored to relocate and resettle in the United States.

It was spring of '94 when my family arrived in Utah, but we didn't journey alone. We were together with close and longtime family friends. In our group, there were two couples who hadn't yet borne children and two couples, each with one child; we all shared a four-bedroom house.

After about a year, we left Utah. We traveled to other states in the Midwest—Minnesota and South Dakota—to join and visit other relatives who were resettled there. We didn't stay long in the Midwest. About half a year later, we found ourselves moving to California, where we lived for four years.

For most of my early years, I was surrounded only by relatives—family friends included in this category. From Ethiopia to Kenya and Salt Lake

City to San Diego—our Nuer communities were close-knit and connected, just as we would have been in the Nuer lands. Aside from my parents, my caretakers were aunties and eldest cousins.

In San Diego, many of the *Nueri* lived in close proximity to one another, and this further facilitated the connectedness in the community. Our mothers would drop us off at each other's houses "so that the kids could grow up knowing one another" and for childcare.

When school was in session, all the Nuer kids would meet at the designated meeting spot, and together, we would walk to and from school. We were a pack, a squad, and though I was attending American public schools, with mostly white, Hispanic, and Asian children, I never questioned my identity as a *Nyanuer*. The power of being within my community naturally supported it.

Life completely changed in 2000 when we moved back to Salt Lake City. For more reasons than one, my family wasn't as connected to the *Nueri* here; over time, we saw less and less of one another. We often lived farther away in predominantly white neighborhoods. Removed from my community, I was more immersed in and exposed to white people, culture, communities, systems.

My parents didn't realize then how deeply our Nuer cultural roots needed to be nurtured and nourished in the face of an opposing outside force. This would prove to be a challenge for us all.

My name has always been difficult for most tongues to pronounce, starting in pre-school (and continuing)! I remember being five years old and feeling confused about why my teacher couldn't just say my name properly. My child brain didn't have the capacity yet to grasp cultural and linguistic differences fully. Looking back, the teachers didn't seem to have any interest in getting my name right either.

Every year onward, every grade advancement, every new teacher, it was the same story. And no correction I offered ever fixed the mispronunciation. Teachers and students alike.

So I gave up trying.

It was much easier to go along with "nick-QUEE" instead of asserting myself in the world as *Nyakuiy.*

This is often the ease with which cultural erasure happens.

I started attending private Catholic school in 6th grade. Baba registered my younger siblings and me, and even though we objected to this switch up, we ultimately had to accept our fate.

At this private, Catholic school, the whiteness was loud, and so was my *Nuer-ness.* And this was the first time I really noticed it. The darkest skin-toned people on earth come from my part of the world, so not only was I physically different from my peers and teachers, but I was beginning to notice the many cultural differences as well: in thought, customs, and values.

I hadn't yet realized how having the cultural support system I had in my early years was crucial for affirming my sense of self. Without my community affirming me and *with* whiteness dis-affirming me, I was lost. I appeared to be fine on the outside, but within I was experiencing an identity crisis.

What I understand now is that I didn't know how to embrace and accept myself as the Creator has made me. I didn't know how to stand firm in my uniqueness, so I lived with the inner discomfort. This discomfort was enough to make me want to run away, to hide deeper into myself, to conform to whiteness, to people please and appease: to become small.

In this school, not only was *I* uncomfortable, but so were my classmates and teachers. And I felt it. Here was where I first recognized that my BEing brought out a particular kind of white uneasiness. My classmates and teachers didn't have to say anything outright; their eyes always told a different story than their words or gestures. . . reminiscent of colonial, imperialist behavior. I felt the mental gymnastics some would perform trying to classify me, label me, fit me in a neat *little* box.

I didn't have the words for any of these feelings, sensations, or experiences at the time; I just knew that all of me was not welcomed and embraced; and that to be accepted, I had to mold myself into someone I was not.

I did that well.

My grandparents' generation was the first to come in contact with Christian missionaries. When my parents married, they had chosen to follow Catholicism. For my siblings and me, this meant that we received the full Catholic treatment with extra additions: baptism, confirmation, first eucharist, altar-serving, singing in the church choir, and of course, attending Catholic school.

I often wondered about my own indigenous concept of God since it was clear to me that Catholicism wasn't native to *Nueri*. I wanted to know how my great-grandparents praised the Most High One prior to the infiltration. My curiosity led me to ask lots of hard questions that were never fully answered. At least not to my satisfaction. I was consistently reminded that only the clergy (read: old white men) had the answers—which is problematic in and of itself—and that if I didn't understand, to pray about it. I was scolded for objecting to church dogma and pointing out the church's tyrannical and violent history, especially toward many indigenous cultures of the world, past and present.

One of the more dangerous mental programs within the church is to view God—my "Lord and Savior"—as a white male. This wasn't verbatim, but it very well could have been. This God was an egomaniac who was simultaneously All-Loving *and* evil; evil enough to send me to the fires of hell, simply for being myself. This felt like psychosis to me, and it felt wrong in my entire being. But it didn't stop the programming from planting seeds of self-doubt and self-mistrust in my subconscious mind.

Not only did I walk this world feeling guarded and insecure from the internalized racism and oppression, for which I later found words, I also walked the world feeling like I needed to protect myself from my own Creator, *Kuoth*. It does a number on the indigenous psyche to imagine and receive The Almighty One as someone who has historically been/

still is the oppressor. God is usually where one goes to find a refuge of comfort; for me, I only found hell.

The only haven of *Nuer-ness*, of safety I could escape to, was at home and the handful of Nuer community celebrations my family attended each year. There was a time in middle school where one of the "uncles" was teaching the Nuer alphabet and some basic spelling to all the kids, and we went for several weeks, but then that stopped. Somehow though, that very bit was enough to be my saving grace.

By the time I reached high school, my life experiences within the social systems and constructs taught me to walk my path to the tune of not enough. I was Nuer, but because I was believed to be tainted with Americanisms, it was not enough. I was labeled "Black," which to my understanding referred to American Black people, but still, I wasn't Black enough. I was a girl and not enough. I wasn't "American" (read: white), so that measured out to: not enough.

All these imperialist-colonialist cultural constructs had warped my self-image. The untruths I internalized made me dismiss, discount, and detach from my cultural sense of self; I believed she was not enough, so I kept her hidden away: small.

Feed the Children. Poverty. Dirty. HIV/AIDs. Lazy. Uncivilized. Starvation. Death. War. Third-world. Refugee. UN. UNMISS. WHO, and other imperialist-colonialist "helping" organizations. White-saviorship. Second-class. Not human. Insignificant. Scorned by God. Minority. In need of pity. Unworthy. Not enough.

My Nuerness and the power therein was drowning in all the propaganda and conditionings, and it would take me a number of years to come back home to who I always knew myself to be.

I attended college in Seattle at a PWI (Predominantly White Institution). I was still answering to "nick-QUEE," but I also decided to try something new and go by *Kuiy*. I had dropped the *Nya* since that was the most difficult sound for most people to access. Subconsciously, I knew a deep reclamation of Self was calling, and though Kuiy still wasn't the most authentic version of me, in a way, I was inching closer.

To my surprise, I found out there was a Nuer community in Seattle. I had a friend who had a friend, and so I got connected. One of the beautiful things about Nueri, is they always take in and accept one of their own. I ended up finding community, and it was like I was being reactivated into loving my Nuerness again. I started to remember who I am as a *nyanaath.*

The cultural anthropology and French courses I took, along with the travels I experienced, were also like gentle nudges for me to see myself and my culture in a new way and from a different angle. Learning about and appreciating the various cultures I got glimpses of allowed me to find a greater appreciation for my own.

I recognized in my studies that language and culture are inseparable and that in order to truly know a culture, you must know the language and vice versa. This encouraged me to increase my proficiency in speaking, reading, and writing in *thok naath,* continuing from where I left off in middle school. I'd say I'm doing pretty great and still have more to practice.

Re-learning to accept who I am, to embrace and love my Nuer self, fully and deeply, was a radical act in the face of such an opposing and often oppressive cultural force. In reclaiming my name, I took back my power, my agency, my sovereignty to choose and be exactly as *Kuoth* made me to be.

The more I saw beauty in myself and my culture, the less the imperialist culture's programming worked on my subconscious mind. I stopped allowing my self-identity to be dictated by anyone else but me. The voices of shame and discomfort about who I am in this skin I'm in stopped taking the lead. In releasing all the ways I learned to be fragmented and against myself, I started opening up to the ways that I actually loved myself. I started to perceive myself from the purest, most sacred place within me, where the *Kuoth* resides, and I uncovered that the (self) Love was always there, underneath the other stuff.

Amid a society that wants to swallow me up whole, reclaiming myself and my roots is my step toward personal liberation, and in liberating myself, I set my entire lineage free.

When I started re-introducing myself as *Nyakuiy*, it came from a place of self-acceptance and self-love. In learning to show up for myself and take up my space in the world, as the Child of the Divine, I found *Greatness* in me. Now, my name has become a reminder of this Greatness; it has always been there, and it will always be there; it was never given by anyone, so it can never be taken by anyone; this Greatness is all *Kuoth*.

With this innerstanding, I am complete in myself and in my Soul. Whole and holy.

Nyakuiy is an indigenous Nuer woman. She is grateful to be connected to and rooted in her ancestry, lineage and believes in the importance of honoring the Ancestors and praising the Most High, *Kuoth,* as a way of life.

She is a poet, writer, intuitive guide, and midwife for Soul-deep transformations. She is passionate about decolonization of the indigenous mind and body for the healing and liberation of one and all.

The potent medicine of Self-knowledge is much needed at this time; she is here for it and is here to bring it forth.

Learn more at: **iamnyakuiy.com**

Special Gift

Personal Energy Reading

This personal energy reading is intended to help you activate your next level of power and potential.
It is an activation point for you to step deeper and higher into your purpose.

iamnyakuiy.com/schedule

Know Thyself/I Am
The Mystery Beyond the Veil
BY PREMA SANDY

"Know the world in yourself.
Never look for yourself in the world, for this
would be to project your illusion."

—EGYPTIAN PROVERB

I AM a Spiritual Pediatrician, and I am here to prepare and support young girls for their Rites of Passage.

I AM a Vision Doula, and I aid women in giving birth to their dreams and visions.

I strive to further redefine myself each and every day.

Yes, **I am here to reclaim what was taken from me when I was a young girl** searching in a system designed to destroy and dampen my dreams and vision for myself.

Yes, **I am here to liberate my Ancestors** from the chains that held us back. The chains that shackled our minds and spirits. Where we couldn't dream or move beyond bondage.

Yes, **I am here to be ME.**

I AM PreMa Antonia Sandy. Daughter of Merle and granddaughter of Cynthia.

I AM a Mother to a beautiful young man.

I AM a lover of all living beings.

I AM all things and no thing.

I AM a multi-dimensional being, and I have come here to reclaim my time.

Do you not see that **I am a physical manifestation of lifeforce energy?**

Do you not see that **I am the daughter of Mother Earth and Father Sky?** My skin is dark like the soil that nourishes and holds all living things together. My skin is dark like it's been kissed by the SUN. The SUN and I are in a love affair.

Do you not see that **my lineage is that of the first woman of civilisation?**

Do you not see that **I carry nations within my womb?**

Do you not see? **Do you not see me?**

I am the first teacher, and I will be your last. I am here to reclaim my time on this earthly plane. This is my time to speak, and speak I shall. I am the elected representation of my Ancestors, and I will tell our story. I will share our journey with you all because we are aspects of the truth dwelling in The Truth. We are aspects of consciousness dwelling in The Consciousness.

I chose to descend on this earthly plane during the Virgo rising under the waning crescent moon in 1981, the year of the Rooster. Yes, I am giving you insight into my energetic blueprint. It's about transparency with me. There is nothing to hide unless you have. I am a recluse in nature, life path 7 doesn't help, but I know my purpose is within the community; thank you, North Node in Cancer. My journey has been a perilous one, and I have many scars to share—too many for this chapter, but I choose to share with you this scar. This scar is so deep it has taken twenty-four years for me to tend to it. The clean-up has begun, and this chapter will seal it up.

Where do I start with my journey? What is my intention, and who am I serving? First, I want to reach out to that impressionable young girl whose dreams are limitless.

I want to reach out to that woman who has clipped her wings and caged her dreams.

I want you to know that your true self knows no boundaries. Your true being cannot be boxed up or labeled by conditions of societal expectations.

Get out. Get out of those boxes.
—LYRICS BY LAURYN HILL

To my 11-year-old Self, I say,

"You are beautiful, funny, lovable, and so unique. There is nothing you cannot do. If you can see yourself doing it, then you can do anything. Your imagination is your vision. Your vision is your imagination. Follow what your heart guides you to do. Even if it goes against what your head, your parents, your well-meaning friends say, for they do not know your intimate journey. But your heart does. It knows where you have been and where you are going. It wants nothing but the best for you and your life. Be at peace with being different. No one is the same. No one was born with the same colour eyes. There are so many shades of each primary colour. We shouldn't condense it down to one when the variety is so vast. No one was born with the same hair type, the same skin tone, the same shaped face, or the same fingerprints. No one. We are all unique and different."

Remember:

You are an aspect of love dwelling in The Love.

You are an aspect of pure consciousness dwelling in The Pure Consciousness.

You are an aspect of Absolute dwelling in The Absolute.

You are an aspect of the Creator dwelling in The Creator.

You are an aspect of your Mother dwelling in The Mother, Mother Earth.

Your bones are her bones.

Your blood is hers.

Your air is hers.

The fire that dwells inside also dwells within her.

You are magical and beyond.

This is for you, Sacred One.

I share my journey with you. I share so that you will never forget. Lest you do, this would be a reminder.

I told you **I am a Spiritual Pediatrician,** and I prepare young girls for their Rites of Passage.

I told you **I am a Vision Doula,** assisting women in giving birth to their dreams and visions.

The veil was convenient; it was my armour. It protected my greatness. It protected my uniqueness. It protected my mystery. It protected my womanhood. It protected that sacred space within my heart that I wasn't willing to unveil. The veil created the perfect illusion of unworthiness. I would wander through the world shrouded in unworthiness, strife, and pain. I knew I was destined for something magnificent, but the pain I perceived in removing the veil would be even greater. No one could convince me otherwise.

I am the third of four children—the sensitive and inquisitive child. The child everyone had to tell, "Stop touching that Prema," because I was curious. I wanted to know how and why things were constructed in "that" way and not another way. "Why did you choose this colour and not that one?" I would question. To some, it was an annoyance but others, like my Uncle Lionel and my Auntie Yvonne, nurtured my mind with books and stories. I am forever grateful to them because they helped feed my imagination. They gave me permission to be as bold as I wanted. Stage. Light and action.

I've always loved writing. When I received my first book from my Auntie Yvonne, *Little Women* by Louisa May Alcott, I was instantly hooked. Jo was my favourite sister. She was gregarious, assertive, fiercely loyal to her family, and so unconventional. I loved her spirit because she knew who she was and didn't take kindly to others boxing her in. I wanted to read anything and everything. I wrote plays and stories from my imagination. I would watch and write as they played out in my mind. I was free to imagine and create whatever I desired. Freedom. I could dress my world in whatever colours, tones, fabrics, and whoever I wished. I was FREE to dream. I knew no boundaries. There were no limits in my world of imagination.

So, when the opportunity came up to write my story, it took me back to those moments where I was free to imagine. I was free to dress my world again. I was FREE to dream. I knew no boundaries. There were no limits.

Now that I am sharing parts of my journey with you, I see the richness and love they instilled in me. It only takes a few good people to plant a seed of a godly tree in soil that is ready to receive. There isn't much you have to do once the seed has taken root, other than guide the shoots, stem, branches, and then it will do the rest. I definitely felt that from my Uncle Lionel and Auntie Yvonne. They were good people. I am grateful for their nurturance.

"You would never make it as a Pediatrician," she vehemently exclaimed with a look of disdain. The look I perceived, through the veil, was a look of *"Who does this young black girl think she is? She should know her place, and it isn't in Medicine."* I bowed my head, feeling defeated. That blow did more than cut; it became my narrative. She was my favourite Science teacher at a school outside of my hometown—a school where there were less than five black people in the entire school, including teachers.

My desire to become a Pediatrician was ignited when I witnessed my older sister give birth to the first grandchild in our family. I remember the night like it was yesterday. My sister, my mum, our aunty (not by blood but through respect), and I were in the labour ward. The contractions were coming faster, and the breathing was getting heavier. Finally, I could hear the midwife saying, you are crowning. My Mum was on one side, my aunty on the other, and I was standing next to the midwife monitoring the progress. I must say, to see such a miracle is breathtaking. I could see her head crowning. "Come on, you can do it."

"Mum, I'm going to die," my sister called out. "You've got this. You can do it."

At 11:13 am, she was born—a beautiful baby girl with a great head of hair and these beautiful brown shiny eyes. I was in love. A man with a white coat, stethoscope around his neck, and a friendly face came round later that afternoon. He asked my sister a few questions while checking over my new love. I watched attentively, making sure he didn't cause any harm to her. My eyes were like a Hawk *watching. . . his. . . every. . . move. If he makes her cry, I'm going to do him in.* I watched as he checked her. I could feel his kindness, gentleness, and compassion towards my sister and her baby. I knew then this was my vocation—I wanted to take care of mother and child.

Writing this chapter has been a painful but liberating experience. As I write, it's 10:18 AM on RA Day (Sunday in the Gregorian calendar), December 6, 2020. The Moon is waning; she is letting go of her load.

After months. . . weeks. . . days. . . hours. . . minutes of feeling paralysed, I'm finally sitting at my desk writing.

So many voice notes to my publisher Astara seeking her reassurance and permission to just be in my own flow. How crazy is that? *Seeking permission to be in my own flow.* I'm feeling it, and that is a complete revelation. I'm laughing about it now, but at the same time, the struggle is real.

Who am I? I am all things and no thing. I have taken many forms, some amazing and euphoric. I have embodied many states of being from joyful to purposeful to euphoric; in contrast to self-doubt, low-esteem, and the deep yearning to escape from life itself. The masks I would wear for each occasion suited me VERY WELL. It was all surface-level.

Even now, I still feel the resistance to sharing how I became PreMA, the Spiritual Pediatrician, The Vision Doula, The Sacred Woman.

Why the resistance? Self-Acceptance.

It requires one to know the total truth about self; to have the ability to tell the truth about who you are—the good, the bad, and the shadows.

> "Be yourself, everyone else is taken,"
> —OSCAR WILDE

Being myself wasn't good enough. My sensitivity was too much. My curiosity was too much. My body was too much. My dreams were too much. It felt like every inch of my being was too much for everyone, so I placed a veil over it. It was stressful and painful being myself. I yearned for belonging, connection, and to fit in. Who do you want me to be for you? What do you want me to do? I would express people's expectations through my thoughts, actions, and feelings.

There's nothing more damaging to a young girl's soul than to create an illusion she has to be someone other than herself to be accepted. It strips away her inner beauty, her dreams, her values, how she sees herself in the world, and her guiding principles.

Well, all that changed when I had to write this piece for *Ancient -Future Unity*. Oh, gurl, yes, the veil lifted, and what I saw scared me. I was paralysed for weeks. I couldn't move. The image of this strong, courageous woman dissolved and melted in front of me. The hologram I had projected out into the world was no more. Instead, my inner child and my inner teenager stood—both shaking out of fear. My inner child crying, and my inner teenager looking at me as if to say, "What do we do now?" I stand there staring at them, shaking my head with my hands to the side, shrugging my shoulders. "I don't know how to counsel or guide you." No one showed me how to explore who I am and be comfortable in my own skin. No one taught me beauty comes from within. No one told me to stop fixating on my body parts and obsessing over my flaws. No one told me there's no such thing as "perfection;" it doesn't exist.

Perfection no longer binds me. Acceptance has freed me. The true nature of life is knowing that everything is transient, imperfect, and incomplete. Nothing stays the same. The past is no longer, it's gone. Holding onto the past and present is pointless and stressful. I stayed too long in the past. It served its purpose as its shaped who I am TODAY. It no longer serves the woman I am and the woman I am becoming. Blaming others for the decisions I made is disempowering. Self-awareness, courage, and support are what I carry with me. Making peace and letting go is the natural order of life.

I want to leave this with you, there will always be people who will make you feel insecure. Just know, they are projecting their insecurities and limitations onto you. I encourage you to be patient and show compassion for they weren't taught differently.

Take one day each week and spend time with your thoughts, emotions, and feelings. Do a body scan using your breath. Turn off all external distractions, be silent, and listen. Pay attention to your thoughts and write them down.

I encourage you to choose a quality that makes you feel beautiful—this might be your kindness—and write a list of the ways you show your kindness. Seek out women who dream big, they will dream big with you. Seek out women who accept the best and worst parts of themselves, because they will accept the best and worst parts of you. Seek out women who are patient and tender with themselves because they will be patient and tender with you. Finally, seek out women who lead by example, for they will show you how to lead.

For years, I hid my truth from others out of fear of rejection. I hid my beauty. I hid my dreams. I hid my values, my thoughts, my feelings, my principles. I hid my passion for writing from the world. Who would want to hear what I have to say? That was—past tense—the narrative but not anymore. No more, I said. I have so much to say, and I choose to speak it. I accept ALL the good, the bad, the ugly and the shadows. I held my inner child so tightly and told her, "You are beautiful, unique and I accept you just as you are." I took hold of my inner teenager hands and expressed my gratitude, "Thank you for being kind, curious and bold. Your dreams are valid and there is nothing you need to change. Hold your head up and trust yourself. Your uniqueness is your strength. I'm proud of you and I love you." And I told myself, "Prema, I choose you every time."

Once that realisation hit, I noticed I wasn't alone but surrounded by a group of women, smiling, and crying with me. I felt my shoulders pull back, and I lifted my head to the skies and screamed. I pressed the green mic button on my phone and spoke my truth to these women. After I finished, I pressed the button to send and put my phone down. My body was shaking uncontrollably from the release. The feeling of vulnerability washed over me. I took deep breaths and embraced the feeling. The fear of no one accepting all of me. The fear of criticism and mockery for not being perfect. The fear of others seeing the real Prema and not liking her. The fear of others not wanting to invest in someone so broken.

I went into the bathroom, took my clothes off, and opened the shower. Whenever I go through a deep emotional or energetic release, water is the element I go to. With my head under the shower, I went to my inner child and inner teenager. As I cried, I held myself in the *Ast* pose (both arms wrapped around each other) and visualised myself holding my inner child. I told myself, "I've got you. You are safe now. I'm here, don't worry." I looked at my inner teenager and told her, "You are amazing. You are enough as you are. I'm here for you, too."

The release opened up a floodgate of memories: experiences of other people telling me who I should be for them, for their ideal, for their reality. But, as a highly melanated girl and fully developed teenager, I wasn't equipped with the tools needed to navigate through the wilderness of my inner world.

I wasn't encouraged to be myself, but I am meant to BE myself. To embrace my body. I'm not just talking about the physical body but the body as a sacred temple. It's an instrument, not an ornament.

It's imperative to know yourself. Otherwise, people will speak their standards into and over your life.

"You either walk inside your story and own
it, or you stand outside your story and
hustle for your worthiness."

—*BRENE BROWN*

I dedicate this offering to the pack who ran in the dark with me: my son Antony, Mummy, my best friend Rehana, love you Sis. Thank you. for being my anchor. RA, Salome, Little Crow, Sameera, Kerry, Carly, Amy, Fliss, Alina, Jess, Vicky, Sistar Queen Louise, Charlee, the Tender Queen, Rosanna, Lisa, Fatou and Warrioress Louise Carron Harris. My Sistar Queen Astara, you have championed me from start to finish. Your unwavering support and belief in my story kept me going. I take a few good ones to believe in you. Thank you. Danielle, my Sistar Queen, I appreciate you for bringing me along and reignited my passion for writing. Thankh you. Kirsten, I must bring you in because you showed me the right dose of patience and accountability. I took longer than others to write up my chapter, but you held me up during the editing phase. Thankh you. Queen Afua for her dedication and unconditional love for the daughters of the Earth, you were a constant reminder of my sovereignty through your teachings. I see and acknowledge your brilliance and divine legacy. And last but no means least, Mama Earth. I give thanks for your presence. You are the first Mother of Creation. I see and acknowledge your magnificence. All things bliss and true, come from you. You showed me I was never going to be left behind.

Special Gift

7-Day Reflection Workbook

These rituals are part of my personal self-care routine.

**drive.google.com/file/d/
1AAb7ujIGOOIAUhIz_2TDWd-OZJG-K51X/view**

Prema Sandy is a self-proclaimed spiritual Pediatrician and a portalkeeper of the womb. She is a certified Sistership Circle and Celebration Day for Girls Facilitator, Vision Doula, Investor and a Moonstruation Educator. She serves as a sacred space holder for young girls and women to reconnect to their creativity and authenticity. Her events, programs, and womb circles explore these principles and offer insights, ceremony and sisterhood to people all over the world. Her multidimensional and practical approach

brings love, clarity, healing and inspiration for that innerstanding and embodiment.

"Wombmen, are the physical manifestation of lifeforce energy. They carry nations in their wombs."

Prema has been blessed to have studied Yoruba cosmology under the respected teacher Baba Ayo from Nigeria/UK. She holds a diploma in Colour Therapy and Sound Healing and is an accredited Transformational Life Coach, Mindfulness Life coach, REBT Mindset coach and Spiritual Coach through Transformation Academy.

Prema's thirst for self-development has led her to study Kemetic cosmology through Queen Afua's teachings, Astrology, Numerology, Human Design, Moon Magick and other heart-led practices, as well as the teachings of the Pleiadians, channelled through by Amorah Quan Yin, KA Ba energies.

While holding these qualifications, Prema strongly believes all women carry the wisdom of womb and embodiment. The highest qualification is the sense of knowing self.

To connect with Prema: **FB: prema.sandy.1, IG: @premasandy**
Visit her website for her offerings: **shupremwellness.com**
Tune in to her podcast I Choose. . . for everyday life stories
anchor.fm/ichoose

The Pussy Portal
Healing With Pleasure
BY TIARA SHARDÉ

I want to dance like a wild woman.
I want to sway and grind and twirl.
I want to feel the wind blow through my kinky-curly mane.
I want the sun and moon to make love to my smooth, dark skin.
I will bring pleasure to what was once pain.
I choose to heal in ecstasy.

I am often asked. . .

"How can Black women heal from everything that we've been through and finally be free?"

My answer is. . .

"You'll be *free* when you honor what's been hidden, pushed down, and held back. Freedom is yours when you reclaim what has been stolen from you, specifically your *magick*, femininity, Divinity, and *Sensuality*.

I didn't always want to display the expanse of all that I am in neon lights for all of the world to see. I had gotten so used to having to hide my magick; heartbreakingly afraid to be big. Yet, there was a very large, creative, and sensitive Goddess stirring deep down inside, and I was overwhelmed at the idea of embodying such a being. The journey of setting *her*—myself, free, is a complicated one. Yes, it's personal and private but also not unfamiliar to most Black women. This tale is not just my own. Housed within me are stories that speak of perseverance and triumph, as well as stories that carry the pain and trauma of the Ancestors who have called me into this physical reality. I am aware now more than ever of their prayers for redemption. Their story tied to my own is yearning to be birthed into this world through me. I speak for them now. I speak for *us*.

Arlene Williams, my Mother, was tall, beautiful, round, and soft, and all I wanted as a child was to be next to her. The "strong Black woman" role was one that she had mastered, having had a full-time career and sole ownership of a successful business in our city. She would leave her place of work and head straight to her store to greet the evening crowd. I would bounce off the school bus, cross the street with my Dad and hang out in the back room of the store until closing. My Mother's hair was always curled just so and had a nice gleam to it from the Lusters Pink oil sheen spray she applied in the mornings. She loved Chanel No. 5 perfume and *nothing* but 100% real gold jewelry adorned her ears, wrists, neck and fingers. And there she sat, every bit the big and beautiful Queen, on a very high wooden stool behind the counter of one of the most successful liquor stores in an oftentimes violent inner city. I would sometimes sneak behind the counter and climb up on her throne. I'd pretend to ring out customers with a bright smile, and a chipper, "Have a great day!"

I imagined myself having conversations with the people who came in like she did. I always saw her congratulating someone on something or other. Or, I'd peek around the thick, heavy curtain that separated the store from the backroom and watch as she gently, humorously, yet *firmly* admonished some man, inviting him to change his life around. She would minister to the people who patronized her store, and she would mourn when one of them fell victim to the streets. One night, my Mother spoke of a dream she had of a customer coming in to rob her, and she had shot him right between the eyes. That same man came into the store the very next day and, greatly disturbed, she told him the details of her weird dream. The man looked petrified as Mom relayed the dream to him and he quickly left the store without his usual purchase.

My Mother was never robbed in all her years of owning the liquor store. Everyone respected her and they would marvel at the fact that all of the liquor stores in the surrounding areas would regularly be robbed—but not my Mother's. If people only knew that she kept a small Bible in her purse, yet had her right hand—sporting two inch long natural nails painted with exactly two clear coats of Sally Hansen's Hard as Nails—under the liquor store counter clutching the prettiest 9mm chrome handgun you've ever seen, while she rung up customers with her left hand dripping in gold link bracelets. She was a firm believer in the "peace that passes all understanding," as well as the *piece* that she never left the house without. I adored her.

My Mother, like so many of our Black Matriarchs, held a trove of family secrets. *"Shhh, don't tell. Don't talk about it."* The family image, what the people thought; all mattered in the Black Matriarch's generation. She held onto, and protected family secrets that didn't even belong to her. And if the secrets of her family couldn't be exposed and healed, she made sure she protected those who desperately needed a hero, a champion. Her experiences had shown her the ways of the world and what horrors could befall women and children, so she dedicated her life to social work as a supervisor in an inner city, for over thirty-two years.

At forty-two years young, my mother didn't really have time for a brand new baby girl, especially one so sensitive, clingy and naturally connected to the spiritual realm. She was determined to shield me from the hands of an unkind world, yet she always made sure that I was aware of the potential dangers. I would stare up at her in wide-eyed horror when she came home and relayed some of the experiences of the children she worked with. So many of them were either used, abused, molested,

murdered or snatched from their homes, and whose fate would ultimately fall under the care of my Mother, and the decisions of the state of
Connecticut. I would never meet these children but I would stay up late
at night with tears in my eyes, praying for each and every one of them. I
decided that my Mother was right, this world was too scary for me and
so, I burrowed deep within myself for safety. She was very protective of
me, her babygirl, however in her protectiveness, she had stunted me.

Life was close to magical when there was love and celebration, like
during the holidays. It was the times in between that were challenging
for me to navigate. I always felt that something wasn't right. I felt that
there was more to life, that I was meant to do something, but what? And
how, I'm just a kid? I grew up sheltered and suppressed in a home with
unresolved cycles of abuse, trauma, and the band-aid that is oftentimes
called Christianity. Due to these experiences, I feel that a family who
hides behind Jesus can never really access the courage it takes to dive
deep enough for healing to take place. In my family, religion became
an inherited and unwelcome silencer which kept the family suppressed,
emotionally distant and angry.

I want to be more than I am now.
I want to meet the woman I am meant to be.
I want to embody all that I am.

I clearly remember the constricting box that I was forced to hide
parts of myself growing up. The parts of me that wanted more connection and nurturing, yearned for constant love from a hardworking
Mother. The box where I was tucked away became a safe and familiar home for me. For years, I had locked my feelings and dreams up
and away from a world I was warned would hurt me. I took all of the
pieces of me that were vulnerable, joyful, and bright and pushed them
somewhere deep down inside where I would be safe. In doing that, I
became aware of this depth within me, and how my energy feels when
I am alone versus how I feel when I'm around others. I haphazardly
grew comfortable and at peace being in solitude. Through trauma and

loneliness, the Divine showed me how to cultivate sacred space in my childhood bedroom.

When a child has experienced a certain level of perceived rejection or outright abandonment, they are more likely to yearn for the reassurance that can be found in emotional connection and physical touch. Holding myself close and praying for peace and love on earth would nurture my spirit enough for me to not feel so isolated. I found that through my surrender to the Divine, and through my own embrace, I was able to go deeper into the parts of myself that I had always kept locked away. Self-pleasure became a very tangible way for me to feel loved, and experience love. My bedroom shifted into a safe and peaceful space where I could lay all my worries and fears down, and be in the presence of the Most High. I would allow waves of pleasure to wash over me while I imagined a life with an abundance of love, unity, and kindness.

Did my Mother know that there was a way she could access this fountain of Divine love that manifests when she connects with her body? Would she, like me, view the experience of self-pleasure as a gift from the Creator that could help her feel safe, comforted, supported? The truth is, my Mother had grown bitter over time. She'd become physically, emotionally and mentally tired from all of the years of hard work, of seeing real-life horrors on the job—all while trying to raise her own children. All while living a life with many struggles and unsuccessfully transmuted pain, yet she somehow managed to keep her head high and her chin up. She was a backbone for so many who may not even remember her name. But I do. I will never forget her name, and I just wish she had known this kind of bliss, had experienced *this* kind of peace in a sacred space of her own design.

The pleasurable temple that I discovered as a young child would later be named by me as the Womb Space, and the Pussy Portal. The spiritual, energic temple that is the Pussy Portal is now the foundation of my work. It had become the map that guided my sacred path as a child, before I fully stepped into the full awareness of what was being built within me and began the process of learning how to cultivate it.

The Pussy Portal granted me access into the deep well of remembrance of who I am destined to be in this life. It made my blossoming psychic gifts grow stronger, and enriched my relationship with the Divine. I was enchanted with being able to see visions, receive downloads from my ancestors and guides, and work in unison with the Divine on clearing my path while spending time in the Pussy Portal. I thought it profound that I was being shown what I was meant to do in this life not from a chapter in the Bible, not from school, but from the teachings gifted to me on the wings of *pleasure.* The ecstasy found in my physical touch and the deep connection that I felt with Spirit on such an intimate level was extraordinarily beautiful and liberating, yet it was at times overshadowed by the fact that I was frightened of what I was capable of. So, I hid the *knowing* that would anchor deeper and deeper every time I embraced my sensual nature.

When my mother passed away in 2016, it was like something was released within me. And, at the same time, something came *into* me. That's when I knew I had to get out of there; my home, my city, the country. It hit me that *I* needed to break the cycle of silence. I let go of just about everything I owned and hopped a flight to Costa Rica which changed the entire trajectory of my life. I found that I had left a traumatic environment and walked into a familiar situation of power, control, abuse, and disjointedness upon arrival. On my third day in the country, I was led to a "going back to nature" group where on the first night, I prophesied a powerful message that later came to pass, and is still unfolding. I parted ways with the group after another three days knowing why I needed to meet them. During that time, I was given Divine insight that there would be several of the group leaving after my departure. I was sent there to liberate quite a few souls out of psychological and spiritual bondage. So similar to the path of. . . my Mother.

I received download after download about my purpose and I also began to see my Mother in a whole new light. I was reminded of all that she was, and is, through me. I thought of all of the women and children she mentored and oftentimes, single-handedly rallied for. She was so closed up and so busy; and *stayed* so busy that she didn't have time to honor herself. The Pussy Portal had freed me in such a profound way. It helped me release trauma and stagnant energy in the body and helped me reclaim my body as my own. Wouldn't it have been nice if Mom knew about the sacred Pussy Portal? There, she would've been able to drop her heavy load and the trove of secrets she held so close. In that space, she would've seen just how much she was loved, honored, and cherished. She could've seen just how worthy she was of peace, freedom, and pleasure. I wanted that for her so badly. I wish that she had that for herself.

I am here to break chains. The insidious chains that keep Black women bitter, traumatized and holding onto a whitewashed Jesus leading a Patriarchal religion that teaches them to remain silent, and hating themselves. As women, our extraordinarily powerful ability to tap into and experience pleasure is a gift from our Creator. My Christian upbringing certainly didn't introduce me to this sensually Divine aspect of womanhood. Isn't it strange that we are taught that we are the children of the Divine, yet we shun the Divinity of our sensuality? It took some time before I decided to honor the fact that my spiritual journey is also a sensual one, and this truth has allowed me to begin healing my sacral chakra, the portal of creativity and sensuality. My hunger for knowledge led me to the feminine and spiritual art of Sacred Sexuality, a structured practice of sensual healing that allowed me to embrace this deliciously juicy aspect of womanhood. I began to understand what I was being called to learn, integrate, and share with others who would soon be called to my unique vibration.

From this moment forward, I fully own my right to pleasure.
I honor my Maternal bloodline when I surrender to my touch.

When I began the sacred process of honoring my sensuality and claiming my throne as a woman, I developed this level of trust in my ability to tap into the intuition of my body. It was this choice to accept, love, and free all parts of myself that also works to free my Ancestors.

With this spiritual tool, I had the ability to renew myself in a way that they never could. As women, we tend to forego our own joy and bliss for the sake of others. We have made a decision, based on survival, to push down the parts of ourselves that make us feel vulnerable or unsafe. However, it's these parts of us that must be unapologetically displayed for our own healing and for those who desperately need to be led by our example. Through my own inner work, I began to realize that it was unresolved trauma and the suppression of self that had caused my Mother to distance herself from expressing and experiencing love in a way that fed her soul. In a way that I could understand.

Honoring and forgiving our Mother is one of the number one ways we can reunite with the Goddess who dwells within. Seeing my Mother as just a woman who had experienced similar fears, traumas, insecurities and struggles as anyone else, made her less omnipotent and more real. I realized that there was so much in her life that she had also pushed down. She had made countless sacrifices for her loved ones when all she truly wanted was peace and love without having had the proper guidance on how to cultivate it. By liberating my Mother from judgment, I liberate myself. Now, I claim redemption for her, myself and my bloodline. By stopping the cycles of suppression and unresolved trauma, I can live out loud.

I am here to awaken and restore the cosmic womb. . .
starting with my own.

I learned that the embrace of self, sensuality, pleasure without apology, shame, or guilt, is our gateway to enlightenment. Society makes women so self-conscious, when our sensual nature is the creative force required for us to birth a beautiful, harmonious world. I give my Mother, my Maternal bloodline, freedom through my *own* liberation. That honey-dripping sensuality that exudes from a whole and healed woman is the sacred essence of her that she has been denied for far too long.

I will no longer deny myself. I tap into the sacred space I lovingly and proudly call the Pussy Portal. I place one hand on my heart and the other hand on my pussy and say:

"I give thanks to the Goddess for all of the love and bountiful blessings in my life. I send love and honor to my beloved ancestors and guides for consistently showing up for me. I reaffirm my value on this Earth and call out to those who align with my purpose."

We have so much magick within us, vast stores of sacred wisdom and cosmic power just pulsating in our womb, waiting to be expressed. Reuniting with the overflow of Divine consciousness that moves through us from the crown of our head, to the galaxy nestled between our legs, is a choice. Sistars, we have tried to thrive in a society that undermines our unique process of spiritual and sensual evolution with their restrictions and toxic parameters. Now is the time to realize that we are not of this society; we are the Creators of Nations. The joy, peace and unity that the world needs right now is birthed by the reclamation of *Wombman*. This rebirth is activated by being willing to *surrender* to the Divine's calling on our life.

I used to run from the enormity of my purpose. I was cool with the healing part, having gotten used to navigating the ins and outs of my mind and soul. It was the spotlight that I shied away from. My journey has been public and far-reaching, yet I had somehow convinced myself that I could live a quiet life. The truth is, I am meant to shout! Flex this throat chakra and air out dirty laundry, liberate those who are unable to speak. Their stories were given to me in whispers of dreams denied and pushed aside for survival and societal acceptance. My Maternal blood-line spoke to me of rape, incest, assault, and abuse. They spoke of how the weight of long-held secrets plagued the hearts and wombs of the women in our family, causing a cycle of pain, spinsterhood, dis-ease, and dissatisfaction.

I feel an urgent need to heal and restore the ancestral, cosmic womb.

The path of the ancestral healer—the high priestess, the Goddess—is one that requires obedience, discipline, and personal sacrifice. It takes courage. Access that courage in the Pussy Portal. In that space, you are safe to reclaim your body as your own. This is where you take back ownership over your body, sensuality, dignity, and your right to pleasure.

So, let the waves of ecstasy cloak you in Divine love and protection. Tap into your inner knowing found in the Pussy Portal and watch the intel come in. What is your purpose? What do you need to address in your life in order to surrender to your path? Are people causing you problems as you go about your Divine calling? Go into the Pussy Portal and affirm your purpose in this life. And then... bust on 'em! Squirt in their eye.

One crucial fact that has been kept from women is the need for the healing that comes from the release of your sacred portal, so now you have an opportunity to reaffirm your Divine purpose and watch joy, peace, and unconditional love permeate this planet. Together, as one, we tell the abusers and oppressors that we are still Goddess, still royal, still worthy despite their mistreatment of us. Those long-held secrets shouldn't have been secret in the first place. The uncles, brothers, family friends, cousins, aunties... call them out. Why do we shun, ostracize and ridicule the victims of abuse while glorifying and praising the abuser? The family creeps get an extra serving of grandma's sweet potato pie and a good-natured slap on the back while your children die slow, repeated and agonizing deaths for the rest of their lives. Now, *that* is cruel, unjust, and un-*Christian*-like.

Ring the alarms! Call them out. We will not keep silent any longer. We call in the healing for our bloodline through focused self-love and obedience. We reclaim our power, our right to happiness, and pleasure. My Mother needed to know she was worthy of a life full of love, ease, and grace. I thank her for her sacrifices by cultivating a life of peace and joy in her honor.

> *A woman who welcomes her sensuality is a gift from*
> *the Divine. May she be anointed with whipped Shea*
> *butter and carried on the shoulders of the Queendom's finest,*
> *most loyal warriors. May she experience earth-shattering*
> *ecstasy so all-consuming that portals of abundance and sacred*
> *wisdom rain down from the ether to anoint the land and*
> *awaken the children of the Most High.*

Decide to come alive through the embodiment and expression of your most Divine self. Share the healing energy with your ancestors as a delicious, loving sacrifice. This is the sacred knowledge of the power of pleasure that has been denied women. We now have an opportunity and responsibility to tune into our body and let it lead us to our expansion.

I allow pleasure into my life as a wise guide, leading me toward a healed and abundant life.

As women, we are expected to embody this independent energy while carrying the weight of our pain, societal limitations, and generational cycles of trauma. However, as enlightened beings, we require a life of delight, so let's just take on the responsibilities that actually nurture our well-being so that we may fully function in our power. Because when women have to be strong all the time, worrying about bills, stability, and safety, our juicy sensual nature is the first to be affected.

I have made the decision that I am done subscribing to this idea of the "strong Black woman" although I honor her for the role she has played in my evolution. I am a woman, a Goddess, and I want all aspects of my life to reflect that *knowing*. I choose to live a life of ease and grace, especially when it comes to my healing. I decided to honor myself and my ancestors in the portal. I free their traumas as well as my own through intentional, sensual release. *And they with the shits!*

Pleasure has been—and still is—the foundation of my healing; not the pain or trauma-bonding that I found myself engaging in simply because heartache was such a familiar friend. If we can invite this new energy into our life, we can align with those who truly honor us. The integration of pleasure and ecstasy in our everyday lives serves to truly show gratitude to our Creator. The women in my community call me The Pussy Priestess for a reason. They have heard me say:

"Play with your pussy, Sis."

And now I say it to you. This is your sacred invitation to step fully into feminine power and grace. The world needs powerful women who are rooted in their spirituality and sensuality to lead as we move forward through time and space. I am enthralled and enchanted with the knowledge that our sensuality is the key to unlocking the cosmic code, the very blueprint needed for us to dive deep into our Magick.

I am your friend, your Sistar Goddess, and your lighthouse, fearlessly guiding and supporting you as we reclaim all that we are.

Let us heal, Sistars.
Let us heal, with pleasure.

My name is **Tiara Shardé**. From the very first moment that I decided to invite the world to witness my journey of healing, claiming my purpose and embodying all that I am, I've had droves of Black women reach out to connect with me. Although I knew the type of revolutionary work that I was called to do, it wasn't until that moment that I realized that the core foundation of what I've been creating is, and will always be for . . . the Sistahs.

I partner with women who are ready to reclaim the magic of Goddess Spirituality and the Divine Feminine Principles to help free them from generational curses, unresolved trauma, and the constraints of patriarchal religion so they can step into their power, enhance their spiritual gifts, and manifest the abundant life of a Goddess.

Creating sacred spaces with the intention of healing and expansion is both my passion and my purpose. I am your mentor, your Sistar Goddess and your lighthouse, fearlessly guiding and supporting you on your spiritual journey.

I am not a feminist.

I am the keeper of Goddess Spirituality, and the Divine Feminine Principles.

I am a spiritually gifted Indigenous woman from Connecticut, an influencer of Divine wisdom and esoteric knowledge, Certified Master Life Coach, author of *Real Goddess Shit: The 7 Step Guide to Manifest the Life of a Goddess,* co-author of *Ancient-Future Unity: Reclaim Your Roots, Liberate Your Lineage, Live a Legacy of Love,* and Founder/CEO of the Transformation Program, and The Pussy Portal Program.

In 2017, my life drastically changed when I took a leap of faith, surrendered to my soul's purpose and hopped a plane for Costa Rica. Over the course of two magical years living in the tropics, I had lost 100lbs and settled into a two bedroom cabana where I underwent initiation after initiation through dreams, downloads and visions. The real activation took place when I began applying this knowledge and shared the light codes of Divine love and wisdom with others. Over the years, I have created and organized retreats, taught workshops, and offered many healing sessions to women from all over the world. . . and yet Spirit wanted more from me.

I was to compile all of the steps I used on my healing journey, the rituals, instructional dreams and ancient practices in one, centralized place for those women who would very soon be called to receive it. This blueprint became the Transformation Program which was birthed on April 20, 2020. The Pussy Portal Program launched in the fall of 2021.

And the rest is HERstory.

It is my joy to share my knowledge and experiences with the world in order to inspire, uplift and connect with people just like me. For those beautiful souls who have heard the call to remember their Divinity and are looking for support, guidance—you are not alone.

I am so excited to witness you embody all that you are.

Learn more at: **TiaraSharde.com**

Special Gift

Like so many women, in the past, I struggled with my desire, as well as the general survival-based need for money. My Christian upbringing instilled the "love of money is the root of all evil" teachings into me and had me shook when it comes to money until. . .

My studies into Goddess Spirituality and Divine Femininity showed me how money literally chases the woman who embraces herself whether she embraces her intelligence, beauty, kindness, or she embraces her ambitious, go-getter nature.

Try this fun and powerful ritual and watch prosperity pour into your life!

mailchi.mp/5c03cf9975b0/alwaysmanifest

The Long Lost Daughter

BY LETTIE SULLIVAN

I am, quite literally, my father's long lost daughter.

We were reunited by a Google search, just shy of my thirtieth birthday. What's funny is that it was super easy because he was always there, still living in the same house he shared with my mother. Still worked the same job from way back in the day. When I found him online he was just a few months into his well earned retirement.

My greatest discovery was how our genetic code is a wonder to behold when it reveals itself through lost family ties. The past, present and future coexist in a dance and Love is a true force of nature. It can be felt even from a distance. Even to those who we do not know personally but feel connected to.

The healing that took place in my life was the identification of behavioral patterns inherited from our family systems and any belief systems that kept me separated from experiencing fulfillment and joy. Once named I could begin to love myself back into wholeness and unify with my Ancestral legacy.

I was only six months in my mother's belly when my parents split up. Neither my mother, nor my father would speak of what caused their breakup. Whatever happened between them, however, was a definite-final-clean and decisive break.

My mother swiftly moved from Chicago to Phoenix and never came back to my dad's to ask him for anything. Apparently, my mother always seemed very sure of her moves, she put God first and then took the leap, fearlessly faithful and determined to make a "way out of no way."

If she had reached out to my father, at least once, she would have found a man ready, waiting with open arms for his child. I believed him when he told me that he always expected my mother to come back one day, he'd never gone anywhere. It never occurred to him that she would never return and that he would never get to know their child. In the times before the internet connected us, it was much easier for people to disappear and not be found.

So now, thirty years later, he's sitting, waiting in a cafe for a young woman he doesn't know—who says she's his daughter—to step through the door. We'd only had two phone conversations.

At the time I was 29 years old, married with two young children, one on the Autism spectrum. I was working as an office manager for a design + build firm in Chicago's Gold Coast. One day my boss had sent me to City Hall to pick up some documents. While my footfalls echoed through the cavernous building, I suddenly had a longing for my father. It was like a bolt of lightning striking me—this profound sense of loss that I'd never felt before. Longing. Sadness. Curiosity.

When I got back to my desk I immediately pulled up Google and typed in his name. This wasn't my first time searching for him, but it had been many years and the internet was growing by leaps and bounds. My heart was racing but my gut was calm. I had a sense of "knowing" that this time would be different.

Buried in the middle of the first page, on the official City of Chicago letterhead, was the image of a commendation from Mayor Daley to a team of people whose efforts were consequential to the city. Someone with my father's name was on that team.

My search then went to that organization's company directory and within fifteen minutes I had made contact! In a snap—a long severed connection had been restored.

When I asked my dad what he was thinking when he first saw me walk through the door of the restaurant, he said, "I knew you were mine as soon as I saw you. You look just like my grandmother."

Our next gathering was at my grandmother's home with my husband and kids. I met my long-lost sister and my nieces and nephew, my great-aunt and my father's mother, the family matriarch.

Grandma stood nearly six feet tall with regal bone structure and beautiful ebony skin, her hair wrapped in a royal blue hijab. When I stood before her that first time and looked into her eyes she said to me, "I worked in the cafeteria for the Chicago Public Schools for over twenty years, and every school year, I looked in that lunch line for your face. It broke my heart what happened with your mother, but I am so glad you're finally home."

That was the start of many weekends, visiting my grandmother, sitting in her living room on the fancy couch with the cushions covered by crinkly plastic. The whole space, seemingly, a time capsule of the 70s 80s 90s. All the different eras represented in my grandmother's living room. My grandmother gave me our family's history and it healed me in ways I never could have imagined.

My dad had actively been working on the family's ancestry.com profile during his retirement. He told me about hours spent exploring the names behind the stories and all the ways that they were connected. We listened about family history not that far removed from slavery times and about my grandmother's many careers. She was often the "first" in many of the things she did in the world. Strong, intelligent, fearless and deeply caring about her family and community. It was healing to hear the stories of this whole other bloodline that was woven into mine.

For the first thirty years of my life I only had one side of my story. By stepping into my rightful place as my father's daughter, I got to activate my father's lineage and all of the remembrance and all of the new understandings of myself, why I did some of the things that I did. It's absolutely amazing what expresses through our DNA! My understanding of Nature vs. Nurture was upended because I am so much like my father that you wouldn't even know that he wasn't physically present to influence my upbringing. Our reunion allowed me to reclaim my soul's inheritance. It changed how I viewed myself and elevated me as a mother, as a wife, as a sister and as a friend. Going from lost to found catalyzed me right as I was looking ahead at a whole new decade of my life.

It was clear that there were dimensions that were yet to be explored now that I felt whole in my humanity and bonded to my full bloodlines, so I began my spiritual journey in earnest. I had been raised with my mother's Christianity but now I was being influenced by the Islamic faith of my father, grandmother and my great-aunt for whom I gave the greeting, *As-Salaam-Alaikum*, when I came to visit. To round it all out, I had also been influenced by Judaism, my husband's faith upbringing, having shared Passover Seders with his extended and immediate family, hearing the stories and practicing some of the high holy days.

In the journey to deeply know and truly love myself I had been weaving in this profound understanding of the nature of Spirit. Eventually, I found myself at the doorstep of the transcendentalist movement, *The Science of Mind* by Ernest Holmes, and the Unity teachings of Charles and Myrtle Fillmore. It was in that decade that my spiritual path revealed itself to me, and I became an earnest student of metaphysics and what one of my mentors, Rev. Michael Beckwith, calls "New Thought-Ageless wisdom."

Having always been a voracious reader, I was finding that I needed to slow down and build a practice to be consistent and disciplined in order to integrate the wisdom and truly LIVE it. Then I put myself in a position to serve in my spiritual community which was instilled in me by my mother who led all types of ministry work. My mother cared for children, prisoners, the elderly and disabled, and especially the homeless. She cooked meals, led classes and Bible study groups, prayed, sang and entertained. She even had a radio program to just minister and to get her message out to uplift and inspire whoever was listening. In today's language, my mother had a regular "IG Live" over the radio airwaves. She was always praying and preaching and singing. In hindsight I am grateful to have witnessed her journey up close, although like many young women I thought I would never do what she did and yet here I am.

Our paths diverged when I began to explore the more esoteric and occult aspects of spirituality. Like any good Christian woman, she feared for my soul and had concerns that the devil was in the details of what I was doing. I wasn't going to argue about it so we were at an impasse for many years. Those were lost years because we kept each other, more or less, at arm's length.

While visiting my second hometown of Atlanta for a class reunion, my ailing mother asked me to pray for her, which was surprising because for the first time she was acknowledging me as a woman of God and more importantly, acknowledging the power behind my prayers. Up to that point, she had been suspicious, though not outright rejecting my belief system. That one prayerful moment with my mother restored my soul. Our kinship as women of God bloomed into the light of day. Those words of prayer turned out to be the last words I spoke to my mother. She passed away just a few weeks later. Fifteen years of wandering on my spiritual path, without my mother's approval, were erased and again the long lost daughter returned home.

The spiritual path is contextualized in many different ways, but most frequently as a spiral. This spiraling path moves inward-upward-downward and in all the four directions. Eventually, you always find yourself back in a new beginning.

At some point in my spiraling spiritual path I became very disillusioned with new-age spirituality. There was this elephant in the room that was wrapped up with all the love and light. Thinly veiled white supremacy, fragility, and privilege that expressed as micro-aggressions and narcissistic gaslighting all wrapped up in a bundle with un-metabolized religious trauma. Unacknowledged shadow, as it turns out, was corrosive for my health and well being and I didn't want to face it.

Ultimately, it was my health that was the signal that it was time for me to make my exit from community service even though my mind and heart didn't want to listen, didn't want to go. But when the writing was on the wall I was left bereft. Where did I go wrong? What do I need to heal? How do I serve? What is my current understanding of a higher power, the God of my understanding? How do I continue to grow spiritually? What do I need to surrender and let go?

In that leg of the journey, I deepened into the arms and the embrace of the Divine Mother principle. The Great Mother Goddess took me into her arms and held me to her bosom. I was able to cry, wail, weep for all of the pain and anguish of separation and the accompanying suffering, confusion and the disillusion.

When my health took a catastrophic turn it gave me plenty of time to lie in my hospital bed and commune with a power greater than myself. I had the experience of being completely and utterly humbled on the banks of the River Styx. During my metaphysical time in the underworld I was able to identify and release the miseducation I received along my spiritual path. To experience a symbolic death and move forward learning to love unconditionally all my teachers, and even those who might have appeared as adversaries. To unconditionally love and forgive myself for my righteousness, misguided interpretations, and my opinions and judgments that contributed to all the seeming misfortune that befell me. It was at 92 pounds, practically skin and bones, sicker than I had ever been in my entire existence that I knew that I had to love and treat myself like a newborn baby. Although my mother was not physically on the planet, I very much felt her there nourishing and protecting me.

Cell by cell, organ by organ, system by system, I regenerated my body temple to restore not just my weight, but the tone, definition, and the strength of my body. Then I had to rebuild my spiritual cosmology and construct a whole new framework for my spiritual journey and keep spiraling through that dark night of the soul period to become the phoenix rising from the ashes.

That Phoenix Rising consciousness led me to a pilgrimage to the motherland. I became the long lost daughter again, and returned home to Mother Africa. My pilgrimage to Egypt was a reclaiming of a legacy of my soul's priest/ess-hood to pick up that thread of my soul's journey into the sacred temples up the Nile River into the Great Pyramid of Giza.

Our voices collectively rising, harmonizing and bathing us in sound waves that rocked my soul to its core essence while my energy bodies dissolved into atomic particles, reformed and swirled back into my physical body system, rocking my world completely and shattering every paradigm I stepped into that King's Chamber with.

Even now, two and a half years later, I'm still unpacking the experience. It was as though I was energetically unified with my ancient self that had prepared for a future reunification. When I reflected that night on the chanting and the rituals as I bathed in Epsom salts and essential oils, I knew that, as a Priestess, the long lost daughter had once again returned home.

Lettie Sullivan is a Priestess of the Sacred Arts and the Creatrix of the Goddess Ministry, whose mission is to anchor energetic activism centered in Love, Divine Feminine wisdom, metaphysical principles, and cosmic time cycles. Lettie is also an inspirational speaker, a professional organizer, a life coach, and a bestselling author.

Lettie's 20+ years of mystical studies, practices and initiations—as well as 13 years in private practice as a Professional Organizer and life coach— synthesized the birth of an online community space dedicated to merging the sacred and mundane with the evolution of consciousness occurring on the planet and to provide a framework for a renaissance in cultural intelligence.

Learn more at: **lettiesullivan.com, thegoddessministry.com**

Special Gift

Sacred Altar Masterclass

Activate Sacred Spaces for Healing and Transformation

**lettiesullivan.com/
offerings/p/sacredaltarmasterclass**

Roadman's Daughter

BY PAULINE TOMLIN

1. The coffee shop

There was no "Thank you for your custom" (order) as *she* exited. She'd been sitting there for some forty minutes. . . in the corner; watching and wondering and dreaming. On every occasion, as someone had left through the permanently wedged-open oak-and-glass door, there had been the obligatory "Thank you for your custom!" trilled in light "sing songy" tones from one or other of the trainee baristas staffing the counter.

It hadn't really occurred to her, until she was twenty or so paces from the establishment; it was a fleeting thought, not that important really in the scheme of things, was it?

Well, what could she expect, she should be used to it, no? she mused. After all, it was common enough. In her fifty-five years in the UK, she *was* used to being ignored: is that the right word? Surely being ignored means being seen, if only fleetingly and then intentionally disregarded. No, this wasn't that. She, the black woman in general, is subject to two extremes of interaction.

A. In fact she couldn't find the word for it, because the only words that came close like repel, or repudiate, deny or rebuff, negate or reject, imply there has been some moment of "seeing," albeit fleeting and then the all too common rejection. For the black woman, the *dark* black woman (not the café-latte "mixed" acceptable-face-of-blackness black woman) there is not even a fleeting glimpse. There's mostly just. . . she stopped to seek the words; they're not visible, not even barely.

OR

B. She is allocated a series of limited, cartoon-like roles to inhabit. In the corporate world, she is made into a token and accepted as long as she remains the "colour hire."

All too often, after proving yourself to be *extra* brilliant and capable, in order to be hired in the first place, that brilliance and capability is shackled. God forbid you have an original idea or go for promotion... oh no sah! That's when the meat cleavers really get sharpened and all manner of slights and indignities are heaped on. Taking away your workspace, rejigging classes, clients, teams, so you're forced to "prove" yourself yet again by turning around underperforming units in unfeasibly short time-frames. Then there's workplace gaslighting and the refusal to put requests in writing. Proffering only verbal instructions in corridors, then denying you were instructed to do any such thing! Yet... you *still* manage, even in those circumstances to pull it out of the bag, but that's when things turn seriously nasty.

Eventually, for the sake of your sanity, scrambling together the very shreds of your dignity, you are forced to make the decision to leave (because, of course, they can't be seen to have fired the "colour hire.") Afterwards, follow the self-mitigating platitudes like, "Well, you can't say we didn't try," or "They still have a ways to go," and then all is well again in *Milkybar land*.

She returns to those feelings of disconnection and loneliness, to existential examinations wondering how and why people can be so cruel. She returns to yet another halt in her cash flow and having to start over, once more thrust into survival mode, to worry and an increased lack of trust. The powerlessness meter is full to overflowing, leaving her bereft and wondering how she can do everything *right*, be the best she can be, do what she was employed to do... and still the outcome (for the Divine Melanated Feminine) is a catastrophic one?

Another layer of trauma bricks are laid... Triggering her past remembrances of the same both in work and personal relationships. There will be the startling resurfacing of generational wounding. With all of this she will sit *alone.* In hermit mode, isolated, and hurt and somehow have to find the fortitude to examine the spewed emotions and heal.

Alone.

2. I'm such a cliché.

You may groan and I won't lie, *yes,* this *is* going to be one of those introspective examinations of the plight of the Black woman in society and why the fuck not?

I can promise you tears and wailing and anger and vitriol, because, guess what? These are the emotions we're given permission to have. So trust me, I'm gonna *swim* in them, bathe in *anger* as if I were completely enveloped in the azure warmth of the Indian Ocean, and wallow in vitriol as if in the blue-green of the Caribbean Sea.

If this makes you uncomfortable, then I suggest you leave now. It will not make for pleasant reading. There will be the *ugly* cry, the muted, stick-in-the-throat-chicken-bone-sharp restrained internal wail Ooh and let's not forget that old staple, just a pinch of stoicism. . .

Ooh I almost forgot the most important ingredient. We can't forget to add the: '*Strong-black-woman-no-need-to-care-about-her-feelings-she-has-none-and-is-not-just-dismissed* pinch for added punch and that provides just a hint of *je ne sais quoi?* to the recipe.

What at all has improved for the black woman since she first stepped on these shores in the 40s? I look around me and I see women like me—some Caramel, some Coffee, some Cocoa, others Coal—single and *alone.* For decades.

SEXUAL AND EMOTIONAL ANOREXICS. . .

Many of our chicks have flown the nest; others of us have none. Some of us lead active creative lives, some (I would warrant *many* of us) are enveloped in a thinly veiled *alone*ness layered with a sickly-sweet mask no one dares or cares to look behind.

I'm standing here in bits—in the middle of a car crash of a life—and I have no one, literally no one who I can talk to about it. No one I can truly be vulnerable with without judgment or the cursory, "You'll be fine, you're strong!" Yes, that old hackneyed trope, which is trotted out when the listener (and I use the term loosely, you understand) is confronted by the fact that you may, surprisingly, have expected reciprocal support within this friendship/romance/siblingship/familyship, whatever this thing-ship is.

3. Out of the Mouths of Babes

My daughter was about 10 or 11 years old when one day she (I can't remember what we were watching, maybe a commercial that featured a black man and a white woman and their darling children) turned to me and said:

Daughter: "Mum, I feel sorry for the Black woman." Long pause. "*No one* wants the Black woman, do they?"

I'm sure you can imagine the stupefied look that I quickly corrected to one of attentive interest. I was surprised but curious to know why and how she had formed such an opinion and what my contribution might have been in its formation.

Daughter: "Well, who does the Black woman have? The white man doesn't want the Black woman and marries the white woman, and the Chinese man marries the Chinese woman, and the Indian marries and wants the Indian woman, and the Black man doesn't want the Black woman, the Black man wants the white woman, so who does the Black woman have?"

Who indeed? Now you tell me, if a 10- or 11-year-old can suss it out, who am I to say differently?

You can't imagine it, but in that moment, my ears pounded with the thunderous sound of my heart shattering into millions of shards.

My baby, that's what she sees when she looks at the mahogany-ness of her mother? A sad specimen of society who no one wants? Which little girl is going to allow herself in her subconscious mind to see that as any kind of role model?

- Which dusky Queen-in-waiting will see that as something to aspire to?
- Which little girl wants to model her vision of herself on becoming society's trash?
- Which little girl dreams of becoming a "Social Housing-living, single, work-yourself-sick" (that's another story) detritus of society, that no one wants and no one wants to be?

No need for the embarrassed internal squirm when the perfunctory "So how do you know X then?" is curiously interjected into polite social gatherings.

Easy then to avoid the *"Oh, so this is your mum?"*

4. Store Policy

I am still followed around department stores. Me, with my salt-and-peppa locs and all that middle-aged wisdom is *still* followed around department stores. The irony is, it's usually a Black man, often in 2020s Britain an *African* from the continent who looks at me with disdain, when the blood in me *descended from the power and will of my ancestors in diaspora veins bubble* and my pointed look dares to challenge his with unapologetic revolt.

Can you imagine? No, I mean, truly imagine the *chip, chip chipping* away at your core. The slow, consistent, dismantling of your humanity and godliness, the very fabric from which you were made. Consider the immense mental fortitude it takes to rise up and above, rise up, and above, rise up and above, rise up and above; always, always having to find the strength to get up, when your spirit is splintering and the fragments scattering on the four winds?

Sometimes, many times, I have *screamed* at God, hoarse and weeping, asking why I, why we, the Divine Melanated Feminine have to carry such a heavy load. I have begged to put mine down, wailing that I can't do this, I'm not strong enough, I'm not able to keep on rising. And each time God says: "You're my child, I am with you. I have not left you, do not leave yourself."

I know Ancestor Maya (may she rest in power) meant well. Her poem is sublimely beautiful in its lyricism, inspired, inspiring, and lauded as it should be. But some days I cannot *rise*. Some days I yearn, plead for at least one moment of peace from the persistent, consistent, steam-locomotive-*chugga-chugga-chugga-chugga* of proving my worth, my validity, my womanhood, my right to dignity, my right to define ME and constantly having to defend ME...

Fighting always, fighting for the right to be the God-given me.

Most days that fight is simply one of getting through the day without losing another shard, another chip, doing my very best to prevent yet another soul fragment drifting off into the abyss.

5. Generations

IMOJEAN

Ruby Imojean was a spitfire. Intelligent, driven, and ambitious. She was the kind of woman who would have been a successful entrepreneur. She did not suffer fools and had a vision for her life. She had plans. But you know what they say about life... It happens whilst you're busy making those plans.

Her first love was a naïve one. Isn't it always? Awed by his good-looking, coolie-fine features and grateful for his *"pretty bwoy"* attentions (after all, he could have had any girl he wanted) Imojean succumbed to his pubescent courtship.

Before she could blink, she was with child... enceinte, ripe and rejected. Educational exclusion and family chagrin were a given. Consequently, Imojean Mini was handed over to well-to-do, upper-middle-class professional teen boy's, good-looking, brown-skinned, coolie-headed family for rearing. Imojean was none of these. Chocolate dark, merchant-class-reared, who was she to oppose this convenient arrangement?'

That was trauma #1.

Starting fresh took a few years. An interrupted education meant Imojean was unfulfilled, but she did what she had to. Fate smiled on her, and some years later she fell in love. This was a true love. A love between equals, a reciprocal love, and she was happy. They birthed three beautiful daughters, and all seemed well in her world. No one could have conceived that the small, moustachioed man with the black, slicked-down hair would cause such a global stirring and affect the lives of so many who barely knew who he was.

And so it was that the love of Imojean's life was sent away. To foreign lands to battle an unknown foe, all in the name of Queen and Country.

His return was tense. He was no longer the man she remembered, the man she loved, the man she had kissed passionately and whispered "Come home safe" to as she waved him off that day. PTSD, is it? Yes I think that's what they call it today. Then there was ridicule and ignorant social chastisement. *"A quicksilver fly up inna 'im 'ed"* chorused as they went about their day. More chagrin, more shame.

He didn't last long. A lack of understanding or care. She did what she could: she loved him.

He died.

And her heart broke.

Alone now, with three beautiful young mouths to feed, she needed more work, more money and so the pretty unit was dissected and thrown to the four winds. To aunts, grandmas, aunts-once-removed-on-father's-side. Fractured.

That was trauma #2.

And so life goes on, Imojean works, strives and provides as her girls grow distant and have vastly differing upbringings, all outside of her control, apart from her nurture and bereft of her guidance. And, like their mother, they are left to navigate their way through life, rudderless, *alone,* and missing a mama's meaningful template to emulate.

It is reflection, time, and space that lead us to wisdom. And Imojean has had no time. Her life thus far is a jet-fueled, perpetual flight from poverty, constantly fleeing the relentless spectre in pursuit, the spectre of destitution and ruin.

Third time's a charm, eh? Nah so?

No. . . Not so?

Still emotionally pubescent, her pubescent emotions succumb once again. But he is already taken and, though able to offer her material comfort, she is still very much *alone*. She is a modern-day concubine, ever ready (she had provided him with the desperately craved *"bwoy chil"* that his barren wife could not).

She is still pursuing that elusive "happy" life that the Divine Feminine is schooled to believe is her duty to manifest.

By now her heart is hardening, and small shards of ice and salt are beginning to form barely there, minute melanomas.

That was trauma #3.

Trauma #4 was unlike the others. He was an introverted, simpler expression of manhood. Safer. His spitfire of a woman will take him places and together they form an easy partnership. She, the fire, he the stabiliser, grafting, providing.

Another three daughters follow. There is a domestic routine, and she flourishes in that for the first time in her life. But life in Jamaica is hard, and the misnomered "mother country" is calling for its loyal citizens in the colonies to come and rebuild Britain. To take their place in a new era of European expansion and expertise and benefit from all the riches that would ensue.

And so whistling and smiling, decked out in their Sunday best, they packed themselves onto ships and sailed the ocean towards the land of opportunity, where the streets were said to be paved with gold.

They were not to know they'd be met with hatred, that they would be despised, that they would be spat at and ridiculed, beaten up and chased. They would be the objects of suspicion and blame both locally and nationally. They would be questioned, doubted, criticised, outcast, maligned, defamed, slandered, smeared, and vilified.

'NO BLACKS, NO IRISH, NO DOGS!'

Father led the migration. Toiling by day and into the nights on building sites, his hands raw, his body ice-water cold, and supervised by snarling guttersnipes, he suffered indignity after indignity to build this new life.

His Master Carpenter skills were relegated to whittling and carving by the fire.

Once more, Imojean was called to abandon her children and follow Mr. to the belly of the beast and create a home in this new world. Once more, her three ducklings had to be scattered to the winds. Each sister missing the other two, now forced to bear the guardianship of strangers no knowing if they be angel or Devil.

That was trauma #4.

Once reunited, the family is still fractured. Papa toils, and Mama makes home and toils within the confines of what society and femininity allow. The girls, wide-eyed and naive, barely have time for their feet to land in this new world when they are thrust out into the *cold*. Work, travel, responsibility, shared burdens; paying board, and absolute obedience are the measure of the day. Childhood is gone. Innocence is lost. The girls are ill equipped to deal with the bitter UK winds.

Mama becomes harsh, Papa disillusioned and tired, fearful of mama's pursuit of expansion and status. His manhood chips away and he desperately tries to regain it through dominance and discipline. Eloise wonders where that sweet father she had in Jamaica has gone, where the laughing singing mother she knew is hiding.

For Eloise, the middle child, that was trauma #1.

ELOISE

Eloise tries to be a good girl, but for some reason Mum chastens her. She feels resented and bullied. Is it because she's not the pretty one? The slim toffee-coloured, hourglass-figured one? The delicate, almost-died-at-birth one? Is it because she's darker and stronger, her character more like Daddy's? She retreats into herself, growing a hurt that explodes into a seething anger when pushed.

Rudderless and afraid, she too is thrust too early out into the biting winds that wail, screech along the narrow alleyways of Britain. After less than a year in school, she is belched into the vagaries of racism and rejection, to work and drudgery. No dreams can take root in her heart, no hope allowed ignition in her belly.

That is trauma #2.

He is handsome, raw magnetism, spirited, and seemingly strong. He stirs places within her she didn't even know existed and is a far cry from the stoic, stable but somewhat argumentative man her father has become. Her mother resents him, loathes him even; perhaps he is a too stark reminder of the flame that once illuminated her chest and has now subsided into a controlling cool resistance.

Eloise loves him. He loves her. It is a delicate, fragile too-young-to-know-how-to-navigate-this love. They are searching for the impossible, for each other to fill the void. Both insufficiently nurtured, both searching, both emotionally ill-equipped. No template, no guidance, no support.

That is trauma #3.

A swelling, a baby, the knitting together of two ill-prepared lives is followed by fatigue, frustration, and fear. Fear of poverty, fear of loss, fear of what will become of the child they have birthed. All that fear means she soon starts to become brittle like Imojean before her. They Ping-Pong back and forth, trying in their own way, to glue this thing back together, for the love is there. But it becomes stale. It sours and becomes magma, white-hot and dangerous.

He retreats and hides in excesses: Women, the "streets," the "fast life." A "Roadman."

Eloise is abandoned, and like Imojean before her, she is *Alone now, with three beautiful young mouths to feed.*

That is trauma #4.

Pansy, their eldest, is a laughing, light, inquisitive little girl. She loves life, but not for long. The joy she intuitively feels and emits is crushed and beaten and critiqued into a timid swallowing of her light within.

Pansy tries to be a good girl, but for some reason mum chastens her. She feels resented and bullied. She is acutely aware of her mother's pain and so, in an attempt to make it all better she becomes the foundation and stability of this unit.

She grows to be bright and creative, a seeker, but constantly tugged back to the "responsibility and support" role she designed for herself so early on in life. This perpetual tug of war between her soul's urge and the role she "should" play creates a life of highs and lows. Abundance, recognition, and stability are elusive.

Love finds her early, like her mother before her. A now-cold Eloise and an extravagant Roadman father serve as poor examples of how to create stability, abundance, joy, and hope. And so Pansy fumbles and seeks, ever the optimist, believing always that "better" is just around the corner.

But, unbeknownst to her, she left home, only to return. To a marriage characterised by her drudgery and support. *Her husband chastens her. She feels resented and bullied.* And yet again the joy she intuitively feels and emits is crushed and beaten and critiqued into a timid swallowing of the light within. The dissolution of her marital connection leaves her, like her mother before her and her grandmother before her, co-parenting. *Alone now, with three beautiful young mouths to feed.*

Decades later, still *alone,* she sits in a coffee shop. And as she leaves, she notices there is no "Thank you for your custom" as *she* exited.

Pauline Tomlin was a bright, luminous child, excited about the world. She was full of adventure and music and singing. She wanted to see, do and experience as much as possible. She knew she wasn't built to follow a conventional path.

Now, as an adult, she is a Divine melanin-carrying feminine who wrestles with her opposing inner forces of strength and control versus wanderlust, nonconformity and eccentricity. She has had many experiences, some which have scarred and some that have illuminated and caused her to grow.

Pauline has managed to maintain a raging fire of hope within her breast no matter how many times she has fallen, no matter how many times she has been brought to her knees. She declares that the old trope of the 'strong Black woman' is perfectly applicable in her own case. Pauline has always believed we are here to connect and this is her deepest desire with any interaction. As such she is a wordsmith.

Words seem to have featured prominently since birth. Ironically, Pauline was often told she used too many, too often. Film, dialogue and narrative enthralled her from an early age and then in later years she used them extensively by becoming an English Teacher. She absorbed and bathed in the written and spoken word, sharing her love and enthusiasm for both with the next generation.

As a child Pauline was an avid reader. She would dream of far off lands, exotic and exciting experiences and imagine her life to be one of thrills, adventure, vibrant light and colour.

Journaling has been her muse, her friend. Writing and words are Pauline's contribution to humanity, through them she hopes to create heartfelt connections and support you as you navigate your journey.

Thank you for the honour of allowing Pauline to share with you.

Learn more at: **insightfulangel.com**

Special Gift

Thank you for supporting this collective of Melanated Queen authors.

As a contributing writer to this anthology and an entrepreneur I would like to offer some form of reciprocation to all you Queens who understand the power and need for the Melanin-carrying Female's voice to rise and shatter her deafening muffling.

So, my gift to you my sis-star is a huge 30% discount off any of the exclusively designed merchandise; Yoga leggings; exclusive Canvas Print of the book cover artwork or Latte Mug with the 'Black woman' poem on the reverse of the full cover design; all of which accompany the *Ancient-Future Unity* anthology.

It's just my way of appreciating the love and support you have shown to us.

"Blissings" & Much love

Use the coupon below:
coupon = AFUWOMEN
to receive your exclusive discount at:
etsy.com/uk/shop/Zanzibarmoonboutique/

Liberation from Trapped Illusions

BY JERMIRA TRAPP

It has always been my dream to be either a nurse, detective, or psychiatrist. I've always loved helping people. I have always wanted to be a positive force for humanity.

My father gained sole custody of me when I was in kindergarten. I grew up on the north side of Chicago in a household with my father, stepmother, and three sisters. My father did the best he could to raise us, but I don't remember ever receiving affection or words of praise and encouragement from him.

Schooling was also not a priority at home, and I only did well enough to barely pass my classes. By senior year of high school, I remember my guidance counselor telling me that my grades were not good enough to attend a four-year university and that the best I could do was go to community college.

While I was initially discouraged, it propelled me to study hard. All my efforts eventually paid off when I received a bachelor's degree from Northern Illinois University in 2006. Ever since I was young, my dream was to become a detective. So after graduating from college, I started applying for law enforcement jobs. Unfortunately, the city went on a hiring freeze, and after a three-and-a-half-year wait, I was finally hired as a police officer in December 2009.

Every day was a struggle in this male-dominated field. I spent my time trying to prove to my co-workers that I deserved the same respect as any of the male police officers. But I was often judged for my looks and received demeaning comments. It was not easy to enter this type of field; nonetheless, I felt a great sense of mission to transform the reputation of the police officers and work to make this city a safer place for its citizens.

Although I had dreamt and waited for this job, it seemed that I was being attacked with negativity in every aspect of my life, and I felt a deep sense of hopelessness. Around this time, in July 2012, a co-worker introduced me to Buddhism. I had always been inspired by his incredible life condition. No matter what kind of difficult situations he had to deal with at work, he always remained calm and positive. With his encouragement and conviction in this practice, on December 15, 2012, I became a practitioner of Soka Gakkai Nichiren Buddhism, a lay Buddhist organization with 12 million practitioners in 192 countries and territories. And so, I began my journey to transform my destiny.

I started my career as a patrol/beat officer. Most police officers are reactive, meaning they only take action when they get a call. But I was determined to be a proactive officer and went above and beyond my duties to ensure my neighborhoods were safe. Because of my determination and drive, I received a lot of negative feedback from my co-workers, who said things like: "Hey kid, you can do all the work in the world; it won't make a difference." I was determined to be that "kid" who would make a difference.

For many years, my dream has been to become a detective. That is why I became a police officer. As a detective, I could really help citizens by giving closure to the victims of crimes. I believe citizens deserve a more humanistic and compassionate form of policing.

You might think that a police officer is never afraid, but I experience anxiety often. The last exam was offered eleven years ago, so I knew the competition would be steep. Many people had been studying since the last time the exam was given, and I had only two months to prepare. To make matters worse, I was convinced that I wasn't a good test-taker. In 2013, I took the Sergeant's Exam, and because of my overwhelming anxiety, I did not do well at all. I lacked confidence. I would have negative thoughts like, "There is no way I can really prepare, the others taking the exam are smarter than I am, and most of the officers taking the exam have much more experience than I have." My anxiety was so strong that my heart would start racing, my arms would tingle, and I would have trouble breathing.

I couldn't stop reflecting on how this had always been my dream. So, in spite of my fears, I chanted the basic prayer (Nam-Myoho-Renge-Kyo), which is a chant that enables all people to bring forth their inherent Buddha nature, like limitless courage, compassion, and wisdom. I moved forward as I studied and prepared hard. Moving forward with the mindset "From this moment on". . . determined to break through the barrier of self-doubt telling me that I could not succeed, finding the courage to fight and win joyfully! I signed up for a preparation course and started waking up every morning super early. The first thing I would do is chant, and then from 5 a.m. to 9 a.m., I would study before I left for work. I was amazed at how hard I worked—I've never studied so hard in my life!

I kept going by grounding myself, and I decorated the walls of my apartment with encouraging quotes from my mentor in life, Daisaku Ikeda, like this one:

> "If you practice faith while doubting its
> effects, you will get results that are at
> best unsatisfactory. This is the reflection of
> your own weak faith in the mirror of
> the cosmos. On the other hand, when you
> stand up with strong confidence, you will
> accrue limitless blessings."
>
> *—DAISAKU IKEDA*
> (MY DEAR FRIENDS OF AMERICA, P. 99)

With this guidance as my compass, I had to fight! The test was on a Saturday. On the following Wednesday, I found out that I was being transferred out of my stressful work environment into a unit that I had been trying to get into for over three years.

I'm also overjoyed to share that I passed the grueling qualifying exam to be considered for a position as a detective.

In July of 2018, while at work and on duty, my teammate committed suicide in his squad car in the parking lot at work. His suicide was the catalyst that inspired my courage to have more one-on-one dialogue with my co-workers. I resolved to be the beaming light demonstrating how, in this "Hellish World," one can be confident, have conviction, and be happy.

In May 2019, I sat in a mandatory department training class listening to the instructor talk about compassion fatigue, suicide, and PTSD. I realized that the department was unaware of the importance of decompressing, the negative effects that dialoguing about incidents with negative people can have, and how replays of traumatic incidents release the same hormones and toxins as if the incident is happening in the current moment. This, in turn, leads to illness within the body.

Officers need to become aware of the long-term effects of unhealthy/negative coping habits such as excessive drinking, eating, gambling, and emotional outbursts; and how these can impact the individual as well as their personal and work environment. We need training on healthy coping mechanisms and how we can integrate them into our daily lives. If we do not have the mental resilience to win and persevere over our mental battles, officers can NOT be effective, productive, and proactive. Thus, unable to provide fully to the citizens that they serve and protect. This is a deep issue; we need to get to the root of it instead of putting a band-aid on a wound that needs immediate/emergency surgery. I am determined to write a proposal to submit to the EAP (employee assistance program) on a holistic approach, offering meditation and other healthy and tangible decompressing coping mechanisms. I'm confident this will help my co-workers be a positive force for citizens. This is not only transformational for the officers, but for the citizens they interact with and serve daily.

In early 2020 while chanting, I came to the realization that my relationships with my ex and my friendships were karmic connections. These relationships helped me to see a lot of tendencies that were not serving me well. They reminded me that the history and love you have with a person is not the most important. You always have to put yourself first... ALWAYS!

You should NEVER seek validation outside of yourself.

I have slowly evolved into being true to my authentic self. My environment is now reflecting those who only serve my highest good. It's quite exhilarating!

I've learned that when I am dedicated to my personal evolution, transformation, and expansion that it automatically impacts the lives of others. When you are seriously dedicated to serving humanity, you will always be positively guided, protected, and forced to step into a higher version of yourself!

As multidimensional beings, our spiritual self exists in many forms simultaneously. It is our responsibility to be aware of all these realities. When I refer to us being multidimensional, an example would be how some people are in a dimension that keeps them stuck in the past, perhaps, trapped in a state of depression and worrying. The "future" dimension can keep us trapped viciously, going through a cycle of fear and anxiety. These are states of consciousness that we unconsciously experience at the same time that many are not talking about.

What I've learned is that the POWER we have is forever PRESENT. It is paramount that we get in the driver's seat; we search inward, at each moment, consciously choosing a new perspective of our reality.

Lil' Mira—Jermira Present—Higher self
(Past) (Present) (Future)

On August 3, 2020, during my cranial sacral therapy session (a form of meditative healing), I envisioned my dad sitting on the couch in sadness, sighing and taking deep breaths. I told myself, "Jermira, stop being mean to your dad, he's in pain and doesn't know better." As soon as I said that, my mom appeared. She overshadowed my dad... she stood in front of me smiling. Immediately I wanted to cry, but I locked my body up and held my tears in. She said, "Baby, it's okay, I am here with you. I've always been here with you." Nancy, the person doing my session, said, "It's okay,

Jermira, I am here." Immediately I screamed and kicked. I experienced an explosion of deep pain and anger.

Tuesday, August 4, 2020 was the day of the funeral. At the end of July, one of my supervisors committed suicide at work while on duty in his office. I did not attend the services. Right before I was getting in the shower, my dad called me. I ignored the call, thinking I can't talk to him right now. Once I got in the shower, my mom came to me and said, "Jermira, you're not mad at your dad because he is annoying and immature; you're mad at him because he kept you away from me." I lost it. Immediately, I cried out deeply in pain at the realization that I suppressed the fact that my dad intentionally kept me away from my mom to cause her pain, *because he was in pain.*

As a defense mechanism for survival, I created this narrative for safety that my dad is immature, he plays too much, and he is annoying. But that was an illusion! That narrative impacted multiple aspects of my life. I had a conflict with men at work who "reminded me of my dad" due to their immature or playful nature. I realized that the true pain and anger toward my dad was because he kept me away from my mom. It felt like getting released from years of imprisonment. I'd been unconsciously suffocating myself.

The next day I went to work with a new narrative. I felt so empowered! I didn't feel anger toward the men who reminded me of my dad. Because those men did not keep me away from my mother—my dad did. I had been suffering at work for over a decade with Illusion.

In Soka Gakkai Nichiren Buddhism, there are three categories of Illusion. The first category of illusion is thought and desire. This category causes people to suffer and distorts perceptions of the truth and is primarily mental and learned.

My narrative was, "I hate men who remind me of my dad: men who are immature, who cut me off when I'm talking, and who goof around at inappropriate times." I also had the narrative in my mind that I couldn't express myself without cursing them out and exploding at their obvious stupidity. I didn't want to come off as being an angry black woman. However, this illusion was making me an "angry black woman." These two perceptions caused me to suffer. To isolate myself, to not speak to officers, I would put myself in positions so other officers wouldn't speak. I had a huge breakthrough at work, and since then, I've been talking to people.

On August 14, 2020, my Sergeant asked me how I was feeling. I told her about my recent breakthrough. "I can see the difference; you look lighter, happier," she said. A few hours later, one of my co-workers from another team said, "Trapp, whatever you're doing keep doing it. You have changed so much so quickly. And it's sincere and genuine—keep up the good work."

Later, she and I had a heart-to-heart dialogue, where we realized that we have a lot in common, especially when it came to our parents. "When we change, our environment changes." She gave me a Beautiful 7 Chakras Energy Stone Essential Oil Diffuser Necklace Hamsa Hand Aromatherapy Fragrance Locket Pendant.

Engraved on the back it reads, "Always remember you are BRAVER than you believe, STRONGER than you seem, SMARTER than you think, and LOVED more than you know!"

Jermira Trapp was born and raised on the north side of Chicago, IL. In 2006, she received her Bachelor of Science in Public Health degree with an emphasis in health promotion and a minor in psychology from Northern Illinois University. Jermira Trapp has been a sworn member of Law Enforcement since December 16, 2010. There is no coincidence that on December 15, 2012 Jermira became a practitioner of Nichiren Buddhism with the SGI-USA. Faith and daily life are not  separate. Jermira's Buddhist practice has helped her become a compassionate, humanistic officer. The Buddhist principle "Faith Equals Daily Life," explains that our everyday activities at home, work and in our communities are where we demonstrate actual proof of our Buddhist practice.

Jermira has received numerous Department Commendations, a problem solving award, and two Joint Operations awards. In 2019 Jermira was the recipient of the Chicago Crime Commission Law Enforcement Excellence by Task Force Award.

Jermira is passionate and dedicated to dismantling the stigma associated with mental health and seeking out professional help.

In March 25, 2019, she published her first podcast episode "Transmuting daily Mental Trapps" where she shares her personal journey as a source of empowerment on how to transmute your "Daily Mental Trapps."

Jermira wants to help people understand how our thoughts, life experiences (especially childhood), feminine and masculine energy, and the power of our subconscious mind impact our daily life. Most people unconsciously wake up every day with the same state of mind, keeping them "Mentally Trapped" in a state of lack, unworthiness, and suffering. The feedback received from her listeners has been the driving force to help her overcome the years that she has felt "covered in mud."

Every word of encouragement has been a reminder of who she is at the core. It is surreal to hear others say how she has empowered them to heal and challenge their old/limiting beliefs. How her voice is inspiring, and they love that she explains things. She is overjoyed and so encouraged to continue on her personal path of evolution and expansion for the happiness of self and others! Growing up she was teased about how her voice sounded, but now she's a force and a voice for humanity! Jermira has the following quotes from her mentor Daisaku Ikeda engraved in her heart.

> *"A great human revolution in the life of one person can change the destiny of humankind and our planet. It is Buddhism, the Lotus Sutra, that encourages and enables people to become aware of their great power, to draw it forth and use it. Buddhism gives people the means to develop themselves thoroughly and opens their eyes to the limitless power inherent in their lives."*

> ____

> *"Courage, strength and wisdom well up in those who consciously take on everything as the protagonist and person responsible for achieving their goals. Unlimited wisdom and ardent resolve arise from a sense of responsibility."*

Learn more about Jermira: **jermira.trapp@yahoo.com; @Transmutingmentaltrapps | Linktree**

Learn about Soka Gakkai Nichiren Buddhism: **sgi-usa.org**

Mind Your Business!

Discovering the Path to "I Matter"

BY KAWANA WILLIAMS

The last twelve months have been busy and swift for me. I have no major complaints about it; however, I have one central observation about it:

I have been *minding my business!*

No, seriously: I have legit been managing and tending to my shit: my feelings, hang-ups, healing, relationships, talents, and abilities.

GETTING UNSTUCK

For almost eight years, I have poured myself into my friends, family, and lover (known affectionately as "Him")—encouraging and healing. During this time, I have watched my family and loved ones soar and improve while I am stuck in the same damned place, doing and being nothing. I mean, sure, I am in school and—fingers crossed with a sacrificed lamb— will be able to call myself "Doctor Williams" within a year. . . So what's the problem?

I have so many talents, yet they all laid dormant because I prioritized everyone around me but me. The moment that I began to include myself in my priorities, my life changed. Not dramatically, but enough for me to notice where I had gone wrong all this time: I minded and was overly consumed by everyone else's business but my own.

THE REALIZATION

Last summer, I reconnected with a sister whom I met through a friend some years back. I loved everything about her. She is a short, chocolate sister with big, brown eyes framed with a big, beautiful smile and wispy hair. She was brilliant in a rare way. As a woman in higher-level academia, she understood my struggle as a doctoral student. We clicked—and quickly. Our conversations would last throughout the day, and within a short period of time, I found myself confiding in her more.

Her personal drama heightened, and I watched it begin to interfere with her life—and a bit of mine. As a friend, I chose to be there for her. I felt that I was reciprocating the energy she had extended to me.

One night, she had an "emergency" and needed help "immediately." Her request inconvenienced me at that moment, as I was diligently working on crafting my dissertation proposal. Despite my irritation, I put my dissertation writing to the side and tended to her.

For almost two hours, I stood outside and helped her process her feelings. I also made it clear that her self-saboteur would be her undoing if she continued to allow it to lead her life and decisions. I felt her energy shift in that instant, but I did not care. I had grown weary of her mess more than she pretended to be. This was not an isolated "emergency" for her, and I felt that she was way too old and intelligent to be stuck in this pattern of self-sabotage as she had been. Nobody was telling her what she needed to hear, and so I chose to do so, thinking it would help snap her out of whatever cycle she appeared to be stuck in.

DISMISSED

I checked in on her for the next three days and noticed how her tone and conversation had drastically shifted from long, detailed, and humorous to short and trite. On day 3, I finally understood why when she made it quite clear that I no longer needed to check up on her. She insisted that I should make sure *I* was okay because I have a lot on my plate that needed tending to. "Take care and be blessed," she said.

The knee-jerk thought in my mind was, "Ma'am: you weren't ignorant to any of this before you made me your unofficial priest/confessional/

Super Save-A-Hoe. So, you throw it back into my face like acid after using me up like a Bill Withers song? To hell with you *and* your bullshit manipulation tactics!"

I felt used. She was left on "Read" in my messages and blocked on social media that day.

What was I going to do with this?

However, in disconnecting with her, I had an important insight: She was partially right. She was rude in her delivery, but the meat of her message was correct:

I did need to tend to my own business.

FINDING MY SOVEREIGNTY

I know I come with my own mess—in fact, I have several of them! This experience was not about placing myself above my friend in any capacity or making her seem like a monster. I realize that as human beings we all have our weak spots and shadow work to tend to. We all have our crosses to bear until they are too heavy to carry. I felt the fatigue of carrying certain crosses because they are heavy as hell! I have learned over time to put some of mine down. She had not, and that is her privilege. My arrogance allowed me to believe that I had to jump up, help her, and set her straight.

That's the gag of it all!

My life was not any better or worse off than hers. But something was unbalanced. My life force was leaking out of me to help her, and it certainly wasn't benefiting me as the other part of this equation. I lost time and sleep over her stresses; she did not. I had been taking over her burdens.

Meanwhile, my work was left undone in my noble attempt to assist with hers. I found out a week or so later that her actions and her reaction to me were just a pattern that she repeated with others. She tended to surround herself with people who she knew could "save" her in some capacity. Her maladaptive patterns had nothing to do with my maladaptive pattern of jumping up to save the day, even to my detriment.

Along with several other of my friends and associates, she became a fervent reminder of what happens when you do not mind the business that pays you. I found myself feeding their needs and wants, encouraging their talents, and cheering them on in their quests for self-improvement. In doing so, one of two things occurred: They had the glow-up of the century, or they were stuck in the very place I tried [and failed] to help dig them out of. But, either way, in extending myself to them, I ignored myself. I began to despise them for it—and to hate myself for accommodating them.

THE REVELATION OF "I MATTER"

Not operating and presenting myself in my full glory is a disservice to me and those around me. At my core, I am kind, giving, loyal, encouraging, comforting, goofy, and honest. I take pleasure in helping those who need it. I don't mind being the shoulder to cry on. I have no problems getting out of bed to keep you company after a bad day. I believe every good friend—hell, every *person*—should do these things. But they shouldn't have to feel obligated to always be there for any person other than themselves. Somehow or another, I never learned to do that or to fully trust that "I matter, too."

All I knew how to do was be there for other people. It is as if I were raised to believe, "I don't matter, but you do." And while that is not the case, that is how I lived and moved in my life for years.

I recall one time explaining to my best friend that I couldn't accommodate her emergency; I felt horrible. She was disappointed, of course, but not with me. I had convinced myself that she was pissed because I couldn't be there for her. Keep in mind, I had the flu and was nursing myself back to health when she called. Keep in mind that she was unaware of this. Keep in mind that while I am one of her best friends, she has other people in her life who she can depend on as much as me. That didn't matter. All that mattered to me was that I could not be there for my friend in her time of need.

Meanwhile, I needed *me!* But why did *she* matter to me more than I did? She would never get out of her sickbed to be there for me in my time of need. Then again, I would never have asked or expected her to. She has always been better at establishing boundaries than I am. And in the twenty-two years that she has been my best friend, I happened to miss learning that lesson from her. The worst part was the knowledge that if I were in the dire emotional or professional straits that some of my friends were in, they wouldn't have the capacity to support me the way I have them.

While my friends may have expected that I be there for them, none of them demanded or commanded that from me. Even to my detriment, being there for others was all my choice—and not a healthy one. I did not *need* to save them; I chose to. I didn't need to extend so much of myself to them, yet I chose to.

I spent time investing in people and their affairs that never manifested into anything for me. I spent so much time encouraging and pouring my energy into friends' needs that I began to negate and forego my own needs. I would call and check on them. I would hug them hard in case they had not been loved properly that day. I would volunteer my time to get them out of the house if they were feeling down. But if you asked me if any of them could reciprocate the love, energy, and encouragement they received from me, the response would be a resounding NO!

I was playing the role of "fixer." But the truth was, no one needed—or wanted—fixing.

COMING HOME TO ME

I had to set boundaries and call my energy back to me—back home to my heart, where I could give myself the love and supportive holding that had eluded me while I waited for others to give it to me.

The humility and soul-snatching that occurred during this revelation changed me for the better. So much so that in the last nine months, I have:

1. Become a Master Reiki Practitioner (Master Teacher to be earned by spring of 2021)

2. Found a shared office suite to conduct my Reiki sessions

3. Been hired for a children's stage play at a prestigious Black-operated theater (postponed due to COVID-19)

I am super proud of my recent accomplishments and for embracing a new strategy for manifesting a fulfilling life. It's surprisingly simple: Be quiet and mind my own damn business. This included creating distance between myself and several sister-friends who may not have the capacity to give me all the love and support that I gave them. And that is okay. . . for them.

I needed to care as much about me as I did them. I needed to feed my passions as much as theirs. I needed to matter to me as much as those around me did.

So I took back my power, and I discovered how to love myself more. I now put myself first, and my life and relationships are so much more fulfilling and authentic.

All it took was for a chick with her own messy-ass life to tell me to *mind my own business!*

So, I challenge you to mind your business and turn toward yourself—there is a world of possibility waiting to be discovered!

Kawana Williams, M.A., LPC, RMT, was born in Carbondale, Illinois, and raised in Dallas, TX; her family relocated permanently to Chicago, Illinois, in 1992. Williams spent her childhood on the South Side of Chicago and moved the Bellwood, Illinois as a teenager. She is an alumnus of Proviso West High School (2001), Fisk University (Bachelor of Music-Vocal Performance, 2007), and St. Xavier University (Master of Art–Community Counseling). Williams was diagnosed with Stage I-C Ovarian Cancer while completing her studies at Fisk, postponing her 2006 graduation;

she received her degree the following year. Williams was inducted into Sigma Gamma Rho Sorority, Incorporated in December of 2006, and into Chi Sigma Iota Counseling Academic and Professional Honor Society in 2018. Williams is a former volunteer lecturer with the Chicago branches of Gilda's Club and the National Ovarian Cancer Coalition, respectively. She is currently a Licensed Professional Counselor, a doctoral student at The Chicago School of Professional Psychology (Chicago/Grayslake), a Reiki Master Practitioner, and owner/operator of My Healing Center. Williams' future goals include doing clinical work with Adolescent and Young Adult cancer survivors and teaching the art of reiki to underprivileged and impoverished individuals worldwide.

Learn more at: **myhealingcenter.net.**

Yin the Beginning

BY CHANTE ZUPANCIC

*What would become of human thoughts had they not
survived will never be known.*

Perception is a matter of frequency.

Where purpose exists, survives rhythmic movement.

*Consciousness is breathing. Witnessing itself,
piped egg-shelled dreams endlessly oozing potential.*

*Torus galaxies infinitely dancing towards the spin created
from consuming itself. An unavoidable fate.*

*The remaining years of earthly survival depended on
which anthems played against the thick web of static of
The "New-Old World."*

*In the later days of the New-Old World (NOW),
scientists were so influenced by the perceived threat
of a black body within their Earth that they attempted
to "correct" it with a few tragic experiments, only to
end up expanding its electromagnetic pull.*

CURRENT PHASE, HARA

Harafolk gather in the belly of an ornate ceremonial cavern climbing with undulating varieties of plant life. Hara women marinate their Earth-enriched skin inside pits filled with bio-illuminated plasma that encourages the release of memories. The melanin-activated extract can be encoded into almost any substance used for rapid propagation and fuel for inter-dimensional travel. There are no wasted experiences; even the gift of ignorance is considered a valuable contribution. Sharing joyous reflections aid in orgasmic birthing rituals while sharing fears prevents them from festering throughout the community.

Sisters fill the hall anticipating the maturity likely to follow the absorption of their ancestral story. Changé prepared her eyes shut, inhaling her mind in rewind. She stood like a giant buzzing stone wrapped with intense focus. A rhythmic pulsation is created from her hands, dividing space surrounding each of them in graceful circular swooping motions.

Let these bountiful healing vapors
remind us of the great composition, our purpose.

May all ancestral memories be blessings
to grow our healing capacity.

May we remember to exist
trusting in the connection beyond our awareness.

Asé

We had no idea the place called the Last Shore existed, but those who were able to tune in felt its pull. We didn't know we had the map inside our skin, inside our blood, within our voice.

Liquid crystals.

Values were quite backward back then. The noise of the world had gotten so loud, so out of control, that it hypnotized the masses. Humans became afraid and uncontrollably hateful toward all things that were feminine, dark, or old. There was a distrust of nature. Even water was thought to be dangerous.